BLACKS IN THE DIASPORA

Darlene Clark Hine, John McCluskey, Jr., and David Barry Gaspar
General Editors

Rumba

Dance
and
Social
Change in
Contemporary
Cuba

Yvonne Daniel

indiana
university press
bloomington and
indianapolis

The paper used in this publication meets the minimum requirements of American
National Standard for Information Sciences—Permanence of Paper
for Printed Library Materials, ANSI Z39.48-1984.

Manufactured in the United States of America

Library of Congress Cataloging-in-Publication Data
Daniel, Yvonne, date
    Rumba : dance and social change in contemporary Cuba / Yvonne Daniel.
      p.   cm.—(Blacks in the diaspora)
    Includes bibliographical references and index.
    ISBN 0-253-31605-7 (cloth : alk. paper).—ISBN 0-253-20948-X
  (pbk. : alk. paper)
    1. Rumba (Dance)—Cuba. 2. Dance—Cuba—Anthropological aspects.
  3. Cuba—Social conditions—1959- I. Title. II. Series.
  GV1769.R8D32 1995
  784.18'88—dc20   94-34363

  1 2 3 4 5 00 99 98 97 96 95

Contents

Preface

So much has happened recently to make the situation of Cuba very grave. We in the United States hear little of the reality most Cubans live. On my last visit, during the summer of 1993, I saw how much had changed since my fieldwork years between 1985 and 1990. The Cuban people's struggle to survive as an independent nation continues with little support or assistance at the international level. There is no comprehensive movement toward humane aid for the Cuban people. They are deliberately isolated in an interdependent world.

But the Cubans march onward, even though they are denied nourishment and look like persons in a concentration camp without barbed wire or bullets. They struggle against external forces that strangle their sources of subsistence and against internal forces that are desperate to see principles sustained. The Cuban people are valiant, and there is no question that their example to the world, against mighty odds, will be recognized in history.

This book looks at Cuba during a stage of cresting development, after the bitter climb up from revolutionary warfare and after two generations of living out a blueprint for a completely new social and economic system. Life was less bleak during the time span covered here. This book presents a view of late-1980s Cuba by means of dance analysis and through the eyes of an outsider who cherishes their ideals of equality. I, like many others in the United States, support Cuba's right to have the kind of government its people choose. I went to Cuba to witness, learn, and analyze its actions as these actions applied to and affected its varied artistic world.

I am indebted to so many people who cared for this project and for me that it is difficult to acknowledge them all. I thank Smyrna Press of Brooklyn, New York, for granting me permission to use Margaret Randall's translation of a poem by Milagros Gonzalez that appeared in *Women in Cuba* (Smyrna Press, 1981). My adopted individual Cuban families, the members of Folklórico Nacional, and the entire family of Los Muñequitos were the ones most strained because of my North American identity; I am grateful to all for their faith and loyalty. My professors, Nelson Graburn, Percy Hintzen, Gerald Berreman, and Olly Wilson, who took their chances with an aesthetic project in the academic halls of anthropology at the University of California at Berkeley, were sources of inspiration. I give special thanks to my mother and my sons, who sacrificed the most that I might complete all phases of this project. And I am eternally indebted to the hundreds of dancers, singers, and drummers in Cuba and the United States who gave of their love of rumba.

Toward positive change here and there,

Yvonne Daniel
Smith College
August 25, 1993

Rumba

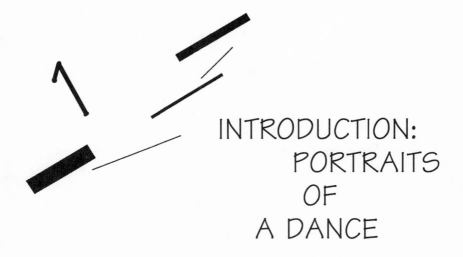

INTRODUCTION: PORTRAITS OF A DANCE

Rumba is a passionate dance, considered beautiful by many. Often the highlight of a community event or social gathering in Cuba, it embodies important elements of life: movement, spontaneity, sensuality, sexuality, love, tension, opposition, and both freedom and restraint. It requires play as well as deliberation. It involves the human body, the human voice, and a tremendous rhythmic sense. And since the Cuban Revolution of 1959, rumba has become even more enigmatic, full of contrasts and contradictions, reflecting life and projecting national goals in contemporary Cuba. The dance looks exceedingly simple, but on close examination it is found to be extraordinarily complex. Using subtle and discrete movements, it appears loose and improvised—and, to a degree, it is. But it is also structured, almost rigid, in its rules.

In examining this important Cuban folkloric dance, I focus on social, economic, political, and religious conditions that shape its structure and meaning. My guiding hypothesis is that social change can generate change in dance and, conversely, that change in dance can be identified, analyzed, and understood in terms of social currents and societal conditions. I selected rumba because of its seminal importance in articulating certain social conditions of contemporary Cuba, where rumba is systematically displayed as a cultural image and enjoys more popularity than other folkloric dances.

The chapters of this book artificially dissect Cuban rumba and examine all of its facets in order to explore its relationship to processes of social change and to illustrate the potential of dance analysis. But before separating its essence into elemental parts, I start with two pictures of rumba that are fascinating, exciting, whole.

THE FIRST PORTRAIT OF RUMBA

The first time I saw rumba danced in Cuba was at the National Folkloric Company's studio in Havana during a regular Friday afternoon rehearsal before *Sábado de la rumba* (Rumba Saturday). The entire company of about forty dancers entered the warm, shaded room and took prescribed positions: the younger technicians in the first rows, the veteran soloists at the rear. The battery of five percussionists and three singers formed a curved line on a stage at the far end of the studio, facing the dancers. Another five or six musicians were seated farther back on the stage, ready to take any part or any instrument on a simple cue. The *claves* (wooden sticks of a Latin percussion ensemble) announced the slow, repetitive basic rhythm, answered by the deep throat of the *hembra* (the lowest-pitched drum) and followed by the *macho* (the middle-register drum); then I heard the sparse, terse commentary of the *quinto* (the falsetto of the drum trio) in playful percussive harmony. The *catá*, or *guagua* (a bamboo or wooden cylindric instrument played with wooden sticks), and the *madruga* (a metal shaker) joined in the musical conversation, and a singer was inspired to begin the syllabic melisma of the *diana*, the introductory portion of rumba singing.

Immediately the dancers began to move in their places. As they waited for instructions from the two leaders of the class, the dancers were trying to maintain their prepared attention stance, but they could not help responding subtly to the rhythms. The movement came from deep within their torsos, through their chests, through their shoulders and arms, and ultimately involved their necks and heads. Their rocking, swaying, and undulating were an accompaniment to the antiphonal singing of a small chorus of men. Suddenly, for my uninitiated ears—but really at the beginning of the compelling rhythmic phrase—the dancers' knees bent and the full force of the rules of the dance consumed the dancers: they began dancing rumba. The instructors had signaled for the performance of rumba to start.

The rhythm was hypnotic as rows of dancers advanced toward me and the musical ensemble on the raised stage. Six dancers proceeded in a single horizontal line, amply spaced across a huge mirrored studio. Their movements brought my attention to the very subtle undulations from the lower spine. The undulations flowed upward and laterally through the sea of bodies. I saw feet moving forward with many subtleties, even within the uniformity of unison movement. The basic footwork appeared like a touch to the side and a return to normal standing position, repeated on alternating sides. In reality, there was a small, weighted push of one foot to the side and a step in place with the same foot, alternating from one side to the other. With succeeding rows of dancers, however, the step was embroidered with small, passing steps as the pattern continued to alternate from side to side. Then I began to notice the dancers' arms, which opened outward and slightly upward, accenting, ever so smoothly, the alternating foot pattern.

The dancers were singing a refrain with the chorus of singers, a short vocal response to the solo singer. Occasionally the shoulders of a woman or man, or of several dancers, vibrated quickly. No knees were straightened; all male and female bodies were slightly lowered in a forward tilt (about a forty-five-degree hip flexion), responding to the rhythmic pulse of the claves. The rhythm acted like an injection that affected the body deeply and traveled upward through the spine, laterally through the hips, and forward and backward in the chest, creating sensuous polyrhythms within the body.

The drums began to speed up, and the instructors signaled a change from the horizontal lines to a large semicircle facing the drums. The dancers' bodies were glistening as they raised their voices in song, smiled, and danced. One instructor, in the closed circle under the resounding drumming, told dancers to watch the *informante*, the other dance specialist who also taught the class.[1] One quiet dancer, who had danced in the back row earlier, came to the center, lifted the edges of her skirt, and began to articulate multiple minute movements of the shoulders, chest, hips, feet, arms, and head. With the slightest bits of energy, she demonstrated the moving elaborated step, gradually building spatial and emotional dynamics and a sense of a soloist's drama. She was in her inner world; intermittently her eyes closed with feeling as she listened and responded to various signals from the quinto.[2] The instructor signaled one of the younger men, and immediately, but slowly, the intense dynamics of a skilled and fiercely expressive body deepened toward the floor with a forward tilt and encircled the dancing diva.

The two dancers smiled at one another constantly, and I noticed how intensely they concentrated. They danced apart spatially, with different steps, but together in relation to one another and in relation to the music. The music was relatively slow, and their accentuation on the afterpulse of the movement, the rebound to a musical accent within the body, was strikingly sensual. Even though they did not make large movements or dynamic changes, the movements grew in intensity. The man circled the woman slowly, deliberately. The woman watched constantly while alternating her body undulations to each side. They danced very close together without touching. He placed a large scarf around her shoulders, still holding two of its edges. They danced even lower to the floor, watching each others' eyes, smiling. They alternated their knees from side to side in unison while slowly rising from the ground. At the same time, the upper body was demonstrating the multidirectional ability of the human torso: forward to backward, side to side, up and down. The man was making wide claps with his knees, and he raised one arm over the woman's head. Now she held the scarf and turned her back toward him, still looking for him across her shoulders.

The rumba music shifted subtly, becoming faster, but the same dance movements prevailed. The instructor signaled the informante again, and she danced momentarily alone. Another young man saw his cue and dramatically advanced toward the dancing diva, holding his head high, his back straight, and rapidly traveling forward on his toes, firing his feet swiftly and tightly, one in front of the other (*pisao* steps). The two dancers watched each other, miniaturizing the basic movements momentarily as they sensed each other, the calls of the drums and the singers, and what I later came to understand as the impending choreographed attack. At that moment, no one knew exactly what was about to happen in the repetitive, undulating, intermittently vibrating kinesthetic exchange. They danced close to one another, he reached to embrace her waist lightly, and both dancers deepened their knee bends even farther toward the ground together. They twisted from side to side and came upward. The man reached to hold the woman's shoulders, bouncing his knees together with wide rebounds. The woman was standing almost upright, slightly tilted and bent forward, noticeably alert, when suddenly there was a pelvic thrust from the man, even from his low position. The dancing diva gracefully but speedily slapped her skirt over her pelvic area, smiled, and spun around, leaving the man undimmed, pleased, and eager to advance again.

Several other couples took turns looking for the possibilities of the pelvic thrust, or *vacunao*. I later learned that this word came from the Spanish verb *vacunar*, meaning primarily "to vaccinate." Cubans coined it to signify this erotic pelvic gesture, the object of male pursuit and female flight that is the aim of the dance. Sometimes it was not the pelvis or hips but a foot, a hand, even a scarf, that made the males's symbolic vaccination of the female. No matter what body part was used, the dancers reveled in mounting the attack and in preparing a defense. Some women came into the circle laughing, holding only one side of their skirts, almost daring the men to attempt a vacunao. When the accented gesture happened, the women adeptly covered themselves with their hands or skirts.

After a time of singing and faster-paced dances, the instructor signaled a tall, handsome man, who was slightly older, more dignified, and seemingly more respected than the earlier partners of the dancing diva. His movements were tight, rapid, and intricate as he traveled around the circle. He would freeze momentarily in implosive holds and quickly start again. His actions answered the beckoning pitches of the leading improvisational drum. The drummer and the solo male dancer conversed in a synesthetic dialogue. The other dancers were quite animated, not only in dancing but also in vocalizing. Challenging comments and encouraging exclamations of amazement rippled around and across the dancing space. At last the tall, handsome dancer pointed a finger toward the floor and grandly exited from the center.

Several male dancers entered the circle in succession. One dancer used his shoulders in a steady vibratory motion as he slowly bent forward to display how evenly he matched the drums with his rhythmic movements. He too used quick locomotor patterns and interspersed them with designs that were momentarily frozen in space. Sometimes he raised both arms high, curving them slightly above his head as he focused downward, listening intently, grimacing with emotion, like a fiery flamenco stance. At other times his body crouched low over a blur of legs in rhythm. One second he was on the ground on his side; the next he was upright, swinging one leg over the other. He was challenged also, but this time by a young female dancer, who had apparently dropped her skirt for this type of dancing. She wore a leotard and tights that clearly showed both the full range of shapes that were the result of expressed rhythm in her body and a female version of the men's gestures.

At this moment the entire circle was filled with excited laughter and shouts; everyone encouraged the young woman to continue her skilled and unexpected display. She followed the drum solo and complemented the rhythmic calls. As she danced, the men were particularly vocal, answering her movements in ridiculing gestures; but when she proved her speed and technical proficiency, they quickly slapped the outstretched hands of one another in fraternal approval. The women cheered her on approvingly, and one woman, older, gave the accepted gesture of challenge, the pointed finger, and entered the center.

Everyone was having fun, competing, flirting, exhibiting their sensuality and skill. The instructor and the informante, the dancing diva, both captivated and pleased, made eye contact after a time and walked toward the drums. The two teachers conversed with the lead musician for a minute, then the drummers played an ending. There was loud and enthusiastic applause for the drummers, kisses and approving touches for the final two female dancers, and much discussion among all the dancers about style and the details of arm and leg placement or agility in the vacunao. I was amazed and puzzled by the analytical exchanges about dancing that followed the almost possessed or totally concentrated states, now so quickly abandoned.

I had no idea of the meaning of what I had just seen, but I was intrigued by this distinctly different dance class. By this time I had observed four days of fabulous dancing in Havana and wildly exciting, contrasting forms, and I had already fallen in love with Cuban folkloric dance. But rumba was profoundly different from the other Caribbean dances I had come to know, perform, and love. Rumba was Cuban, not African or Spanish; and as I realized later, there was an attachment to it among all Cubans—white, black, or brown (as some North Americans would say).

Rumba was filled with an incredible excitement: within the danced steps themselves, between the dancers as males and females danced together, between challenging male dancers, between the dancers and the musicians, and between the dancers and the spectators. I felt a powerful rhythmic contagion; I saw the intricate and subtle gestures and sensed the feelings within many dancers; I heard the hypnotic challenge of instruments and song and, later, the voiced connections between performers and spectators.

I bombarded myself with questions. Why was this dance so compelling? What was the difference between it and other Cuban dance traditions, such as *Arará*, *Palo*, and *Yoruba* (of Dahomey/Benin, Kongo-Angolan, and mainly Nigerian origins, respectively)? Profoundly rhythmic shoulders propel Arará dancing, and percussive, pulsating footwork initiates Palo dancing. Hypnotic rocking, torso undulations, and exquisite gesturing characterize Yoruba dancing. Was the difference between rumba and these exciting, sensuous, and dynamic dances a result of the supposed opposition between the secular and the religious? Did Cuban rumba relate to other "Cubanisms" in Cuban modern dance or in ballet?

The company director, who was sitting with me, noticed my puzzled expression and told me that what I had just seen was distinct within the Cuban dance experience. Though rumba is technically difficult and is danced mainly by one social class and one "racial" group, it is cherished by many and acknowledged as intimately and fundamentally "Cuban" by most Cubans. It is one of four popular and representative creations from Cuban social dance of the nineteenth century (the others are *conga*, *danzón*, and *son*). A movie called *Rumba* made by Cubans Oscar Valdez and Hector Vitria and distributed fairly widely in the United States in recent years, documents the pervasive popularity of rumba as a well-known and specially regarded dance among old and young, dark- and light-skinned, rural and urban Cubans.[3] Even more important for my analysis of social change, however, is that rumba has been selected by Cuban authorities (either the Ministry of Culture, the directors of the national dance companies, or the organic educational process of the Cuban Revolution—no one is quite sure which entity is fully responsible) as important dance material. Since the Revolution of 1959, rumba has emerged as a symbol of what Cuba stands for among its own people and what Cubans want the world to understand when the international community envisions Cuba and Cubans.

Before seeing rumba in Cuba, I had read about it in Janheinz Jahn's *Muntu* (1961), and I had heard about it while dancing *salsa*, or *mambo* in California and New York.[4] At certain changes in the music, my dancing partners in the States would lead me in a switch of rhythms, but none had danced what I had just witnessed in Havana, and none had danced for so long a time—about one and a half hours. I recalled the warning given me by a friend and colleague: that I would be astonished when I saw real Cuban rumba.[5] I had now connected happily with a distinct dance tradition, and my quest for meaning began.

THE SECOND PORTRAIT OF RUMBA

My next encounter, with a different kind of rumba, took place in the town plaza of Matanzas, an important cultural center northeast of Havana. It was a regularly scheduled Saturday performance of rumba that used the shaded overhang of the municipal theater and the adjoining cobblestone streets as a staged veranda. About thirty to one hundred people, at varying times, gathered there on a gray, overcast afternoon. From my perspective as a newcomer in Matanzas and as a novice in public rumba dancing, rumba took on a different character. The intense, physical activity that I described in the first portrait was experienced and observed in the second, but the second portrait compounded external factors. After experiencing many similar events, I discovered rumba's second portrait; this one is more participatory, while the first is more spectator-oriented.

It could be argued, of course, that I experienced a unique rumba on this occasion because of how I was viewed. I was acknowledged as a foreign visitor, and I was made aware of how delicately influential my U.S. nationality, my association with Havana's Ministry of Culture, and my membership in the National Folkloric Ensemble could be. Irrespective of how I was viewed, the unique situation that is reflected in this second portrait did not change the nature of the dancing. The situation of the second portrait defined the character of most rumba events.

I arrived in Matanzas within hours of the scheduled event, having been told previously that I had not experienced "real" rumba without seeing *rumba matancera* (rumba from Matanzas Province). Matanzas officials from the Ministry of Culture were there, awaiting a group of international visitors, not me. They formally greeted me as another foreign visitor when I was presented to them by the directors of the leading rumba group of Matanzas. This switch, wherein instead of being introduced by the Ministry of Culture to the leading local personnel, I was introduced to ministry officials, was a result of my having been adopted and incorporated already, even though superficially at that time, into a large extended family of Matanzas. I was offered a reserved place in the audience for foreign guests, on the first of two rows of chairs that marked the circular performance space, and I was introduced to several leading Cuban researchers, staff workers, and photographers. After a while, however, my new family encouraged me to go "backstage" among the several groups of musicians and dancers who had gathered under the shaded overhead of the building for the occasion.

People were assembled from many families associated with traditional rumba, including some from Havana. There was a great deal of hugging, kissing, and gossiping, accompanied by drinking. At first I felt that the rum they shared was part of the routine of Cuban welcoming; I realized later that it was also part of most rumba events. In this particular circumstance, the kind of rum that was circulated boosted the activity to a different level. It was Havana Club Añejo, a special seven- to ten-year-old rum. People who were scheduled to perform, dignitaries from municipal and cultural administration agencies, and I shared full swallows of this warm, smooth, very strong rum. (On other occasions, rum of lower quality or beer was consumed.)

This rumba took an unusually long time to begin. The approximate time announced for its beginning came and went. People were socializing—not simply the spectators, but the performers as well—and it was hard to gather members of each group into one place. Finally, an announcer began the program.

Several rumbas were sung without dancing, but eventually a series of rumba songs were danced. At times the sun appeared in its full brilliance, the kind that produces blisters on exposed backs, but on this day the sun alternated with huge dark clouds that, in combination with the waiting and the delay caused by the foreign visitors, accounted for growing tension.

The combined music/dance activity, presented by alternating groups, occasionally included family members from the spectator space. There was a sense of a scheduled program among these traditional specialists, but the dynamics of each ensuing dance caused more audience participation than I had seen in professional settings in Havana. A spirit of competition enveloped each succeeding couple and was augmented by many shouted comments from the audience. Members of several rumba groups, including Havana's Compañeros and Matanzas's Muñequitos, Afro-Cuba, Obbatola, Perico, Niño de Atoche, and Portales de Cárdenas, were scattered through the audience, and I can only surmise that they shared a friendly, respectful competition as well as individual jealousies.

As the afternoon wore on, it became apparent that the visiting dignitaries were not coming, and some ministry officials left. The consequences were that the occasion was almost totally Cuban and almost totally unsupervised. From this point on, what occurred approximated what I call spontaneous rumba, even though officially the event was a prepared rumba performance. (For a discussion of the distinctions, see chapter 4.)

The first songs and dances established a kind of quick review of the rumba literature. Probably more important, they affirmed a sense of honor toward the renowned specialists who were present.

The next section of the program highlighted younger groups, which were organized formally as amateurs. But most of these youngsters were members of the families of recognized musicians or dancers of rumba and were quite phenomenal. Drummers exchanged positions to demonstrate individual virtuosity; singers displayed extraordinary skill in a cappella style; dancers amazed local spectators with unlimited flexibility and astute rhythm.

These teenagers tried to play and sing original pieces based on the musical structures and styles of their parents and grandparents. They did not attempt to play standards because the oldest living members of some of the first rumba groups were present and because these standards are still in the repertoires of those masters. The young musicians were carefully scrutinized all afternoon, even amid the talking, laughing, gossiping, smoking, and drinking that occurred during every piece. Sometimes a father or uncle took over a drum to demonstrate a particular technique or to push the pace of the composition.

The young dancers danced the routinized steps in an improvisational form, at first as couples. They executed the classic style, then proceeded to emphasize contemporary elements of choreography. They even interspersed break dance steps and the moon walk step associated with Michael Jackson and introduced acrobatic double and triple flips. They also danced with some of the veteran *rumberos*, sometimes fathers with daughters or aunts with nephews.

The next event featured adults, with both men and women as lead singers, often interrupting or overlapping one another to start their own improvised versions. When one woman led a traditional song that is associated with men, the crowd noisily and excitedly approved. At another point the rhythm shifted into a *conga*, a distinct dance/music form in Cuba, and members of the crowd burst into dance without leaving their places. I was surprised that nonrumba music/dance was being performed at a rumba gathering. This piece ended with the crash of a bottle and a fight between two men, who had to be separated and taken away by the police.

The rumba resumed, women and men dancing with raw challenge. Each rumba piece started relatively slowly, with the tempo increasing greatly by the end. Ecstatic cries and critical shouts came from members of the audience, who also participated with encouraging movements and gestures, bouncing up and down in time to the music or waving outstretched arms upward repeatedly.

Many rules that I had begun to understand as de rigueur for rumba dancing were broken: a female dancer stayed in the circle dancing as the men challenged each other; older people danced as soloists within what is considered couple forms; and men, almost ruthlessly but with much laughter, vied for position to lead the dancing and singing. Many participants and observers had been drinking heavily, not only from the unexpected supply of rum intended for the absent foreign visitors but also from local concoctions of alcohol and lemon juice. But up to this point the drinking seemed not to affect the fine music production or the outstanding dancing agility.

The best example of the kind of intense feelings that heightened through the afternoon came when some of the men set up empty rum bottles in a line and pushed their young sons (six to eight years old) to dance rumba between the bottles without knocking them down. The father of the winner received a full bottle of rum and initiated a series of outstanding male solo performances. Older men brilliantly executed precise, polyrhythmic, aesthetically pleasing innovations, showing absolute virtuosity within exquisite and incredible creativity. Here, rumba dancing and music truly reached great heights.

The crowd had reduced the plaza's dancing space to a mere five- or six-foot-diameter circle as it pressed forward to witness each step. The audience cheered or criticized each performer and took sides in evaluating skill. The performance spot also had changed, having slowly shifted from the official location near the theater's veranda directly onto the cobble-

Guaguancó tradicional matancero, a
traditional rumba, performed by Ana Perez
and Diosdado Ramos, members of Los
Muñequitos de Matanzas, in rehearsal,
Matanzas, 1987. Photo by Y. Daniel.

stone street, the usual site of historic nineteenth-century rumba. Time, on
the other hand, had expanded beyond the usual limits of a few hours for a
planned performance for foreign visitors. The approximate five o'clock
ending of a usual prepared performance was extended to seven o'clock.

Neither singers, musicians, nor dancers seemed to want to stop mov-

Columbia profesional, performed by Domingo
Pau at *Sábado de la rumba*, Havana, 1985.
Photo by Y. Daniel.

El vacunao 1, performed by Bárbaro Ramos
and Ana Perez of Los Muñequitos de
Matanzas, 1986. Video frame, Y. Daniel.

ing; the audience of participating spectators shouted and gestured, continuing their participation as well. Pushing and pressing became the rule. Then suddenly a male performer, apparently upset at what someone had shouted or insinuated, rushed across the dance circle to physically attack another male. Fighting broke out in several places; dancing and music stopped almost immediately as neighbors separated the angry combatants. Soon everyone was encouraged to leave the plaza by armed guards, alerted, I presume, by the interruption of music and the shift in character of the noise. It was dark now anyway, and thus rumba matancera ended.

THE PROBLEM

I had planned to study dance in Cuba, but not rumba. As I saw more professional and amateur rumba and heard more of its history, however, and especially after seeing the public rumba just described, I realized that rumba could be viewed as an indicator of social conditions and perhaps of governmental efforts to change attitudes. It would be possible to analyze variations within rumba types, to examine the development of the Rumba event, then to investigate both the aesthetic and the social reasons for the changes I had noted. So I decided to look at rumba historically and developmentally, from before the Revolution to the present, in urban and rural environments, among the young and the old, among more and less privileged Cubans, among whites and blacks, and among professionals and amateurs.

I discovered that Rumba had shifted from a spontaneous, improvisational event that included a set of rumba dances and other dance forms to a choreographed public performance executed regularly in cultural programs throughout the island. It had also evolved organically as a Cuban music/dance complex without artificial shaping or preconceived structuring. Rumba, a dance of predominantly lower-class black Cubans in the nineteenth century, became the focus of a two-week national festival after the Revolution and eventually was institutionalized in monthly public activities.

The National Folkloric Ensemble of Cuba, the Conjunto Folklórico Nacional dancers, musicians, and administrators, along with several Ministry of Culture officials, took advantage of the pervasive popularity of rumba over other folkloric dances and instituted Rumba Saturday as part of an embracing cultural education program as well as an entertainment program for foreign visitors. These Saturday performances, beginning late in 1979, celebrated rumba as a national symbol and, among foreign visitors, as

El vacunao 2, performed by Teresa Polledo and
Johannes García of Conjunto Folklórico
Nacional, Havana, 1990. Photo by Y. Daniel.

La bañista, performed by Lourdes Tamayo of
Conjunto Folklórico Nacional, 1994.

an international image of Cuba. Consequently, rumba emerged trium-
phant over other dances that are generally easier to perform, dances that
involve a larger cross section of the total population, and dances that emphasize more communal participation.

Since decisions in postrevolutionary Cuba were made either by Presi-
dent Fidel Castro or by specifically work-designated groups as a unit and
approved by other designated groups, no one individual can be named as
responsible for the selection of rumba as a major cultural symbol. What occurred is the product of a series of responses to sociopolitical conditions
after 1959. Before the Castro victory, ballet had received tremendous support and acclaim in Cuba, but neither folkloric dance nor modern dance
had been much supported or encouraged. Certainly neither had been promoted at a national level. With the Revolution, a shift of support toward
rumba occurred. This interest in rumba cannot be interpreted solely as an
interest in artistic concerns; rather, it represents a concern for previously
denied Cubans and their immediate importance to the new government.

The need to reinforce the goals, objectives, and hopes of the Revolution prompted the government through its ministries to use all aspects of
social expression and to embark on a selection process. They rejected attitudes and guiding ideas associated with the elite stratum of society and pro-
posed new ideas and images that stressed investment in human resources:
commitment to equality and social justice, guaranteed access to shared
resources.

With all departments of government actively embracing such goals, the
Ministry of Culture interpreted its responsibility as the support of Cuban
expressive culture that reflects, embodies, or promotes identified national
objectives (see Giurchescu and Torp, 1991). For dance, it formed and developed national companies to display and publicize national attitudes,
ideas, and beliefs through traditional and modern songs, instrumentation,
and costuming as well as dance. Afro-Cuban rumba, as a symbol of the inclusion of lower-class expressions within the Ministry of Culture's programming, was promoted to assist overarching national principles that would
benefit all sectors of the population. Rumba, apparently more than other
Cuban dance traditions, expressed an identification with African-derived
elements that make up Cuban culture, represented the interests of workers, and solidified the participation of the Cuban artistic community in the
social advance of the new political system. This situation of rumba in Cuba
became the focus of my research.

In a complex social system and with a cultural expression that is more
meaningful to one sector than to another, the challenge of creating a national symbol is great. Despite the glorification of an African and European

heritage or "working-class" values within rumba, it continues to be a dance primarily of black or dark-skinned Cubans, with relatively little participation by mainstream Cuban society. In the appropriation and formal presentation of rumba, the dance not only demonstrates Cuba's identity with the masses of workers who have enriched Cuba with their indelible influence; it also displays Cuban attitudes and prejudices. A long and forthright process of education and institutional support is necessary to make ideological and institutional change meaningful, that is, to have change understood and embodied. This is precisely a portion of rumba's task in contemporary Cuba.

DIFFERENTIATING RUMBAS

The Spanish words *rumba* and *rumbón* refer to a collective festive event, a gala meal, a carousal, or a high time. They are synonymous with some Bantu and other West Central African words used in Cuba, such as *tumba*, *macumba*, and *tambo*, meaning a social, secular gathering with music and dancing. Fernando Ortiz, the major scholar of Afro-Cuban folkloric traditions, defines *rumba* as a dance of Cuban origin with African antecedents and lists other derivatives that mean "to gather and dance" or "to have a party," e.g., *rumbanchear, cumbanchar* (1924:406-11). Argeliers Leon and Olavo Alen, Cuban musicologists who have studied the music and dance of these events, agree that the precise meaning of *rumba* is difficult to determine, but it is found within those words of African origin that point to a collective party, unrelated to religious ritual (León, 1984a:153; Alénb, 1987:1).

Rumba developed during the 1850s and 1860s in places where free blacks gathered to communicate their feelings or comment on their struggles and where enslaved Africans were permitted to congregate after work. Particularly with the abolition of slavery in Cuba after 1886, *los negros humildes*, poor Afro-Cubans, moved to urban areas and joined poor white Cubans looking for jobs, which were more plentiful near the ports than in rural areas. Both light- and dark-skinned groups adjusted to the particular conditions of free women and men in a society based on color and class and participated together from time to time in communal gatherings such as rumba. This was the Rumba event, spontaneous, "real" rumba; it corresponds to the second portrait described above. (For clarity, I refer to the Rumba event with upper-case *R* and to the dances and music with lower-case *r*.)[6]

Rumba is also the name of a dance, a rhythm, and a group of related dances, together called the rumba complex, which evolved in the nineteenth century; it was described in the first portrait above. Types within the rumba dance complex were transported from Cuba through much of the world, to Spain in the nineteenth century, to the United States in the 1920s and 1930s, to Africa in the 1940s and 1950s (see Ranger 1975). Related dances are found in other Caribbean and Latin American settings, but they are not part of the rumba complex of Cuba, though they share similar ambiances and movement patterns: the chase of the female or the bumping of a dancing couple, for example as found to some extent in the *samba* of Brazil, *malambo* of Peru, *zembra* of Argentina, *porro* of Colombia, *cumbia* of Puerto Rico, and *bandamban* of Suriname.[7]

Rumba was and is associated with African communities in the Americas; however, in its most commercial form it has also been associated with whites and a style of ballroom dancing called rhumba or *rumba de salon*. While both dance variations use traditional rumba rhythms, the popularized ballroom style does not resemble the original Cuban dance, sometimes contrasted as *rumba del campo*, or rumba from the countryside. Rumba dancing flourished in urban and rural areas where Cuban workers of all colors and from many occupations rendezvoused and shared their creole heritage in music and dance.[8]

According to Ortiz (1951:433) and Rogelio Martinez-Furé (1982:114-15), the current authority on Cuban dance traditions, rumba may have begun as remembered fragments of songs and steps from Africa among the Ganga or Kisi people in Cuba, generalized ethnic groups of West Central Africa. Jahn suggests that the dance came from the Sara peoples of northern Nigeria, who sometimes dance with rows of boys in front of rows of girls, getting closer and closer until they touch and then separate from one another (1961:82).[9] In present-day Zaire there seems to be a history of similar dances; an old traditional BaKongo dance called *vane samba* seems to relate directly to rumba's antecedents. In this dance, men and women dance in a circle with cloth strips attached to waistbands around raffia skirts. As the performer kicks and throws his or her legs, the cloth is thrown up in the air and toward a member of the opposite sex. The cloth is intended to touch a person and in this way to ask the person to dance in the circle. The last person chosen stays in the circle to choose the next performer by throwing or "giving" the cloth again (Bunseki Fu-Kiau, personal communication, 1991; Malonga Casquelourdes, personal communications, 1989, 1992).[10]

The antecedent dances that most closely relate to rumba in Cuba are of West Central African or Kongo-Angolan origin—from what today comprises Zaire, Angola, and the Congo—and are called *yuka* and *makuta*. Cubans refer to them as Congolese or Bantu dances. A characteristic feature occurs when the bodies of a dancing pair meet or almost meet at the navel, a movement that relates directly to rumba's vacunao. From the musical perspective, there are additional connections between Kongolese traits and Cuban rumba. For example, drummers characteristically use wrist shakers in both yuka and rumba, particularly when boxes are played as drums.

It is believed that Rumba grew out of the social circumstances of Havana, the capital city (Ortiz, 1951; Martinez-Furé, 1986; Pedro, 1986; Leon, 1984a). Havana was the center for large numbers of enslaved Africans by the end of the eighteenth century, and slave barracks became focal points of anguish and protest (Knight, 1970, 1978; Klein, 1967; Martinez-Furé, 1982:114-15; Hernandez, 1980:49). Rebellion was difficult and dangerous, but protest in a disguised form was often expressed in recreational music and dance. These recreational events occurred at prescribed times or on predetermined occasions during the era of slavery. In fact, throughout the Caribbean and plantation America, enslaved peoples often imitated and satirized elite society in dance and music for personal recreation (Emery, 1972: 39-40, 45, 48, 98-101, 108-9; Bremer, 1851 [1980]; Moreau de St.-Mery, 1796 [1976]:44-51).

With the end of slavery, poor black workers continued to lament their meager opportunities and depressing conditions and expressed their frustrations, as well as their joys, through dance and music. *Solares*, the large houses that were divided into crowded living quarters and where poor Cubans were forced to live, served also as meeting places to relax, play, and dream in song, dance, and poetry. These solares offered spatial solace as they distanced poor blacks from continuous racial prejudice and the unjust realities of political impotence. Martinez-Furé says that rumba came from the solares and was "a vehicle of liberation and protest" (in Chao Carbonero and Lamerán, 1982:114). From the solares, Afro-Cubans expressed their personal successes or failures in love relations, satirized government practices, and gradually fashioned the dance/music complex called rumba. Poor Cubans, both dark- and light-skinned, created a music and dance of their own, neither totally African nor totally Spanish, that utilized singing, drumming, and dancing in specific configurations and within specific rules.

Different types evolved depending on the circumstances of particular locales. One type, which developed in the urban areas of Havana and Matanzas provinces (there is much debate on exactly where), involved couple dancing. Another type, a male solo form, was produced in rural areas; it may have reflected the huge imbalance between males and females during the slave trade (cf. Moreno Fraginals, 1984:10-14). In the rural areas of Matanzas Province, especially near sugar mills, large African populations congregated both during and after slavery. The male solo type of rumba may be the result of the influence of the Carabalí (southeastern Nigerian male secret societies), which brought a tradition of male dancing to Cuba (Cabrera, 1958; Blier, 1980). Or the solo rumba may be part of the continuum of competitive male dances from Africa (Emery, 1972:27-29).

The rumba complex spread slowly throughout and beyond the country. Almost seventy years after its supposed beginnings in Cuba, rumba was taken to a trade fair in Seville, Spain. At the Chicago world's fair in 1933-34 (Jahn, 1961:84), rumba gained its first recorded performance outside Cuba.[11] Rumba, along with other Latin American dances, gained great popularity in the United States and Europe in the 1930s. Latin dance surfaced again in the international popular dance fads of the 1950s, and again in the 1970s and early 1980s.

In 1934 a movie called *Rumba*, starring George Raft, joined a series of feature films highlighting music and dance of Cuban origin as well as Raft's dancing ability. Filmed dance extravaganzas were created as part of the burgeoning U.S. interest in "exotic" dance, and Katherine Dunham's all-black dance company was commissioned to perform in a general Caribbean style, including rumba. The filmed dances were often variations on the original or traditional Cuban rumba.[12]

OBJECTIVES AND CARIBBEAN DANCE RESEARCH

The Hollywood version of rumba popularized the name of the dance internationally, but it also created misunderstanding and facilitated misinterpretation. In succeeding chapters I take the dance, rumba, and examine it from many angles to point out, ultimately, its meaning in contemporary Cuban society and its connections to nonaesthetic aspects of Cuban social life. The analysis demonstrates the kinds of influence rumba has, what it does and can do in particular settings. In the process of analyzing this one case, I also identify some of the ways dance is important and useful in contemporary societies. The consequences of expressive culture, the connections between a dance and seemingly divergent aspects of human social activity, reveal much about artistic forms and the societies from which they come.[13]

My study of rumba revealed how sparse the research has been on dance in Caribbean anthropology, which is curious when so much of Caribbean social life involves and accentuates dancing. In Cuba, dance is part of national, community, and family life. Political meetings and national holidays often emphasize dancing in parades and at rallies. Dance is instrumental in communication between the human and spirit worlds in the beliefs of many religious groups of Cuba. Furthermore, dance is a forceful and exciting mode of entertainment that generates income from tourists for a government in dire need of foreign exchange. Recreational dance serves to balance difficult daily conditions in a technologically limited and politically isolated society. Since dance cross-cuts so many spheres of Cuban life, it was surprising to find so few anthropological studies on Cuban dance.

My examination of rumba traces its development as expressive culture and looks at the social arena for explanations and consequences of change. Therefore my objectives are twofold: to provide an informed dance ethnography for the Caribbean region and to examine the relationship between dance and social change. This study analyzes the development of both Rumba as an event and rumba, the dance/music complex, with their variations and innovations since 1959. It shows how change in the dance indicates shifts in social currents and attempts to change cultural attitudes. Investigations center on three main factors: the use of dance and dance events for public ritual and ethnic and national identity; the manipulation of dance and dance events for special visitors or tourists by governmental agencies and entrepreneurial factions; and the removal of dances from their original religious context, the use of secular dance as an instrument of change. This study crystallizes the ways in which dance mediates the contradictions between ideals and reality in Cuba. It is about the dynamics of contexts as they are expressed in dance. It illustrates social conditions, constraints, and currents in Cuba from 1985 to 1990. It addresses artistic and anthropological issues through a careful examination of one kind of dance in a society of people who love dancing.

METHODS

It is by dancing that one can fully understand dance. By dancing Cuban dance traditions as an observing participant, by sharing critiques of Cuban dance, and by interviewing Cuban dancers and nondancers, I accumulated basic understandings of Cuban dance, rumba in particular. In these ways, discussions and evaluations were evoked, not only of dance criteria but simultaneously of expressed concerns in Cuban life. These methods, the mainstay of my investigation, verified discoveries made as a result of the more traditional anthropological approach as a participant observer.

Dancers who not only have earned their living by dancing but also have trained in anthropology have always impressed me. I have often recounted the story of Katherine Dunham's interview with representatives of the Rosenwald Foundation (for Caribbean research funding) in which she danced in an effort to make them truly understand the complexities of dance research. I have also witnessed the growth of interest in African dance through the performances of Pearl Primus as she, also artistically and anthropologically, examined dance cultures. And in my early studies I read the works of Joanne Kealiinohomoku, Drid Williams, and Judith Hanna, all of whom danced and were trained anthropologists.

I was also impressed by specific writers, apart from dance or anthropology, and their sensitivity to artistic forms within the mechanics of research. I gravitated toward Steven Feld's methods (1982) for the investigation of music in cultural context and Robert Farris Thompson's methods (1974, 1983) for sculptural and danced art (also see Salvador, 1975, and Graburn, 1976 and 1977, for visual art), and I have tried to use their studies as my methodological and inspirational models. These researchers focused on performed expressions that embody basic premises of a culture. Feld related mythology, human and natural sounds, social ethos, and sentiments and emotion in the understanding of Kaluli singing in Papua New Guinea. Thompson emphasized movement, encoded gestures, mythology, and proverbs in an explanation of African sculpture and masked dancing. Feld recommended that researchers establish a co-aesthetic relationship with the people of a culture, a sharing of aesthetic values and evaluations between investigator and informants through performance, which I had intuitively started doing. He played jazz for Kaluli consideration and enjoyment. Thompson played drums with African musicians-dancers (personal communication, 1977) and showed videos of dances for evaluation by several groups.

Dancing, which ultimately requires an observing participant rather than anthropology's orthodox participant observer, was the focus of the work and the main activity of the work. For the most part I danced in classes and in private as well as public spontaneous situations in which I was praised, evaluated, criticized, corrected, or ridiculed according to Cuban standards. When I was imitated, I discussed North American standards; when I was corrected, I had the opportunity to ask why. Feld suggested such interchange for a "more ethnographically informed or humanly sensitive understanding of other visual, musical, poetic, and choreographic systems" (1982:236). I also presented my own videos, films, and slides of Cuban dance and shared African-American styles of dance from the United States to elicit Cuban comments and evaluations.

I recorded examples of all forms of Cuban dance: ballet, modern, popular, and folkloric. I recorded as many dance events as possible, including performances, spontaneous dancing, rehearsals, and some audience response. I would have preferred to record classes where discussions of goals and criteria took place, where variation and criticism abounded, but this was curtailed early by administrators of dance companies who were fearful that taping or filming would violate Cuban choreographies in some way or, at the very least, exploit them for financial purposes. All dance segments were recorded by means of video 8, super-8 film, or 35-mm still cameras. Often I was able to show on television monitors what I had just recorded; thus I was able to hear, see, and feel aesthetic response, concern, interest, or disagreement. I was able to record accompanying music separately.[14]

I danced seven hours a day, six days a week, for most of one year. Equally important, I relied on discussions with Cubans about my dance experiences. I recorded few interviews and did not take copious notes. As a U.S. citizen in Cuba, I constantly feared that my work would be subject to counterrevolutionary charges or could inadvertently implicate others in problematic situations. Since I had no idea what my research would ultimately reveal, I kept a diary, made notes on particular interviews, and taped music, but I mostly videorecorded dance examples. The question I used most frequently was "What does rumba mean to you?" For this reason, the present text has a limited number of direct quotes. The voice of the Cuban people is not absent, however; nor is it a unitary call. Rather, because of my shared dance experiences, I can relay Cuban voices through details and intimacies within rumba analysis. In so doing, I write out a harmonious song of complex social life.

I lived the life of an average Cuban worker who happened to be a professional dancer in the National Folkloric company, training daily in chorus, gymnastics, and modern and folkloric techniques; observing rehearsals of traditional repertoire and new works in progress; and attending concerts, performances, and events that featured the company's dancers. In addition, I attended many events in Cuban life: national and cultural holidays, house parties, *toques de santos*, or religious festivities given in honor of the saints, and so on, where dancing took place. To augment my understanding of Cuban dance, I interviewed and studied privately with dancers, dance teachers, and dance researchers. I held informal discussions with other visual artists, musicians, art administrators, community members, and tourist industry personnel (people who outside Cuba would be viewed as booking agents, presenters, or entrepreneurs). These activities, in combination with my professional and personal background, yielded enormous data and understanding, as well as complex complications.[15]

When all the data were collected, I used the holistic framework of Allegra Fuller Snyder (1974, 1988) to organize material and to begin to analyze how dance interrelated with other spheres of Cuban social life. While I did not follow her example exactly in terms of its divisions within each level (according to time, space, and energy, as Cashion, 1980, approximated, for example), I followed Snyder's levels, which are several straightforward perspectives on the organization of dance material. While the levels are not mutually exclusive, the process of analyzing the data in terms of specified levels was instructive. I achieved an integrative assessment by first separating out important complementary factors and then identifying contrasting or contradictory issues. The framework's most important advantage is that it inhibits narrow, squeaky-clean fits. The framework forces the analyst to contend with contradictions or agreements between levels and to understand them in the reality of a dance—which, in this case, proved exceedingly helpful. I have interspersed the data derived from Snyder's levels throughout the book and have placed the labanotation in an appendix.[16]

While the process of analysis is static and freezes the dance artificially in the mind or on paper, it was helpful as a methodological step in understanding the whole of rumba. Dancing intensely for such an extended period in Cuba made me mindful of the difficulties in dissecting the whole of dance. The rich wholeness that I and other dancers and spectators often experience, i.e., that which the dance contains, is often lost in written analyses. The understandings gained through an emphasis on connections, process, and reintegration, however, offer added knowledge of, and hopefully appreciation for, the dance.

I begin in chapter 2 with a discussion of Cuban dance culture. This overview of the many dances that Cubans have inherited, created, and experienced documents Cuba's rich historical heritage and outlines the milieu in which rumba surfaced and in which it continues to live.

In chapter 3 I concentrate on people and examine the many world views within segments of the Cuban population. I present a glimpse of Cuban society, 1985-90. Those who love to dance, play, and sing rumba are seen within their contemporary ambiance.

In chapter 4 I present a specialist's description of the rumba complex, both music and dance. I detail rumba's structure: the types of dances; the actual movements; the dynamics of space, time, and energy that propel rumba performance; instrumentation; song style and form; and the secular ritual rumba exists within. I discuss types of performance practices and analyze public display and ritual intensity.

Chapter 5 turns from the dancer's or musician's concerns to identify social processes that connect society, the dance, and the dancers. It explains the linkage of dance and anthropology through rumba, taking my accumulated information and positing rumba as a symbol in contemporary Cuba, irrespective of the intentions of its advocates.

Chapter 6 concludes the book with an evaluation of rumba's efficacy and discusses the potential of dance that is consciously directed toward human and societal development.

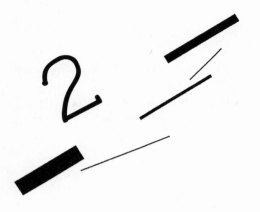

CUBAN
DANCE
CULTURE

It is important to see how rumba fits into Cuban life and to understand how it has fared in the history of the Cuban people. This chapter serves as a window onto the shaping of Cuban culture. It identifies the pattern of social interactions in Cuba, including dance and dance events, and discusses the formation of Cuban dance culture through a survey of those cultures that formed Cuba's dance matrix (see Kealiino-homoku, 1974:99-106). This overview of Cuban dance history will help the reader understand how rumba differs from other Cuban dances.[1]

THE PATTERN

The yearly cycle in Cuba is marked by set events, holidays, and festivals. The national calendar records this annual cycle, but a composite of other cycles, presented in the world-view circle, creates Cuba's culturally determined ordering of events, social, religious, and political (see Snyder, 1974:213-20, and 1978).[2]

The Cuban year begins on January 1 with celebration of the triumph of the 1959 Revolution and ends with New Year's Eve. The political and economic sphere of activity evolves from the anniversary of the Revolution to the year's first sugarcane harvesting and refining season (*zafra*), celebration of the Cuban worker (*Días federales*), the second sugarcane processing season, and the closing and opening of the cycle (*el año nuevo*).

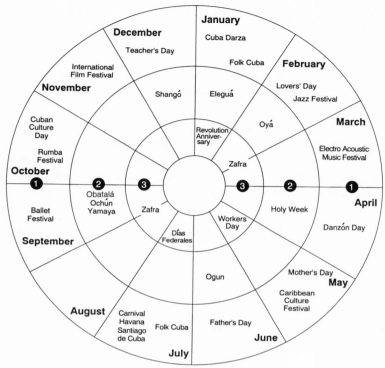

THE CUBAN WORLD VIEW

The religious cycle follows the general span of the year, whether seen from Christian, African, or Jewish viewpoints or from those of other practices, such as forms of Buddhism and yoga. The Cuban world-view chart reflects only the most visible religions, since to a great extent the belief system that characterized Cuba during the period of research was generally atheistic.[3]

Within the annual cycle, rumba is seen quite often. No other dance has such well-designated spots on the calendar. Rumba occurs reguarly or sporadically depending on the world-view and social position of the Cuban who is questioned, but in calendar time, rumba occurs frequently throughout the year.

CUBAN DANCES

For an overview of Cuban dance, particularly as it existed in 1986-87, I present the array of dances from the emic view, in the chronological order and historical framework that Cubans generally use when summarizing their dance culture: antecedent dances, national dances, and other influences. (I leave the analysis of rumba for the next chapter.) Olavo Alén (1984a), the Cuban musicologist, has organized the music of Cuba and its dance into five complexes, and Susan Cashion (1986), a North American dancer and anthropologist, has prepared a taxonomy of all the dances of Cuba. I have used both perspectives and the results of my own investigation in formulating a chart that situates rumba within Cuban dance culture (see the Cuban dances chart). I use Alén's terminology for musical organization (danzón complex, son complex, rumba complex).[4]

ANTECEDENTS

Indigenous

Indigenous culture in Cuba (and the Caribbean) has been documented through archaeological evidence, (see, for example, Steward, 1948) but more so in writings on the colonial period (for example, Dirección Política de las FAR, 1971; Knight, 1978; Bremer, 1851 [1980]; Carpentier, 1946 [1979]; Hernandez, 1980). After the arrival of the Spanish in 1492 and before the extermination of the indigenous peoples, many of the *conquistadores* vividly described the dance practices they witnessed in official reports and diaries (see Knight, 1978:1-22, and Hernandez, 1980:1-10).

The Spanish called the dance forms of the indigenous people *los areítos*, meaning Indian or indigenous dance and song (Hernandez, 1980). The purposes of these dances were to raise the spirits, bring success, and please the gods. Dance was based on an oral tradition of chorus and poetry that led to processional, choreographed dancing. Some choral and group dances used large groups of five hundred to one thousand men and women. A leader (*tequina*) began locomotor patterns (walking, jumping, hopping, stamping, turning, leg lifts), and everyone followed and imitated his step. At times, dancers held hands or locked elbows as they danced in procession; at other times they danced individually. The dance was very structured; dancers proceeded and then retreated a set number of steps. Utter exhaustion constituted the end of the areíto. That might take four or five hours or all day and night (Ortiz, 1951 [1985]:270; Hernandez, 1980:1-10).

Cuban Dances

ANTECEDENTS

Amerindian	Haitian
Areítos	Tumba Francesa
Spanish	Contredanse
Zapateo	
African	
Yorubá Complex	
Kongo Complex	
Arará Complex	
Carabalí Complex	

NATIONAL DANCES

Danzón Complex	Rumba Complex
Danzón	Yambú
Danzonete	Rumbas del Tiempo de España
Danzonchá	Mama'buela
Son Complex	Papalote
Son	Muñeca
Montuno	Gavilán
Guaracha	Karinga
Changüí	Guaguancó
Sucu-Sucu	Columbia
Mambo	Giribilla
Chachachá	Batarumba
Mozambique	Zapateo Cubano
Casino	Chancleta
	Campesino
	Doña Joaquina
	Zumbantorio

OTHER INFLUENCES

Haitian	North American
Gagá	Modern Dance
European	
Ballet	

The conquerors considered areítos pagan, boisterous frolic and did little to understand the special ceremonies. Rather, they made a concerted effort to change indigenous life and to teach new and presumably better ideas. They persuaded, then coerced indigenous peoples to live in a system of slavery. These peoples' dances are no longer performed in Cuba.[5]

Spanish

After the Spanish entered the area in the last decade of the fifteenth century, indigenous culture quickly disappeared as it encountered superior military strength (in horses and armor), the debilitating effects of *encomienda* organization (plantation lands that were organized originally for the profit of colonial armies), and the annihilating consequences of disease. The Spanish began to settle Cuba in 1509. Spain offered its countrymen land incentives for four years of settlement work in the Americas (Guerra y Sanchez, 1964 [1970]:22-33) and promoted colonization with land grants to powerful and influential explorers, military men, church officials, and landless workers and sailors (Dirección Política de las FAR, 1971:24). The Spanish Crown closely associated conquest and settlement because of its earlier success in distributing conquered lands to the Spanish poor (Knight, 1978:23-50). The rulers had learned from their African adventures that people do not easily give up lands that are destined to become their own. Settlement created physical and emotional barriers against potential threats of invasion.

After serving their indentured years, however, most of the Spanish settlers left Cuba for the mainland, interested in Aztec and Inca gold. Some did stay to raise cattle on large ranges and learned to plant tobacco and grow citrus fruits, peppers, and various staples in the lush and productive soil.

From the fifteenth to the eighteenth century, Cuba was developed in *latifundios*, primarily large cattle ranges given as land grants, and *estancias*, small provision lands. Lands allocated and divided in this way created a national foundation of both large- and small-scale proprietors, most of them attached to their own lands, raising livestock, cultivating small plots or ranges, and trading hides, cattle stuffs, and agriculture products with the ships that came once or twice a year. These settlements were significantly different from later English, French, Dutch, and Portuguese entries in the area. Other colonials came purely for exploration and exploitation, paying little attention, at least for many years, to long-term settlement. According to Franklin Knight,

> The pattern of society existing in 1509 in Espanola (Santo Domingo) also presaged the future for Spanish colonization in the New World. At the top in social esteem and in political power wielded through the village councils were the arrogant Spanish settlers. These were a variegated group, dominated by Andalucians. . . . Contrary to popular belief, only a few of these immigrants were criminals. A substantial number were decent, honest, hard-working individuals who were out to seek a

fortune or to find a better life. . . . The Spanish men who ventured to the Indies represented a cross section of their metropolitan society and a wide range of the medieval motivations for territorial expansion and military strife. . . . Entire families moved with wives, children and servants following the men to maintain the structure and organization of the expansion taking place since the middle of the fourteenth century on the southern Iberian frontiers. (1978:27-28)

For many years, Cuba, unlike the non-Hispanic Caribbean islands, had a predominantly white settlement, primarily around the earliest ports of the island: Baracoa, Trinidad, Sancti Spíritus, Havana, Bayamo, Santiago de Cuba, and Santa María de Puerto Príncipe. A fairly long history of farming, ranching, and family life was established before the introduction of sugarcane or the plantation system. With the introduction of sugarcane between 1590 and 1600, an important demographic change began; however, the social impact of sugar plantations in Cuba was exceedingly slow. Elsewhere in the Caribbean, sugar production and consequent slave population density had created a black majority. In Cuba, sugar was not as common nor as profitable as cattle until the nineteenth century. Although some areas were demographically African, Cuba maintained a large European-American population well into the twentieth century (Ortiz, 1963; Guerra y Sanchez, 1970; Knight, 1970, 1978:93-120; Mintz, 1964, 1971, 1975; Klein, 1967).

It is pertinent in discussing Cuba's Spanish heritage to mention the black persons of Spanish descent. These Spanish Africans were brought from Spain to Cuba; thus African influence came from Spain as well as from Africa. As Knight states,

Africans had accompanied the Spanish explorers and colonists to the Caribbean from the beginning of the age of exploration. An indefinite number arrived with the expedition of Nicolas de Ovando in 1502. By 1516 Spanish-speaking Africans—most likely born in Spain—had already outnumbered the true Spanish colonists. . . . The Spanish Crown abandoned the cautious scruples that had inhibited the selling of non-Christians in their American possessions, and in 1518 Charles V sanctioned the monopolistic commerce of non-Spanish-speaking Africans shipped directly to the Antilles. The trans-Atlantic slave trade then began in earnest. (1978:46)

Between the sixteenth and mid-eighteenth centuries, Spain gave less attention to the island territories than to the gold-filled mainland. The Hispanic Caribbean thereby experienced economic isolation and an increase in the free colored, or mulatto, sector.[6] The free population of color, a result of intermarriage between Africans and Europeans, increased as a demographic entity mainly by liberal slave codes on manumission, as part of Catholic belief and Hispanic practice. As Cuban sugar production increased in the eighteenth and nineteenth centuries, however, the need for massive slave importation grew and slave populations began to outnumber free mulattoes and whites (Mintz, 1964:xv-xvi, xxiii; Williams, 1970 [1984]:46-57).

The Catholic Church and the Caribbean slave plantation environment set boundaries of shape, structure, and form in Cuban dance. At first, Cuban dances of Spanish heritage were variations on forms from Andalucía and the Canary Islands (León, 1984a:95-118, Hernandez, 1980:12-20; Chao Carbonero and Lamerán, 1982:23-27). These dances were products of evolution; their forms changed slightly, but they remained significantly close to their European origins. It should be emphasized that their European origin was mixed with North African culture before coming to the Americas and that in song and dance, the Spanish had already combined elements from Spain and Africa (Alén, 1984). As Ortiz has stated (in Carpentier, 1946 [1979]:48), "Songs, wild dancing, and music came and went, i.e., flowed between Andalucía, the Americas, and Africa, and Havana was the center where the rainbow's hottest and most polychromatic hues blended" (my translation).

Public dancing occurred on secular festive days, for marriages of the elite, military victories, notices of royal births in Spain. In Havana's Plaza de las Armas on saint's days, people celebrated in processions; each *cofradía* (trade guild, fraternity—black or white—or local organization under a patron saint) would advance toward and dance in front of, sometimes inside, the church. Dancing to Christmas carols within farces and comedies was authorized by the church until the middle of the seventeenth century (Moreau de St.-Méry, 1796 [1976]:65; Labat, 1724, vol. 2:54).

The dances, related to sixteenth- and seventeenth-century European dance forms (*chaconas* and *zarabandas*), are described as "languid dances, always sensual, where the dancers 'appear to offer their bodies or give themselves' by raising a handkerchief or picking up an apron with two hands and raising it to the neck, on the shoulders, on the hand and going on tiptoes like a Creole rumba dancer might do today with the edge of her dress. . . . The flirtatious girl . . . raises her skirt while dancing in front of the youth she most likes" (Carpentier, 1946 [1979]:49; my translation). Other descriptions tell of four men and four women making shaking or wiggling gestures, presenting certain attitudes and looks, giving embraces, and pressing belly to belly (Hernandez, 1980:16).

These descriptions provide evidence of an important element of African dance that came from Spain as well as from Africa: separation of males and females while dancing. This element contrasts with one that later became characteristic of many dance forms in the Caribbean islands, including Cuba: partner dancing. African style allowed the male to pursue the female and allowed the female to permit momentary closeness; but it did not allow holding on or dancing together in a closed position, i.e., as partners, as was typical of Spanish heritage or European dance.

Accounts dating from the eighteenth century document another type of Spanish influence. *Zapateo* was one of the most typical Spanish dances in Cuba, and in a very limited fashion it continues today. Zapateo is an entire dance but also a particular step within the dance that developed as an integral part of dance traditions in many parts of Latin America, including Mexico, El Salvador, and Argentina. The dance's name comes from the Spanish word meaning shoe, *zapato*, and refers to the rhythmic sound of shoes beating against a wooden floor (exemplified most notably in modern theatricalized flamenco dancing). This form originated in the Gypsy culture of southern Spain, the region of the Andalucian settlers of Cuba, and in Cuba it became a rural or *campesino* form primarily.

In contemporary Cuba, zapateo is a historical dance performed to commemorate Cuba's Spanish origins, but it is not danced by the general public (see the Cuban dances chart under "National Dances"). It is now preserved by cultural institutions that operate at the professional and amateur levels, providing opportunities for zapateo to be recognized and remembered. Unlike rumba, however, it is not promoted in festivals; nor has it been performed routinely within any segment of the population in contemporary times.

Another group of Cuban dances cited for their Spanish heritage and continuing today are *las rondas infantiles* (Hernandez, 1980:19). These children's dances are choral forms that utilize circles, lines, and zigzag floor patterns, often encircling one child or more than one in the center of a circle. They have a collective character and are performed by girls, boys or mixed groups.

African

Cuban dances of African heritage are evolved variations of African dances that come from many cultural areas within Africa. The dominant Spanish culture of Cuba in its early stages set boundaries of shape, structure, and form for the dance, but African culture from Africa (as opposed to Spanish-African) had an immense influence on the content of dance structures. New World plantation owners did not have the resources or the inclination to comply with Old World Spanish directives that affected daily life. Therefore African influence flourished and became more pronounced than might have been expected.

Enslaved Africans had a continuous influence on Cuba after 1518, and particuarly after 1700, through 1886 (Moreno Fraginals, 1977 [1984]:5; Knight, 1978:48). During these years, massive numbers of new arrivals kept a persistent and forceful garden of African culture growing wherever and whenever they could in the nooks and crannies of overwhelming colonial authority and restriction. These numbers gave Cuba limitless possibilities of direct African influence for more than two hundred years.

Cuba really began its huge increase in slaves and sugarcane production in the aftermath of the Haitian revolution (1791-1802), when there was great speculation in sugar processing as well as great fear of black insurrection (James, 1938; Knight, 1970; Deschamps Chapeaux, 1971; Duarte Jimenez, 1988). On one hand, plantation owners tried to deculturate the slave population, to strip it of identity, cohesion, and dignity, so as to secure a work force that was totally dependent on the white planter class (Moreno Fraginals 1977 [1984]; Deschamps Chapeaux, 1971). On the other hand, the planter class organized slaves into preestablished ethnic groups to provide a source of self-protection against possible slave rebellion. This organization was initiated for economic reasons, to maximize production and increase colonial profit, but over time it was done for other reasons. The authorities thought that factionalism among enslaved ethnic groups would lessen the danger to outnumbered whites, so black *cabildos* were tolerated. Cabildos were homogeneous African ethnic groups that, like Spanish guild associations, operated as mutual aid societies or lodges. Eventually cabildos consolidated multiple African ethnic groups and solidified African culture in Cuba (León, 1984a:11-15; Cabrera, 1958 [1970]).

African cabildos in Cuba conserved several African languages, ritual practices, belief systems, dances, songs and chants, and instruments and instrument-making techniques. They contributed to the crystallization of certain African dance/music concepts in the Americas: that music and dance are not primarily entertainment forms; that music and dance are interdependent; that their structure utilizes both set and improvisational elements; that complexity and depth are built by the layering and interfacing of small, simple, diverse units; that the human body is paramount (Alén, 1984a:1; León, 1984a:7-32; Millet and Brea, 1989:7-11; cf. Wilson, 1981:1-23).

Though we know that some dances, such as *ziripá* (Ortiz, 1951 [1985]:431) and *juego de maní* (Ortiz, 1951 [1985]:396-429; Leon, 1984:71-73), did not survive the centuries of resistance and assimilation that Africans experienced, four major branches of African influence in Cuban dance have survived: Yoruba, Kongo-Angolan, Arará, and Carabalí (Ortiz, 1951 [1985]; León, 1984a:13; Thompson, 1974; Martinez-Furé, 1986).[7] In Cuba these terms are major equivalent roots of Afro-Cuban culture; in Africa they refer to cultural groups, territories, linguistic groups, and ancient kingdoms. Yoruba influence is primary in the western and northwestern regions of Cuba and secondary in eastern Cuba. Kongo-Angolan influence is primary in the central and eastern regions, secondary in the west. Arara is found in the northwestern and eastern regions. Its dance culture is similar in Cuba to Yoruba culture, and the two groups share common dances. Carabalí is found mostly in the northwest (Dailey, ca. 1950:180; Hernandez, 1980:20).

Día de los Reyes dancing is important because this festive occasion provided early examples of distinct African nations or cabildos which were transported to the Americas. This annual celebration facilitated the slow process of transculturation where Spanish and African cultures meshed to form a new Cuban culture. On the Day of the (Three) Kings, January 6, Epiphany of the Catholic calendar, the church and Spanish civil authorities encouraged a collective praying in the streets with music, dance, and masking. This was a substitute for the earlier celebration of Corpus Christi in May, which was deemed too serious an ecclesiastic event to permit black festive participation (León, 1984a:35-37). On Día de los Reyes, processional displays were presented to governing captains, their entourages, and church officials in return for gifts that had been given to slave and free black workers as Christmas presents. Each cabildo was organized to perform its special songs and dances as representations of the group. Lucumí, Congo, Náñigo, Mandingo, Arará, and so on dressed in costumes with peacock feathers, tutus, high silk hats, face paints, sailors' uniforms, grass skirts; they marched and danced to the drums of their "king" and "queen," personages who were selected to lead each cabildo. The celebration was the most festive occasion for the enslaved peoples of colonial times, as they were essentially free for the day. They joined free blacks and celebrated their ancestors and heritages to the extent that they could.

Through the years, Afro-Cubans have danced in festive and symbolic clothing to suggest their allegiance to neighborhood collectives (Ortiz, 1951 [1985]:273-90). Groups called red bands and blue bands (*bandas rojas y bandas azules*) performed staged battles (Martinez-Furé, 1961; cf. Morán in Chao Carbonero and Lamerán, 1982:155-56). These dances of African origins combined parading, group battles with mock competition, and dances of male pursuit and female coquetry. Remnants of competing bands are found around New Year's Day in Matanzas in the form of competing rumba groups that often wear red and blue coordinated outfits.

Competitive dances developed and continue to be performed at various contemporary events, such as the opening or closing of festivals, New Year's celebrations, and particularly national and provincial carnivals. Many of them take their names from the Kongo-Angolan branch of African influence, congas or *comparsas*. In contemporary Havana on July 26 and 27, the carnival comparsa, also called *conga de Habana*, occurs. Groups organize floats and parading bands to march in front of a centrally located, raised stand of onlookers. At the climax of this spectator event, prizes are awarded to the best musical and dance groups. In Santiago de Cuba on July 25 and 26, commonly called *conga de Santiago*, the more traditional form of conga or comparsa continues its participatory but still competitive dance and music display (Evleshin, 1989).

Each African branch in Cuba has a tradition of religious dances. Often these dances reveal an intra-African syncretism, the transformation over time of differing African religious and ethnic traditions owing to their proximity and interaction. Separate cultural traditions were affected by the ruptures of slavery and utilized the often parallel structures of neighboring religious systems (Walker, 1980:32-36). For example, in Africa, Kongo-Angolan belief did not focus on cosmic spirits, or *orishas* (MacGaffey, 1968; Thompson, 1981), but Cuban descendants of Kongo-Angolan culture have syncretized some of their spirits with those of Yoruba and Dahomean belief. The shared deities perform dances that are similar, though there are stylistic and rhythmical differences. In these African-American systems, devotees call upon the deities in prayer, songs, drumming, and dances, giving themselves to ceremonial possession by ancestor and cosmic spirits for the resultant spiritual experience and congregational advice (see Walker, 1972).[8] Ortiz reports the similarities and sharing that occurred in Cuba (1951: 381-87, cf. Barnet, 1961 and Feijóo, 1986).

One other distinct group of dances comes from a pronounced African heritage: Carabalí, or Abakuá.[9] These dances, which find their legacies in secret societies from the Calabar region of Africa, have been transported, replicated, and transformed to a certain extent to fit the social environment of Cuba (Cabrera, 1958 [1970]; Sosa, 1984; Blier, 1980). Abakuá dancing reenacts stories of mysterious beings who communicate through postures, gestures, movement motifs, and the intangible expressiveness of the *íreme* (*diablito*, or spirit) masks. The masked dancers command respect and awe; they affirm secret society attitudes and values. Their dances in the *plante*, or society meetings place, are some of the most intensely moving of all Cuban traditional dance forms (Chao Carbonero and Lamerán, 1982:95-101).

Haitian

Many history texts neglect the importance of Haiti in the cultural development of other Caribbean islands, and as a result the existence of Haitian dance in Cuba comes as a surprise to many. Haiti has exerted great influence on Cuba because of two major migrations of Haitians, one at the end of the eighteenth century and the other at the beginning of the twentieth century.

Those from the first migration trace descent from French colonial families. Many French plantation owners brought their families and their slaves from Haiti to Cuba. As a result, several Cuban provinces are associated with Haitian roots as well as with the formation of Cuban culture: Camagüey, Matanzas, Santiago de Cuba, Holguín, Guantánamo, and Granma. As the Haitian revolution grew imminent, there was an exodus of French colonials, Creole plantation owners, and both African and Creole slaves. This first wave of French or French-Haitian influence centered in eastern and central Cuba, but with a significant thrust in one western province, Matanzas, where French colonials from Louisiana Territory in the United States also participated in the migration (Pedro, 1986; Knight, 1970:12; Fernandez, 1986; Alén, 1987a:9-15). It is the eastern provinces and the French-Haitians, however, that are mainly responsible for several Cuban dance traditions. Cuban authorities of the Spanish Crown authorized immigration of French families both from Haiti and Louisiana. They encouraged white settlement in the eastern regions in hopes of increasing the racial balance of that area (Alén, 1987a:12-13; Knight, 1970:33, 68-72, 181 ff.).

When French and Creole colonists (French people in this case who were born in the Americas) fled Haiti, they brought the *contredanse* to Cuba. The name *Contradanse* quickly became *contradanza* owing to the encouragement with which the French were welcomed in eighteenth century Cuba and because of the popularity and excitement of the dance itself. The French migration to Cuba brought elite culture with entertainment and recreation as important social activities. Dance schools taught line formations and circle figures, imitative of court dancing in Europe, which was heavily influenced by French culture.

Africans and black Creoles who came with the French colonists brought their version of the contredanse also. Drums, poetic song, antiphonal song form, and imitations of colonial elite dance were the elements that had already begun to transform the contredanse while in Haiti; line dances were performed to drum batteries, later called *affranchis*. This French-Haitian dance structure, in Cuba during a period when Cuban culture was not yet formed, became a new ingredient for the growing recipe of Cuban dance. The French-Haitian ingredient is called *tumba francesa*, the distinct musical and dance tradition of black French-Haitians (Alén, 1987a; León, 1984a:21-23; Rigal, 1991; Gordo, 1985).

NATIONAL DANCES

During the nineteenth century, Cubans gradually gained a voice in their own affairs. Cuba's distinctive culture was shaped during this century in the midst of a cattle-breeding and cash crop economy, a developing sugarcane industry, and an emerging coffee industry. Because of the interest in and possibility of enormous profits in sugar and coffee, colonial Cuba was in the difficult position of confronting opposition from the Spanish court. Cubans could not count on Spain as a market or as a funding support as time progressed, and Spain could not count on Cuban colonials for allegiance or income.

Cuba's position as a nation became clear as a result of concerns that were different from other Caribbean islands and because of the creolization process, the formation of something new from disparate parts owing to particular environmental conditions and political and economic interests. As noted, when other Caribbean societies were trying to develop markets other than sugarcane and were decreasing the use of slave labor, Cuba was more interested in sugarcane production, sugar refinement, and the consequent slave labor force that these types of production entailed.

By the beginning of the nineteenth century, the elements of foreign cultures within Cuba had formed definite affinities and positions with relation to one another. Many elements meshed, then crystallized to form a new creole culture. From the dance perspective, the result was the fashioning of new dances with a new style, dances that were neither African, Spanish, Haitian, nor indigenous American but national and creole.[10]

Cubans developed the European contredanse and its Cuban derivative, contradanza, to create a completely new form, a Cuban form, *danza*. The contradanza, like the minuet and quadrille, had used passing and turning formulas that led couples in line and circle formations, usually with bows and greetings. This was the kind of group dance that was practiced in Cuban dance schools of the eighteenth century. Danza, on the other hand, allowed independent couples to hold each other throughout the dance and to use individual couple floor patterns. More important to the new style, Cubans slowed down the tempo and added more hip accentuation as a result of a gliding or sliding step. This demonstrated taste and preference but also the blending of an African emphasis on body part isolation (hip, in this case), a European musical form, and a French-Haitian dance structure.

Danzón, another Cuban creation, developed danza through slow tempo, subtlety, and sensuality. It was and still is a dance and music form incorporating a walking sequence that alternates with a danced sequence every eight measures. The walking or resting period, a musical section, gives the dancers time to adjust to dancing in a humid, tropical climate and permits socializing among the dancing couples. It also allows time for sexual tensions aroused by close partnering to subside.

In their beginnings, danzón and danza generated prejudice and antagonism against Afro-Cubans and their music/dance. A controversy ensued over the Cubanisms of the dances and the immorality they suggested. As critics remarked, "For some time . . . we have been reading your pretended defense of *la danza* and *el danzón*, dances which you and others call Cuban, when they are really a degeneration of the African *tango*. . . ." "Mothers who have daughters, inspire in them an aversion for dance. Make war against all sensual dance. Ask for the *lancer*, the *rigodón*, the *quadrille*, and the *cotillion*, but never *danza* nor the inferno of feelings which are called *danzón*" (Faílde, 1964:145-46, 153; my translation).

Danzón became the national dance of nineteenth-century Cuba (Carpentier, 1946 [1979]:189; Martinez-Furé, 1986; Moliner, 1986; Urfé, 1948, and n.d.). The overwhelming tenacity and popularity of danzon demonstrated the integration of Spanish and African elements in the late nineteenth century. Danzón symbolized the unique position of Cuba in its confrontation with Spain during its War of Independence in 1895-98. Artistically it marked a separation from colonial domination and the emergence of independent Cuban thought.

The danzón complex—danza, danzón, danzonchá, and danzonete—is a group of social, popular, couple dances that reflect elite society of nineteenth-century salons. The salons, however, were those in which Afro-Cuban musicians played a significant role as accompanists for dancing and in which African movement characteristics were accentuated and ultimately accepted. The mulatto and black musicians who played in the orchestras of the elite interspersed rhythmic motifs, alternative instrumentation, and improvisation. These compositional and stylistic elements changed the feeling and form of European music in Cuba and effected change in the dances as well (Carpentier, 1946 [1979]:106-19, 231-42).

Cubans look to the *son* complex as one of the most pervasive of Cuban expressions in both the music and dance systems (see Alén, 1987c; León, 1984a:119-45; Carpentier, 1946 [1979]:192-95). No one is sure of its date of origin, but evidence points to the mid 1800s, around the same time the rumba originated. Son signifies a particular kind of rhythm, instrumentation, manner of dance, and song style in Cuba, but generally refers to popular dance music that distinguishes the general Caribbean area (Carpentier, 1946 [1984]:192).[11] It has its origins in open-air, collective occasions among rural folk and the cattle-farming families in Cuba; but it can also be played with a minimum number of people, a man with his guitar usually, both in urban and rural areas.

Sones evolved out of the intermittent reunions and celebrations among small agricultural workers with their need for recreation. They used string instruments: guitar, *tres, bandurria,* or all three; a *botija* (ceramic jar that is blown like a jug) or a *marímbula* (a plucked percussion instrument); and eventually the *bongos, maracas,* and trumpet. The song form employs a repeated chorus or refrain (*montuno*), which alternates with a soloist's verse. Lyrical improvisation on varied topics used to be standard, but a closed or set part of a son was introduced before the montuno, which gave the topic and main idea of the song and limited the possibilities of variation later.

Many Cubans claim that son is the national dance of Cuba because more Cubans dance son and its variations than any other Cuban dance. Based in partnering and spatial designs, this originally rural form combined with dance currents of the urban salons to produce a dance/music form that included the zest and fervor of Cuban rural workers when they relaxed as well as the sensuous, close partnering and lilting style of the salons. Although son began with rural farmers, today it is not limited to any segment of the population or region of Cuba (Orozco, 1984:363-89).

Son, in its development at the beginning of the twentieth century, opened the closed partnering of the previous ball and salon dances and allowed individual couples to alternate between closed couple position and independent but still very closely related positions. When the thick-textured polyrhythms and the embroidered improvisational playing of standard orchestras and bands were added, it became the founding skeleton of Latin American social and popular music/dance.

Today what is called *salsa* finds its antecedents in the son music/dance complex of Cuba. Mambo, *chachachá, mozambique,* and *casino* are twentieth-century dance types within the son complex, with slightly different style and slightly different rhythms that affect the feeling of each dance.

The dance form that evolved in contrast to the son complex of the salons and dance halls was *la rumba* (Alén, 1987b). It was a dance of the lower classes performed primarily in the streets and barrios of urban areas. It included political comment on the life conditions of enslaved and free but poor black and white workers. It appeared in the middle of the nineteenth century, but it is not known which type evolved first or where this occurred. (See chapter 4 for its full description and analysis. Also see Ortiz, 1951 [1985]:426, 432-33; Hernandez, 1980:49-53; Chao Carbonero and Lamerán, 1982:113-122; Alén, 1987b).

In addition to creations from the public, folk, or social sphere, Cubans created a unique variant of modern dance for the concert stage. After the Revolution, amid the effort to define that which is Cuban, the movement and technique of the Cuban National Modern Dance Company, or Danza Nacional, was organized (Guerra, 1989; Geraldo Lastra, personal communications, 1986, 1987; Victor Cuellar, personal communication, 1987). The predominance of torso-initiated movement and undulations in both ordinary Cuban motor behavior and extraordinary dance movements came ultimately from the matrix of dances that emerged as Cuban creole creations, as *Cubanía* or Cubanness.

Simultaneously there was a conscious search for and reformulation of the techniques of Martha Graham, Doris Humphrey, and José Limon to fit Cuban tastes and style. This move, led by Ramiro Guerra, choreographer of the pioneering modern dance company, included Eduardo Rivera and Geraldo Lastra, among other choreographers and dancers. (For reviews of Cuban modern dance development, see Hernandez, 1980:136-40; Cashion, 1988:15-28.) The folklore of Cuba was used as thematic material, and the folkloric dances (Yoruba, Kongo-Angolan, and so on) were used as movement motifs that were fully embroidered and developed, as in "Suite Yoruba" and "Okantomi," by Cuban choreographer Eduardo Rivero.

These elements make up only a part of the imaginative and innovative repertoire in the Cuban National Modern Dance Company today. A great deal of interest in learning this unique concert style has arisen in recent years from Finland and Switzerland to Mexico and the United States.[12]

OTHER INFLUENCES

Several other cultures have contributed to Cuban dance, especially Haitian (as opposed to French-Haitian), North American, and non-Spanish European cultures. Some have made significant impressions on Cuban dance systems. What has resulted is not new or creole creations but dances that are Cubanized.

Haitian

In addition to the first wave of Haitians and French colonials, interisland migration reports often showed Haitians moving to Cuba for jobs in the sugarcane industry, in particularly large numbers during the first quarter of the twentieth century (Pedro, 1967, 1986; Knight, 1978:173; Fernandez, 1986). These Haitians are now Cubans, but many of them still identify with their historical heritage in Haiti (Gordo, 1985). Their cultural expressions are regarded as Haitian expressions that give their influence to Cuba, that is, as Haitian-Cuban forms. Haitian-Cubans emphasize *gagá*, a dance tradition different from the French-Haitian tumba francesa, and gagá is recognized throughout Cuba. Cuban musicologists and ethnologists have examined the French-Haitian contribution to Cuban music (e.g., Alen, 1987a) and are now studying Haitian influences on Cuban culture, including dance (for example, La Casa del Caribe and Instituto de sciencias; see Pedro, 1967, 1986).[13]

European

Within the hierarchical structure of Cuban society during the nineteenth century and through the first half of the twentieth century, ballet was the style of dance that was revered ideologically and supported financially. Folkloric forms were ignored in the concern sphere, and modern dance styles were fledgling, avant-garde endeavors. European-American influence on Cuban dance was demonstrated in urban centers, primarily Havana. Bourgeois and elite patrons were entertained in formal concerts. Ballet training for wealthy and predominantly light-skinned students in private academies resulted in recitals, cotillions, coming-out parties, and benefit performances for hospitals and universities. Classical training usually involved study in Europe or the United States until the formation of the Pro-Arte Musical Society of Havana in 1918 (Hernandez, 1980; Cashion, 1980).[14]

Despite its elite history, ballet in Cuba has been praised for gradually embracing the goals of the revolutionary masses. A *New York Times* article concluded some time ago that ballet's discipline, hard work, and dedication to a task are what contemporary Cuban ideology supports (Copeland, 1978). Contemporary Cuban ballet gives striking examples of the social changes that have occurred in Cuba in terms of the racial segregation that existed before the Revolution. Black and mulatto ballet students and professional dancers are found in significant numbers and status within ballet organizations today. But a heavy preferential cloud still surrounds ballet when it is compared with folkloric and modern dance. That is due in part to the long history of professionalism within ballet but also to the deference given to its established star, Alicia Alonso. Mechanisms to minimize these conditions, such as equal intitutional status of all dance companies and comparable salaries for principal dancers and members of the corps, are also present.

North American

During the first half of the twentieth century, Cuba was used as a playground for U.S. business, diplomatic, and artisitic communities. North American trends, fashions, and styles permeated Cuban radio, press, film industry, and literary circles. These currents brought changes in Cuban popular music and dance that were admired both domestically and abroad and were quickly integrated into North American movies, the record industry, and, later, television.

North American promoters and producers ultimately diluted Cuban social and popular dance forms for commercial purposes. Authenticity in terms of regional variation was disregarded; often any Latin-looking dance was called a rumba or a conga (see Veloz and Yolanda, 1938; Luis, 1942; American Rumba Committee, 1943; Shahin, 1944; Rodriguez Savon, 1945; Barry, 1953; Astaire, 1955; and Dance Guild, Inc., 1956). The characteristic thick, intricate, rhythmic texture of Cuban percussion decreased; costumes were not always indicative of each region. In fact, people did not differentiate between nations, between Cuban rumba, Brazilian samba, Haitian meringue, or Trinidadian carnival dance, for example. Eurocentric versions of dance became standard. Social music and popular dance were commercialized for popular consumption both in the United States and in Cuba.[15]

Conversely, in the concert and educational arenas, dance from the United States was instrumental in the development of authentic Cuban forms. The pioneers of American modern dance, one of the two indigenous arts of the United States,[16] focused on the body's natural movements and the portrayal of the psychological aspects of human life, as well as on independence in terms of content and form, sound and movement. What was considered interesting and exciting in the ballet era of the nineteenth century was eclipsed by choreographies that were often rhythmically irregular and angular, off balance and asymmetrical, and alternating or shifting in feeling.

Doris Humphrey[17] was an indirect but important influence on Cuban modern dance because she worked intensively with José Limon, who later worked in Cuba (see Mahler, Guerra, and Limon, 1978). She was a famous teacher who influenced many North American professional dancers, including two who traveled to Cuba and influenced Cuban dance and dance training for more than forty years: Elfrida Mahler and Lorna Burdsall. Mahler was praised as a teacher who trained a great many Cuban students in the "American" art of modern dance. Burdsall became a member in the early years of the Cuban National Modern Dance Company and has influenced choreographic and technical aspects for over thirty years.

Cuban dance also was influenced tremendously by international interaction, particularly from Elena Noriega of Mexico's National Dance Company. She was another influential teacher who brought North American modern dance concepts and technique to Cuba (Hernandez, 1980:137).

(In summary, from a dance perspective, Spanish, African, and Haitian cultures were particularly important to Cuba because they formed its dance matrix. These cultures had more than an influence on Cuba; they were instrumental over time in the very formation of Cuban dance culture. (Indigenous dance was not significant in the creation of Cuban dances.) The dances came from these differing people and shifted slightly or evolved in Cuba's new environment in terms of instrumentation, costuming, staging, accoutrements, or accompanying systems of belief; but essentially the dance movement retained the native identity of the dances.) Some, like Abakuá and *orisha* dances, remained intact owing to secrecy and the absolute desire to guard and maintain an important measure of ancient culture. Others, like tumba francesa, continued an evolution that would have occurred, although differently, in their native lands. These dances provided the important germinal layer from which a distinct Cuban culture grew and produced new forms.

Ortiz (relying on Herskovits, 1941; cf. Pratt, 1992) used the term *transculturation* to refer to the processes of destruction, retention, reinterpretation, and interpenetration of cultures in Cuba (1940 [1963]:98-103, 1950, 1951 [1985]). Transculturation included the destruction of indigenous cultures; retention of some Spanish, African, and French-Haitian elements; and reinterpretation and interpenetration of others that supported the new forming cultural entity. All matrix cultures pronounced their distinctness to one another annually in the early years of Cuban culture formation. Later, political and economic isolation created an interdependent social sphere. Diverse dance cultures became the core of an integrated whole in a Cuban aesthetic and artistic system.

The emergence of new Cuban dance forms from this dance matrix demonstrates the human need to express ideas, attitudes, and feelings in dance movement that are meaningful to the space, time, and values of individuals and groups with these heritages. New forms, from contradanza, son, and rumba to ballet and modern dance, signaled a reality that integrated the island's history and its present in human movement. These Cuban creations were further influenced by other dance currents from foreign lands.

CUBAN
PEOPLE
AND
RUMBEROS

This chapter focuses on differing world views in contemporary Cuba that have developed within segments of the Cuban population because of Cuba's colonial history, distinct socioeconomic environment, and unique political status. These world views differ in terms of dance and thereby present distinct evaluations of rumba.

THE PEOPLE: A MÉLANGE OF WORLD VIEWS

The simplest way to reveal Cuban world views and the behavioral patterns they produce is to describe typical situations in composite form. I generalize Cuban world views based on categories of people I came in contact with from Havana to Caimito in Havana Province, in Camaguey in the central provinces, and in Santiago, Media Luna, and Barrancas in the eastern provinces, Oriente. These contacts augmented and crosscut my main connections within the artistic community.

At the time of my research, Cuba was isolated from the United States and Europe but well connected to the Soviet Union and the East European nations. I saw evidence of long-term settlement of Soviet workers, mostly in Havana but also in other large cities throughout the island. These Soviet workers formed my first particularized world view in Cuba because, interestingly, they represented the ideal political-economic perspective of most Cubans and yet their life-styles (which I viewed as a fellow long-term foreign worker) reflected little of Cuba's social views and values. They lived and socialized in rather closed communities, although a few fraternized with Cubans. Many Cubans had traveled to the Soviet Union for extensive technical training, and a few of these women and men had married Soviet citizens and returned to Cuba. A great many young Cubans spoke Russian, and many Cuban households displayed Russian dolls or nested painted bowls as emblems of their contact.

For me, the Soviet presence in Cuba seemed to create a transparent veil over the island's Caribbean culture. I thought that the Soviets were responsible for the officious pretense I found among older Cubans, an attitude that sometimes faded the bright spirit I had come to know throughout the Caribbean. This aura of officialdom and bureaucracy may have been a recent example of creole culture, a result of thirty years of Soviet-Cuban contact, but the veil may in fact have been very Cuban, because it certainly characterized many Cuban business, academic, and political-military settings.[1]

After work hours, however, and at home, Cubans were more stereotypically Caribbean: open, easygoing, friendly, optimistic. Even though they had limited resources, they never ceased to amaze me with their thoughtfulness and creativity.

I distinguished several Cuban world views: those of the party member, the *pionero*, the *campesino*, the *Habanero*, the foreign worker, the student, the expatriate, the religious leader, the hustler, the bureaucrat, the elderly person, the artist. Each category experienced the world differently, from a slightly varied perspective.

The general Cuban world view was also influenced by a regional outlook. Over the years, many of Cuba's thirteen provinces have competed with the capital city of Havana for contacts, growth, and development. For example, five provinces as well as Havana Province now have dance training centers, but it is in Havana's center, at the national school, that the best students from each region train. In this manner, *Habaneros*, Havana, and the things of Havana acquire prestige; Havana-trained dancers and graduates, for example, gain higher status than others. Among the three folkloric dance companies of Cuba, all of which have equally talented and trained professionals, there is rivalry for recognition as Cuba's national company. Many dancers and observers evaluate Folklórico de Oriente and Cutumba as highly as Havana's Folklórico Nacional and view the Havana-based company as regional, equivalent to those of Santiago de Cuba. As elsewhere in the world, regional pride creates differing points of view.

The world view that I found to be shared by most Cubans was that of a worker involved in constructing a society, a society whose resources were

Ciudad-Habana
La Habana
Matanzas
Villa Clara
Sancti Spíritus
nar del Río
Ciego de Avila
Camagüey
Las Tunas
Holguín
Cienfuegos
Isla de la Juventud
Granma
Guantánamo
Santiago de Cuba

C U B A

thor's Havana neighborhood,
86. Photo by Y. Daniel.

Author's home away from home,
Santiago de Cuba, 1986. Photo by
Y. Daniel.

shared and whose members were cared and provided for. That certainly was the paramount view of adult Communist party members and their younger counterparts, the pioneros, or members of the children's organization. Campesinos, or rural workers, and students also seemed convinced that the official party platform was correct, and they were quick to articulate Marxist teachings and Fidel Castro's public pronouncements, which guided most Cubans' behaviors and attitudes.

(Until 1990 these workers and students could point proudly to standards of living that were shared more equally throughout the nation than ever before. They could see that the vast majority of Cubans now had nutritious foods, basic rural or urban housing, competent as well as free medical and dental care, and full access to basic education and specialized employment that guaranteed income for necessities and desires. They could point to the government's carefully organized concern for children, the aged, and the infirm. They understood that critical needs were provided by state organization and national resources; state organization positioned them within Cuban society and provided security, such as it can be in a small, struggling, independent nation.

These workers and students diligently behaved according to idealistic principles of the Revolution. They reached for the full integration of society with planned access to and interaction among the general public (*el pueblo cubano*), the scientific, educational, administrative, and ideological communities, and the artistic community. They answered critics by explaining that problems in every aspect of Cuban life cannot be solved in thirty short years; with more solidarity, support, and commitment and with less local counterproductivity, domestic criticism, and especially less international obstruction, any problems could be rectified. From this common point, other concerns became more or less important depending on the social position of the Cuban involved.

Other workers—in airports, hotels, factories, cane fields and construction sites, for example—were also aware of complications that sometimes contradicted party ideals. While they recognized that cases of rape, drug abuse, homelessness, prostitution, and child molestation, which ravage most large industrialized nations, were virtually absent, they saw, on a practical level, the uncomfortable and ultimately devastating effects of poverty, dependency, and political impotence. They saw that officials and managers showed preference to certain relatives, particular nationalities, or specific prestigious people when scarcities should have led to objective decisions, as in housing distribution. They saw that the power of position afforded opportunities to exploit co-workers and foreigners, as with the increasing problem of robbery in laundries and locked hotel rooms. They saw problems of harassment and occasional theft in customs operations and postal services. Discussions of such problems were sensitive and problematic, occurring in organizational meetings in workplaces (*asambleas*), at home in neighborhood problem-solving meetings (gatherings of the Comité por la Defensa de la Revolución, or CDR), and in a more general sense, in discourses on rectification plans made by Castro and other national leaders.

Some Cuban workers were disillusioned after more than thirty years of diligent effort. They wanted more justice apportioned and more rights protected. They saw little discrepancy between personal freedom and social justice for all.

Foreign students, foreign workers, and expatriates, or long-term foreign residents, influenced another aspect of the Cuban perspective. While they were not Cubans, they often lived for long periods almost as Cubans (from one to ten or more years, with five as an average for foreign students). On one hand, they received equal education, medical care, food, and housing, the same as Cubans. Therefore they were not categorized as tourists or foreign visitors; they were treated as virtual Cubans. On the other hand, these foreign residents had access to additional and differing foodstuffs, clothing, and other imported items that continued to be in short supply and were often denied to Cubans. These items were stocked in separate stores (*diplotiendas*), restaurants, and hotels, reserved primarily for tourists, but the status of long-term workers allowed all foreigners special access. Such circumstances permitted a high degree of intrigue and exchange between Cubans who did not have access to particular items and foreigners who did.

This type of interaction was not officially encouraged; in fact, Cubans who were in the company of foreigners or tourists were often investigated and sometimes harassed for possibly "doing business" with them. Yet when one casually observed Cuban streets, one could not help notice that almost every Cuban, young or old, had items from the stores that were said to be off-limits—tee shirts, North American and European jeans, and so forth. As a result, some Cubans decried their limited entry and their harassment at the doors to hotels and diplotiendas by guards and police, when their non-Cuban co-workers and fellow students could enter, participate, or have choices more easily. In this situation, the Cuban hustlers were revealed. It was they who changed money on the black market and pressured tourists for money or material items. It was they who persuaded the long-term foreign students and workers to assist them in buying purchases from off-limit stores. These hustlers represented a small part of the total population, but other Cubans shared their point of view. "Doing business" was increasing with each successive trip that I made to Cuba.

Another differing aspect of the Cuban world view was apparent among the diverse religious leaders and devotees. The official world view did not give positive value to religious orientation. In fact, persons with religious connections often found it difficult upon completion of their studies to secure a place in a university or a job of their choice. While this situation was discouraged and the practice of religion was not illegal (particularly after 1985; see Castro, 1985a), it was not generally advantageous to be associated with religious organizations of any kind. One valedictorian of a high school class, for example, was persuaded not to enter theology school despite her profound interest in religion but to study medicine instead.

On the other hand, Afro-Cuban religions were officially acknowledged as folklore and culture rather than religion, and as such, association with some of them was accepted to some degree. Many *santeros, paleros,* and Christian priests, pastors, and especially spiritists were becoming more open in the practice of their faiths.

The reality of varying religious views was felt only with time in Cuba. It was faintly seen and weakly heard within ordinary social situations or short tourist or specialized visiting (which is why I am often skeptical of various political and economic commentaries on Cuba by those outside of Cuba). Yet many dedicated individuals and small groups of faithful believers maintained a religious orientation and resolved their daily dilemmas within religious acts of prayer, confession, baptism, divination, initiation, and contemplation. Their world views were not tremendously influential, but their mere existence in an atheistic environment was impressive.

In addition, Cuba contained persons with the typical views of differing generations, but these views were made more curious by Cuba's special social situation. The older generation had seen vast changes, living under capitalism, socialism, and communism. It could attest to an improved quality of life for more Cubans and to a diminished gap between the haves and the have nots. The older generation could also attest to a decrease in personal freedom, and it looked with interest at the consequences of *perestroika* and *glasnost* in the Soviet Union and of life conditions in postrevolutionary Nicaragua during the years of my research and shortly thereafter.

The younger generation had grown up under the new programs of the Revolution and espoused the best revolutionary ideals and objectives. It was also the product of a contemporary world filled with recording stars, tape recorders, tee shirts, jeans, VCRs, and CDs. The nation was accordingly shocked when national radio and television reported that one of the finest products of the Revolution, a party member and recognized young leader, had been accused of using position and power to accumulate houses, jewelry, furniture, and bank accounts. Castro revealed this discovery in July 1987 on national television and discussed its seriousness publicly.

Because the arts were woven into national concern, dancers were integrated within national life and had come to share a basic world view with most other Cuban artists. Like civil servants or rural workers, dancers and musicians gave to society the product of their labor and received care, support, and security; dancers studied, trained, created, and performed and in return received food, shelter, clothing, medical care, professional education, performance opportunities, and salaries. They also received recognition and thanks on national holidays, particularly on Cuban Culture Day, October 20, and Teachers' Day, December 20. Over time, however, the reciprocity that occured did not yield total equality.

Like most artists, dancers enjoy excitement, stimulation, and exchange in order to create works that are capable of affecting people or of attracting and maintaining their interest; artists need to develop an aesthetic view within themselves and to fulfill their potential. Dancers and choreographers need interaction in the global society, of which they are completely aware. Those in Cuba lamented their sparse interaction with non-Cuban artists and hoped for expanded opportunities to experience foreign choreographies and other developments in the world. More than thirty years of sparse contact with the international artistic world had concentrated development of Cuban artistic forms, but it also had affected creativity. This situation was not good for national development because it planted seeds of discontent within a vocal and potentially powerful segment of the population.

There were wide variations in the views of party members, students, factory, field, and long-term foreign workers, each generation, religious devotees, dancers and other artists, but most Cubans shared a common daily work pattern or schedule. They worked hard with increasingly meager resources. They started the work day with a long walk, a crowded bus ride for ten minutes or for hours, a frantic bicycle ride, or, with luck, a car ride with associates from work. In Havana, Cubans once rode buses for one or two blocks rather than walking in the sun; now they wished for a bus—anytime. Many Cubans worked near their residences, but often, to secure employment, they took jobs from forty-five minutes to two hours away, using three buses each way. Each bus ride involved a waiting line, or *cola*, and often the cola caused delays and tardy arrivals at work. There was a cola for practically everything, and everyone accommodated to this fact.

Work days usually began at eight o'clock. Some Cubans, a traditional and professional rumba dancer perhaps, or a worker in a tourist industry, had a swing shift beginning at one in the afternoon until seven, or from three until eleven. Often workers were asked to volunteer additional hours to fill in for sick workers or simply to accomplish specific tasks. It was not uncommon to have workers working double shifts of sixteen to eighteen hours. Workers did so in order to stay in good standing with supervisors, administrators, and party officials, but also because they knew if they had emergencies or problems in the future, co-workers would cover for them likewise.

Work was hard and demanding, no matter which category of worker one might describe. In the fields, work was backbreaking, and many Cubans could recount how, at one time or another, they had to assist in the grueling zafra, harvesting the sugarcane. Work in offices was often frustrating and confusing as well. There was poor telephone communication, and it was not uncommon to get wrong numbers. People let phones ring ten to fifteen times before answering, mainly because it was considered impolite to stop a conversation to answer the phone. It was also frustrating when deficiencies in supplies and machinery presented themselves. Often flourescent lighting was inefficient, and a lack of standard materials, such as paper and pens, inhibited basic business practices. When problems arose, there were no easy solutions and everything took a great deal of time to organize and resolve. The greatest testament to Cuban solutions was the number of 1950s cars that continued to operate. Somehow mechanics had managed to patch and repair these vehicles and to use them continuously since the late 1950s. Average citizens had learned to recycle many products. Seemingly insoluble problems did get resolved in Cuba with time, patience, and ingenuity.

Although the pace of Caribbean life is relatively slow, there was tremendous fatigue and tension among all categories of Cuban workers. Many Cubans could not sleep for long at one time; they took naps for an hour or two and then resumed activities in full swing. Women were physically tired from the amount of walking and heavy lifting it took to complete the innumerable necessary chores of household management. A limited supply of water, gas, and electricity restricted what could be accomplished in any day. Meals, clothing, and cleaning were done by hand for the most part and took a great deal of time. Most hours of the day and evening were consumed in walking to secure food and other items and standing in line. Men either did heavy manual labor for at least eight hours a day or worked all day and then studied and prepared papers all night (with old typewriters on rough—although ecologically efficient—paper made from sugarcane).

They awoke again to a schedule that often required working all day and half the evening.

The Cuban manner was to appear exceedingly efficient in the work atmosphere, but when things broke down and deviated from the expected, many Cubans were casual and calm, filling the time with swallows of strong, sweet coffee, running personal errands, gossiping, or flirting. Lunch time and coffee breaks were often used to shop for the big meal of the day, to look for one particular item, or to attempt to accomplish one bureaucratic task. Dealing with bureacratic rules and with the bureaucrats themselves could take days. To resolve serious issues, it might be necessary to wait months or years. Hundreds of pieces of paper (receipts, requests, permissions) were catalogued and stored by every family to prove certain conditions and to ensure forward progress in long, arduous bureaucratic processes.

Breakfast was usually *café con leche* and bread or crackers, with eggs and milk for children. Lunch time was the focus of the morning, and variations of rice and beans with meat and water were standard. Pork was preferred, well fried or roasted, but chicken, beef, and, less frequently, lamb were available to complement huge mounds of delicious *congrí* or *morros y cristianos* (respectively red or black beans and rice). Rural workers and rumberos often preferred soup (*potage*) as the lunch meal and rice for the evening supper. Cuban soups were nutritious and tasty, with beef, chicken, or pork bases and a multitude of tropical vegetables: *malanga, boniato, papas, plátanos,* or *berenjena* (a kind of potato, sweet potato, white potatoes, bananas or eggplant respectively); *ajiaco* was the ultimate mixture.

Fish was plentiful but not preferred by many individuals. Egg dishes were not considered suitable for guests; an egg entrée such as an omelet would signify that the hosts were not doing well (not able to get out to shop for meats and other food or not working at the moment) or that there were inadequate supplies of meat in the stores.

The Cuban diet was rich in carbohydrates and adequate in protein, and Cubans consumed enormous quantities of sugar in sweets, coffee, and rum. Many Cubans smoked strong, unfiltered cigarettes and cigars. There were usually abundant varieties of fruits, but not many varieties at any one time. Green, leafy vegetables were rare; they were usually imported and supplied to hospitals and the aged first. Generally, Cubans experienced continuous shortages.[2]

Music, however, was always available from the two television stations and several radio stations. As elsewhere, television was a major source of entertainment, education, and information. Cultural programming for

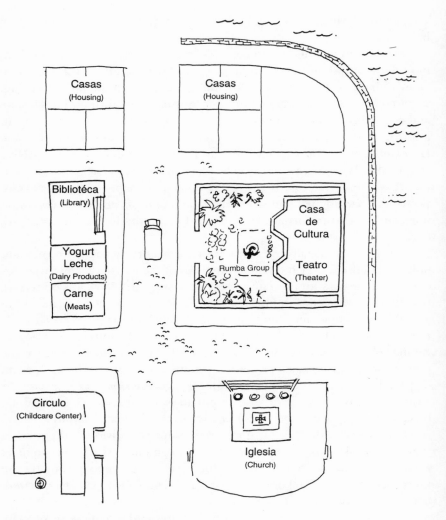

Rumba in context. Drawing by
Mary Parks Washington.

children and adults gave way to more popular soap operas and variety
shows. Television was on as background entertainment nearly all of the
time in most households, sometimes in addition to the radio. A large portion of Cuban programming was news reporting.

A walk in the streets (see the idealized drawing of the rumba context)
was always accompanied by music from the surrounding houses, except

close to the sea where the wind and the waves filled the ear. Popular music from Mexico, Spain, and the Eastern bloc countries played intermittently, while Cuban music of all types was presented almost continuously. Cubans were quite familiar with rock, disco, reggae, hiphop, and jazz and with their national stars as well as many international performers. They were acquainted through television, but mainly through the *casas de cultura* programming throughout Cuba. By seeing so many performers at either local culture houses or repeatedly on television, Cubans had an intimacy and acquaintance with most artists, which was unusual in the North American context. The reason was not simply that Cuba is an island or a small "third world" country; it was a consequence of a very high literacy rate (slightly more than 96 percent), vast educational programming in schools and neighborhood meetings, and participation in and exposure to innumerable cultural events at the local level (Paulston, 1971:375-98).

I noticed that Cuban men and women brag about their children, even though they are quick to discuss the value of small families. Mothers spend as much time as possible with their children and are seriously affected when, for example, married children cannot live close by. When Cuban fathers are around their children, and that is fairly often, they are quite attentive and openly affectionate. Marriage occurs either formally in a civil or religious ceremony or informally in consensual union. Within the home, it produces a variety of family structures: nuclear, extended, matrifocal, and patrifocal, as well as extended matrifocal families. Since the Revolution, divorce has been fairly frequent and that, in addition to serial marriages, can produce many cases of interrelated families (for Caribbean family studies, see Herskovits, 1941; Simey, 1946; Henriques, 1949; R. T. Smith, 1956; Clarke, 1957; M. G. Smith, 1962; Solien, 1971; Martinez-Alier, 1974; Marks, 1975; Larose, 1975; Laguerre, 1975; Sudarkasa, 1980; Barrows, 1984). Fathers often take pride in their children from second marriages and more casual unions, but generally they also take care of them by giving some portion of their monthly salary to the children's mothers.

Cuban parents look forward to two occasions centered on their children: graduation from university and their daughters' fifteenth birthday. Special parties mark both events, but the *quince años* is a feature of traditional Latin society that has maintained its importance. Families save and borrow to make the fifteenth birthday special with new clothing (from underwear to formal gowns) and a picture album to document the event. Dinner is often arranged at a state villa that has been preserved for such occasions. Family and friends dance for the evening at the expense of the parents.

Visiting seemed to be the most important part of Cuban social life.

There were daily visits among family members and almost daily visits with friends. There were numerous short visits to announce what was available at different markets each day or visits to sell items acquired from stores outside the neighborhood or from tourist shops. One week people were looking for children's shorts or tee shirts, the next week shorts and tee shirts could not be given away because everyone wanted socks or women's oversized shirts. What was desired changed from week to week, depending on availability or lack of specific items. There was always a demand for shoes, deodorant, toothbrushes, razor blades, and soft-lead eyebrow pencils or makeup powder, but the most esteemed items were food staples.

By the time people were able to relax, it was very late, but they relaxed with gusto under gorgeous starlit skies. Evening activity for most Cubans was divided between cultural activities, household chores, and relaxation. There was a wide variety of performances at culture houses or theaters, at artists' and writers' meetings, or at classes (for example, Russian and English languages or José Martí's poetry), and there were ample movies to choose from. Outside of classrooms, people read, studied, and joined with others to discuss issues. For example, there was a lively group on Haitian culture in Cuba that met regularly. Speakers for the evening discussions were scholars, but the audience was made up of everyday people who wanted to know more about Haitians, Cuban history, or Caribbean culture. One such lecture drew a film editor, a tourist agency worker, a translator, Haitians living in Cuba, a singer, a visiting scholar, a tourist, and a few unidentified others. On special occasions—for dating couples, holidays, special Saturday nights—evenings were spent in clubs and hotels dancing casino and disco. More commonly, Cubans talked and drank at home with *aguadiente*, the fresh or homemade rum, and commercial beer when these were available. Or they got pedicures and manicures and attended to religious obligations.

Night time in Cuban rural areas was physically beautiful, but the social beauty of urban Havana was astounding. Nights were filled with warm family interaction, televisions and radios blasting, checkers and chess games under soft street lights, packed buses belching dark fumes as they wound through narrow streets, and neighborhood guards standing patrol every few blocks. People communed with each other safely in small apartments and crowded homes. Buses were packed even in the wee hours of the morning. Children were up and out late in the evenings, as they spent a great deal of time with adults and they were not excluded from most activities. Only occasionally were there cries in the night. Normally, nights were filled with sea breezes near the coast, mosquito nets farther inland, informed discussions among friends, quiet reading alone, and romance.

The state provided private conjugal spaces (*posadas*), where couples could rent a room with bath by the hour. Their use was not confined to night time, but at night there were lines of couples drinking in outdoor cafélike areas or kissing in the shadows of a courtyard as they waited their turn. These spaces closed down when there was no water but otherwise stayed open most of the day and night. Because indoor space was at a minimum, because there was little privacy from family members, and because there was scrutiny from neighborhood committees and political party members most of the time, couples meandered outside and embraced in thousands of small parks and plazas or along the *malecón*, the sea wall.

RUMBEROS

(*Rumberos* are ordinary people as well as extraordinary artists, and they must attend to a daily life quest and struggle in the same manner as other Cubans.) However, work for rumberos usually means rehearsals and performances. In rehearsal, discussions take place regarding analysis of previous performances, the order of songs for the next show, costumes, invitations, confirmations, and the itinerary of the group. The director of the group, whose position rotates among members of long standing and respect, relays requests for necessities to Ministry of Culture functionaries and technical staff members. Old songs are rehearsed and new ones are arranged; the drummers and singers check their parts.

There is rarely a week that does not include rumba. Incredible as it may seem, children of rumberos are encouraged to imitate the dance steps, repeat the rhythms, and sing the refrains from their first year. Teenagers go to school, help with shopping and household chores, meet with friends at various cultural events, but also practice rumba frequently and routinely attend performances of family members. Adults eat, sleep, attend to household chores and practice or perform rumba. Everything revolves around practicing and performing rumba. In the same manner that most Cubans spend a great deal of time shopping and preparing foods daily, rumberos spend as much time practicing, traveling to prepare a show, performing shows, and traveling back home.

Rumberos travel to towns and hamlets throughout the provinces. Travel is by bus and usually takes two to four hours in each direction. The trips are spent quietly, except on the return, when the mood of the performance carries over to the bus. At these times, rumberos sing for each other, switching from rumba to Santería songs and creating a Rumba ambiance in the aisles of their transport.

Rumbero families often, but not always, look forward to *santo*, "making their saint or making their heads," i.e., formal initiation into Santeria, the Afro-Cuban religion of Yoruba heritage. It can be a lengthy process taking years, but the intense study of ritual chants and rhythms by rumberos introduces the possibility of religious influence on rumba dance and song. The same is true of Abakuá song, dance, and drumming; many, if not most, male rumberos are fully acquainted with the dance/music elements of this secret society tradition; its rhythms and practices provide meaningful resources for improvisation in rumba.

Families of rumberos share and combine many of their resources. When guests come, hot coffee is prepared in tiny demitasse cups with cold water to follow. If one household does not have coffee, a family member quickly runs across the patio to an aunt, grandmother, or neighbor to borrow some. When a visitor arrives, one household prepares the main course, but perhaps another provides the bathroom and shower, and yet another provides ironed sheets for a bed. Friends and relatives feel no inhibitions about asking to borrow things. Apparently there is equal exchange, as only a few people are known not to give things back or to selfishly refuse to share.

When shopping for their own families, rumberos buy gifts especially for children. Children are cherished and tenderly cared for. A standard greeting includes "and how is the baby?" Even children from the father's "other family" are welcomed, fed, and affectionately entertained.

With enormous amounts of time involved in preparing and performing rumba, rumberos have become astoundingly expert in their craft. Most of the time, rumberos are animated, excited, and involved with the interplay and exchange of song, drumming, and dance. It is almost unbelievable to hear or see the tremendous virtuosity, subtleness, and creativity displayed.

At other times, rumba has become automatic, effortless, and routine, and it is amazing to see and hear such fantastic technique revealed from unconcerned, nearly uninvolved, expressionless faces. Most trained musicians and dancers can attest to the extraordinary skill they witness in a traditional or professional rumba group, yet fairly frequently it appears that musicians especially are not truly there. What is so highly charged for the spectator-participant at times appears boring, almost unimportant, to its creators. They reveal an attitude of musicians everywhere, one of someone who plays a performance that simply pays the rent. Still, on most occasions their performance stimulates and nurtures the creators and practitioners of the craft.

PROFESSIONALIZATION

Between 1959 and 1962, the desire to protect cultural expressions was articulated in the formation of national dance companies that would present major dance traditions within Cuban culture. An evaluation of the objectives and goals of the Revolution took place at all levels of society, including the Ministry of Culture, and lo cubano, cubanía, or Cubanness became a guiding perspective (see the chart of dance organization in Cuba, 1987).

The government provided space in Havana for ballet, modern dance, and folkloric forms. Alicia Alonso's ballet company was nationalized, and it has maintained its special position as a prerevolutionary cultural representative of Cuba with its own company building and space for the training of ballet dancers. Danza Nacional was formed in 1959 to support the continuity and development of Cuba's distinct variation of modern dance (see chapter 2). In 1962, Folklórico Nacional, the major professional rumba group, elevated dances of the streets, barrios, and religious centers as part of the national artistic treasury. Over time, Cuban folklore obtained prestige commensurate with the presumed legitimacy of ballet. By extension, rumberos were elevated as well. (For another Hispanic example of the intricacy of social class and importance of dance/music, see Quintero Rivera, 1986:49-65).

The formation of national dance companies assisted other government objectives by providing jobs and salaries for workers. Many artists, like rumberos, were organized according to their specialties and were given jobs to preserve the many dance treasures of Cuba; their responsibility was to share diverse national traditions with fellow Cubans, as well as with foreigners. They were paid not only for performance but also for the time it takes to create works, to prepare and rehearse performances, and to train and maintain proficiency in their disciplines.

As Folklórico Nacional became more professional, its specific needs for appropriate space caused a shift from a beautiful but spatially inadequate building (the present home of Ballet Nacional on Calzada Street) to a more suitable building with a very large patio (the present home of the Folklórico Nacional on Calle 4, between Calzada and Calle 5). The major reason for this change was Rumba presentation. In the former building, the proper performance of rumba, but not of other dances, was almost impossible considering the participation of the audience and the size of the company. The spatial necessities of Rumba impacted, even dictated, this change along with spatial requirements for tourist activities. The dance shifted from its original locus, street corners, where it often shared attention with parallel activities of traffic, business, and socializing, to its secondary quarters, the professional stage, to another home, the theatrical patio.

By 1980 Folklórico Nacional began the regular Rumba Saturday, where, through dance/music, the public recognized and acknowledged

Dance Organization in Cuba, 1987

Ministry of Culture
Armando Hart, Minister of Culture

Programming
Lecy Tejeda, Director

International Relations
Theater & Dance
Vicente Pauso, Director

Amateurs
Ramon Barata, Director

Theaters & Dance
Choos, Director

Artists

Professional
Ballet Nacional
Alicia Alonso, Director
Danza
A. Mederos
Folklórico Nacional
Teresa Gonzalez, Director
Ballet Camagüey
Fernando Alonso, Director
Folklórico de Oriente
Antoñio Perez Martinez, Director
Cutumba

Professional Music, Dance, Theater, Visual Arts Schools
Enseñaza Artística
(Artistic Training)
Havana Province-Cubanacán
Nadia Beregüer, Director
Santiago de Cuba
Guantánamo
Isla de Joventud
Villa Clara
Etc. for all 13 Provinces

Traditional
Los Muñequitos
Ricardo Cané, Director
Afro-Cuba
Francisco Zamora, Director
Obbatola
Pedro Tapanes, Director
Arará/Perico
Calimete
Niños de Atoche
Benito Aldamas, Director
Aburý Okán
Caidije
Bonito Patois
(Etc. throughout every province)

Amateur (bona fide)
Provincial
Casas de cultura
groups of chemists who dance,
groups of medical students,
groups of dancers who train with
professional and traditional dancers
as coaches, etc.

Municipal
Casas de cultura
neighbors in classes of dance,
groups of hotel workers, chemists,
international students, engineers,
or any lovers of dance who
organize together for instruction and
performances, etc.

Venues

Theaters
National Theater
Administration of all theaters
Ballet
Modern dance
Theater
Orchestra
Folkloric dance

Carlos Marx Theater
Spectacles, extravanganzas
mainly

Lorca Theater
Ballet
Opera
Theater

Mella Theater
Modern dance
Folkloric dance
Orchestra

Cuban culture, Afro-Latin heritage, and the Revolution's new values. Development of company personnel, performance opportunities, and artistic vision permitted a focus on traditional rumba as the one dance that received different, if not special, treatment.

It is safe to presume that both the artistic direction of Folklórico Nacional and the officials of the Ministry of Culture agreed to let rumba emerge and to allow its focus to continue. The artistic directors, with the consensus of company members, instituted Sábado de la rumba. Teresa Gonzalez, director, and Rogelio Martinez-Furé, ethnographer, both of Folklórico Nacional, have been identified as the two persons most responsible for the rise of rumba. They have used all opportunities to validate folkloric contributions in Cuban history and, in this manner, have been instrumental in the emergence of rumba as a national symbolic dance. In effect, rumba was singled out for specific presentations and special choreographies. With efficient administration and satisfactory space after the Revolution, the professionalization of Rumba became a fact.

It is conceivable that in the early postrevolutionary years spontaneous Rumba may have been considered problematic. It attracted large groups of emotionally charged people at unpredictable times, caused congestion of certain areas, and was associated with fights, drinking, and public revelry, which the new government probably sought to control. Rumba events caused a demand on rum and beer as well, and it is possible that some people complained about noise and that police were called on occasion. By organizing where Rumba could take place agreeably and successfully, the government, through the Ministry of Culture, moved to structurally safeguard one of its major dance/music complexes and incorporate it and Cuban artists nearer the core of official Cuban culture.

INTERNATIONAL RUMBEROS

Interest in Cuba has increased despite the sparse contact between Cuba and other nations. North American and European dancers (and many members of the public) have wanted to know what has happened to Cuban dance in the past thirty years. What does Cuban technique look like? What kind of new forms have developed in this historically rich music and dance center? What is the Cuban artistic response to dance performance elsewhere? The Cuban government and dance company directors have matched such interests with professional performances outside Cuba and international dance festivals within Cuba, allowing an interchange of dance performance and dance training. A new group of rumberos has developed as a result.

International students, the new rumberos, have been both enthusiastic and somewhat disheartened with regard to their experiences in Cuban dance workshops. They have saved substantial sums of money to make the trip and to pay for lessons and have been anxious to take classes in rumba, the first level of classes offered in folkloric dance workshops. While they have been critical of the pace of classes, the range of abilities found in a class despite the advertised levels, the class sizes, and on some occasions the inappropriate facilities, such as tile floors to dance on, hundreds of dancers from all over the world continue to flock to Cuban dance/music workshops annually (and some twice a year). They relish the time and contact with revered specialists and the opportunities to perform in Rumba Saturday.

There are, then, several segments of the Cuban population with differing points of view and differing evaluations of rumberos and rumba. Officials, white-collar workers, and light-skinned Cubans generally pay nominal respect to rumberos, but they do not participate in the dancing or drumming, and they exit quickly and politely when they are coerced to attend a Rumba event. At other times, dark-skinned Cubans and other Cubans of varying backgrounds playfully and excitedly dance to the rumba clave when it intersperses a popular song (Daniel, 1991). What is apparent is the ambiguity of Cubans and their evaluations of the creators and performers of rumba. Yet it remains true, as Rogelio Martinez-Furé says in quoting the popular saying, that "without rumba, there is no Cuba; without Cuba, there is no rumba."

PERFORMANCE
OF
RUMBA

THE RUMBA COMPLEX

Rumba as a dance/music complex involves specific drumming patterns and instrumentation, special songs, a particular song form, three basic types of dance, and, above all, elaborate improvisation. Three basic dance expressions developed as the rumba complex, all of which have identifiable rhythmic bases and rely heavily on pantomimed themes of seduction and competition: *yambú, guaguancó,* and *columbia.*[1] It is believed that all three emerged during the 1860s among dark- and light-skinned urban workers who congregated in the poor, crowded living quarters called solares, and also in a more limited fashion on rural plantations.

While 80 percent of the enslaved population lived on plantations between 1840 and 1860 (Knight, 1970:48, 59-60; Klein, 1967:151-52, 158), the urban environment was still a source of African cultural expression and skill. Both enslaved and free persons of color worked alongside Europeans and creole colonials in the urban centers and in almost identical occupations (Klein, 1967:194-226). In Havana and Santiago de Cuba, free people of color and whites worked as skilled and semiskilled laborers. Males were cigar makers, day laborers, carpenters, masons, stonecutters, and musicians; females were seamstresses, laundresses, cooks, house servants, and midwives (Klein, 1967:203-5). On both the eastern and the western sides of Cuba, there was an active shipbuilding industry and copper mining, which was supported by the Spanish Crown. In both industries, skilled slaves were hired out by their master for profit; but they also worked for wages, and the urban centers and port cities were where they congregated.

With the legal end of Cuban slavery in 1886, but also even before slavery ended, through "temporary" and permanent runaway situations, African and creole slaves left rural situations of slavery to look for employment, sometimes posing as free people of color within the urban environment of taverns, ports, schools, universities, and militia of the island.[2] Most found themselves in urban housing that was arranged around a central, common patio area. The Catholic practice that prevailed and the legal framework of the Spanish Crown had provided for regular nonwork time on Sundays and holidays when dancing and drumming were permitted during daylight hours, even for enslaved peoples (Knight, 1990:124, 128-29).[3] In towns and cities, free people of color, free and indentured whites, and slaves—that is, both whites and blacks, light- and dark-skinned Cubans—found moments of recreation together in outdoor patio areas. Their desperate, insecure, and difficult situations were momentarily forgotten or made somewhat more manageable through periodic singing and dancing (León, 1984a; 151-52, 163; Alén, 1987b:1-2; Rogelio Martinez-Furé, personal communication, 1986; Moliner, 1987:40; cf., Ortiz, 1951 [1985]:432-33).

Rumba evolved from several dances that can be traced to western, Central African heritage; particularly, the BaKongo, Lunda, and Luba of Zaire have been known historically to share dances that focus on a gradual closeness of male and female dancers and the touching of bellies or thighs (Malongo Casquelourdes, personal communication, 1988; Bunseki Fu-Kiau, personal communication, 1991). Dances like *makuta* and *yuka*, rumba's antecedents that still survive in Cuba, contain distinct characteristics: a dancing pair that dances in a circle, independently and yet in relation to one another; dancing to three drums and a wooden box with commenting spectators; and particularly the touching of the belly or thighs (see Ortiz, 1951 [1985]:394-395; León, 1984a:73; Chao Carbonero and Lamerán, 1982:91-92). These characteristics became important in the evolution of rumba style and form, especially the emphasis on the bumping or gesturing toward the navel (see chapter 2). The Bantu words meaning navel or belly button, *mkumba* and *mukumba* seem to link *makuta, yuka,* and rumba in Cuba with other Caribbean dances that have similar characteristics (see chapter 1, notes 7 and 9).

Rumba has been incorporated into the repertoires of ballet and modern dance groups. Alicia Alonso, prima ballerina of Cuba, has performed a pas de deux based on rumba. In *Ad Libitum* with Alonso and Antonio Gades, the ballet world of Cuba acknowledged the importance of rumba: a balletic stylization of rumba, a suggestion of rumba, was presented *en pointe*, with toe shoes. Geraldo Lastra, one of the founding dancers and choreographers of Danza Nacional, the National Modern Dance Company, used rumba, its famous personages, and its history as a theme for a major choreography that was premiered in 1988, just before his death. He addressed Folklórico Nacional members with his ideas about rumba and its importance to the heart of Cuba. He also stressed the importance of Folklórico Nacional members as representatives of rumba in rehearsals (1986–87).

In theatrical settings, where control could be maintained over outside influences and distractions, rumba developed as political culture. Preferred images and messages were crystallized into dramatic and poignant presentations, and rumba was directed, shaped, and molded to fit, emphasize, and mediate specific objectives. Certain songs became standard in national company programming and through-composed compositions (not improvised) became routine, with concentration on national heroes and homages, themes of liberation, solidarity, and freedom, and so on. These topics can overshadow themes of personal love, risqué elements, or sociopolitical commentary from historical, traditional rumba.

Rumba used to be less structured and more spontaneous. Instruments were gathered, enough voices to sing parts were accumulated, and people danced and sang when they were inspired. Rumba was a form of the moment, and often songs were composed on the spot, so that spontaneous creations were the object of the form. But postrevolutionary professionalism led to manipulation of rumba form. It condensed the time of a Rumba event to fit theater time and audience concentration time. It also crystallized specific visual images through elaborated costumes and designed sets, cultivated special voices and technically specific instrumentation to accompany selected interpretation of dance styles, and framed and packaged the dance form on stages and special performance patios.

Rumba changed from limitless to limited time. When rumba is examined in terms of speed, duration, and occurrence, rumba has increased in speed, takes more time to prepare, and occurs more frequently than before the Revolution. Faster types predominate over slow types, and therefore actual performance takes less time. People often say that they prefer the slower forms, yet faster forms are performed more often and consume more time within one program.

There has been a shift from small, contained space to wider, larger space in the move from street corner to concert patio. Now people gather around the plaza of casas de cultura when they anticipate rumba performance on Rumba Saturday. There may be two to twelve persons (often children) watching the technicians setting up or the performers unloading instruments. When the singing and drumming begins, people on the streets join the rumberos, enlarging the group to twenty or sixty persons. At international and tourist events, the audience is generally large (from twenty to

The Rumba group. Drawing by
Mary Parks Washington.

two hundred or more), and tourist performances exhibit multiple couples
dancing simultaneously. With the inclusion of more than one couple dancing at a given time, more space is needed.

Competition and opportunism that exist in the choreography are extended to personnel in performing groups. Often these elements are exhibited in good-natured joking; however, since the rewards for outstanding performances are opportunities to travel, to represent Cuba internationally, and to have international artistic contact, artists compete vigorously. There is a great deal of competition for such opportunities and the consequent prestige. Keen competition builds tension, especially when professional jealousies cross family ties within rumba groups.

Before the Revolution, energy patterns in rumba were smoother, more connected, sustained, and soft. Filmed versions display subtle, discrete virtuosity, as in the performances of Nieves Fresneda of Conjunto Folklórico Nacional, the senior exemplar of most Afro-Cuban traditions, and Dolores Perez of Matanzas, the acknowledged traditional dancer from Afro-Cuba.

Since the Revolution, the flow has become more forceful and percussive, as exhibited in the styles of Johannes García and Nancy and Margarita Ugarte, first dancers of Folklórico Nacional, and in the swift, slick style of Folklórico de Oriente company members. The predominance of male energy is characteristic, even within the couple types. Males take more space, have more numerous and larger movements, and execute more aerial and floor movements than females do.

Nonetheless, rumba choreography has not changed in major ways. Although the basic step travels more and covers larger distances, the circular shape of the rumba space has not changed and the proximity between the male and female dancers remains a constant. Most of the torso-initiated movement that uses the center of the body as an axis (axial movement, such as undulation) continues with little change. The slight changes emphasize high rather than low body orientation, partnering, and more touching beween male and female dancers as a result. That means a slight shift of emphasis from subtlety toward explicitness. What has not changed in either type of rumba presentation or within any rumba group since the Revolution is the generation of high, explosive, contagious energy as rumba is performed. This constant is found not only in the performers but also among the spectator/participants.

DANCE FORMS, TYPES, AND VARIATIONS

The rumba complex comprises three fundamental dance types and several styles and variations (see the rumba complex chart). In yambú, which is also called *rumba de cajón* (box rumba, referring to the use of boxes in place of or in addition to drums), the mood is danced seduction. Guaguancó is a faster dance that involves the vacunao, described in the in-

Rumba Complex

FUNDAMENTAL TYPES	STYLES
Yambú	Matancera
Guaguancó	Habanera
Columbia	Santiaguera
	De salón (ballroom)
	Del campo (traditional)

VARIATIONS
Rumba del Tiempo de España
Batarumba
Giribilla

troduction. There is a chase that is often described in metaphorical terms of a rooster stalking a hen. Columbia, traditionally danced by male soloists, is the fastest of the three basic types; it displays virtuosity, male prowess, and danced competition.

Rumbas del tiempo de España (rumbas from the time of Spanish colonial control), or *rumbas de los viejos* (rumbas of the old people), make up a separate category in Cuba. It includes old mimetic rumbas that vary between yambú, and guaguancó rhythms and fall somewhere between the two in tempi. *Giribilla* is a variation that has shifted the music/dance form toward a separate musical form, primarily because of its incredible speed. The music is played so fast that it was once described as the bebop of the rumba variations. *Batarumba,* one of the latest innovations, weaves into traditional rumba the vast array of Yoruba religious songs, rhythms, and dances, thereby creating a dense creole fabric.

Rumba is a dance of couples primarily, but in one type, ideally, it uses a series of male soloists or one male soloist. Dancers come to a center space, usually in front of the drums, in an overtly virtuoso articulation of polyrhythms within the body. Regardless of which type of rumba is performed, the dancers remain constantly aware of the drummers and often listen keenly to the commentary and evaluation of onlookers. Dancers are watched for specific style, specific steps or feats, and sometimes a competition occurs between dancing partners or between consecutive dancers. Usually in yambú and guaguancó, one couple dances while others observe. As many as five couples may come forward to dance simultaneously, but this is rare and reserved for tourist performances. On a few occasions, a man will release his female dancing partner to his *compañero* (good friend, coworker). Dancers complete the dance with the singers' ending, or earlier if they are tired. The drummers usually close the rumba form.

The objective of the dance depends on the type of rumba that is performed. In yambú, the mood and aim are danced seduction. The main rule is that the dance must retain its sense of pure flirtation and the male must never make the gesture of capture toward the female. Both the man and the woman display sensuality and attempt to rhythmically demonstrate the sensuousness of the woman and the attractiveness of the man. Both actively partake of an enticing chase, displaying charm and poise. They often dance very close to the ground and use a scarf to accentuate their movements. The man may wrap his scarf around the woman's shoulders and bring her close to him while barely touching her. Occasionally the woman puts her scarf around the man's neck.

In guaguancó, the slightly faster rumba, the vacunao, or vaccination, is the goal. The objective is for the man to pursue the woman and to execute a vacunao or vacuna by gesturing with his hand, foot, or, most often, a pelvic thrust toward the woman. This stylized vaccination derives from the unabashed love of both dance and double meanings in Cuba. The choreography involves opportunism and depicts a man quite similar in behavior to a rooster chasing a hen: preening himself, puffing his chest out, strutting about, and relentlessly pursuing his potential mate. The woman, like a hen at times, is uninterested, tries to evade and avoid him, but is eventually attracted to him and allows him to dance nearby. In her choreography, she shows off her skill, ability, and attractiveness; she competes, blocking the man's attempts. She dances with grace and seductiveness but always tries to avoid the vacunao. She escapes the vacunao by protecting her pelvic area with a covering gesture while sustaining the rhythm and maintaining a seductive attitude.

In columbia the aim is perfection of form and style, interchange, bravado, and competition. As the fastest of the three types, it displays virtuosity in rhythms, stylistic form, creativity, and musicality. It features the male dancer in all his glory and provides the forum for danced competition. Columbia is danced in a series that encourages each man to dance in virtuoso style and puts everyone in competition. The columbia dancer kinesthetically relates to the drums, especially the quinto (the highest-pitched drum), and tries to initiate rhythms or answer the riffs as if he were dancing with the drum as a partner. Some dancers dance with machetes, knives (*cuchillos*), or bottles (*mañungas*); others (especially members of Portales de Cárdenas) attempt a couple version that uses extraordinarily fast guaguancó movements with columbia rhythms.

In all three types there is a gradual heightening of tension and dynamics, not simply between dancers but also between dancers and musicians and dancers and spectator/participants. Yambú and guaguancó are more literal, situational, and representational; columbia is more abstract. They are all fundamentally sensual but have been viewed in the literature as basically pantomimic (see Ortiz, 1951 [1985]; also see the labanotation for the three types in the appendix). As Fernando Ortiz says,

> La rumba es esencialmente pantomímica, la simulación del cortejo amoroso hasta su peripecia orgásmica, y siempre se desarrolla estilizando con crudeza o con sutil comedimiento ese diálogo de los sexos. Pero fuera de su afroide trauma esencial, ha adoptado en Cuba otras expresiones miméticas a manera de adornos anecdóticos complementarios. Todavía los viejos *rumberos* criollos, que quieren mostrar "erudición" y lucirse con antiguas *rumbas*, reproducen algunas de éstas que tuvieron cierto sentido pantomímico. (Rumba is the essential of pantomime, the simulation of loving courtship until its orgasmic episode, and always the dialogue of the sexes is developed in stylized raunchiness or with subtle comedy. But beyond its essential African plot it has adopted other mimetic expressions in Cuba in a manner of complementary anecdotal decoration. Still the old creole rumberos [singers, drummers and dancers of rumba], who wish to demonstrate "deep knowledge" and to illuminate it through old rumbas, reproduce some of those which have a certain pantomimic feeling.) (1951 [1985]:432)

Ortiz believed that rumba was influenced by commercial trends of the early twentieth century that distorted the grace and subtleness of traditional rumba (1951 [1985]:432; cf. Jahn, 1961:62-96).[4]

Rumba del tiempo de España was probably Ortiz's model; at least in its form today, it includes some of the most pantomimic rumbas. They have a variety of themes and always use the rumba step, whether the mime is about taking a shower or hunting blackbirds. They are said to be old stories acted out playfully in dance form. They make up a separate group because they are not simply couple dances with themes of seduction or solo virtuoso displays but reenactments of traditional folktales and solo characterizations.

One of the most popular of these dances is *Mama'buela*, the tale of a grandmother, or *abuela*, who finds her grandson playing and dancing in the streets when he should be in school. The part of the grandmother is usually played by a young woman dressed as an old woman with a walking cane. The boy is usually a man dressed in shorts, a sailor's suit, and a bow tie. The grandmother scolds him as she hobbles on her cane. He appears to tell her of his joy in dancing rumba and how he does not want to return to school. He pretends to begin to return to school, but she catches him loitering and dancing again. He even tries to dance with her. Eventually she takes pity on him, dances a bit with him, and becomes enthralled with rumba also. When he makes the vacunao gesture, she goes into shock and faints. They leave together with the grandson fanning her. The narrative is acted out in danced pantomime: they are a dancing couple, and throughout the story they are dancing rumba steps.

In *la muñeca*, the doll rumba, a doll comes to life and dances rumba. She wants onlookers to play with her, to imitate her moves and to dance rumba. In *caballo*, also a pantomimed rumba, there is a man with a broom. The broom is transformed by the imitative gestures of the dancer into a horse which must be tamed. The rider tries to mount and is wary of approaching the wild horse. Gradually the horse is tamed and the dancer, turned horseman, rides comfortably. All of the actions are performed while traveling in rumba's basic step and alternating with basic mimetic gestures. In *papolote*, or kite, a scarf or string is imaginatively tied to the waist of a woman and a man holds the string. He may wind up the "kite" and let the woman soar in the distance or he can pull in the string and bring the woman close to him. The woman dances rumba during her role as the kite, usually dancing in the opposite direction of the man. The imaginary string makes the dancers compensate for the wind that seems to pull at the lines.

Probably one of the most popular rumbas in this style is *Lala no sabe hacer na'*. In this rumba, the words indicate that Lala does not know how to wash clothes, iron, take care of babies, brush her hair, or cook. The pantomime of daily work chores and the effort to prove that the woman can or cannot do these "womanly" duties usually results in whistles, flirtatious comments, and double meanings. As the woman mimes the work activities, she is dancing a very seductive rumba, even getting on her knees (in mopping the floor or washing clothes) and accenting hip circles. The ending implies that all Lala can do is dance rumba. Dancers who perform this rumba well today are considered expert; they receive the most applause and praise for executing rumba's fascinating movements.[5]

All of the mimetic rumbas are relatively slow in tempo and narrative in style. In various ways they focus on attractiveness and seduction. The slow rippling of the body and the hypnotic repetition of the drums make rumba del tiempo de España fascinating to watch and fun to dance.

Of the two contemporary developments in the rumba complex, one is based on an old form, giribilla, which is one of several almost extinct variants of rumba, according to León (1984a:164-65) and Alén (1987b:7). Giribilla has shifted rumba, the music/dance form, toward a singular musical form, primarily owing to its incredible speed. According to informants in Matanzas, giribilla is faster than columbia. It uses the guaguancó rhythm, yet musically it resembles columbia because of its speed.[6] It is seldom danced now, however (Matanzas and Havana informants, 1987, 1988). I heard one rumba teacher complaining to a lead musician as a rumba class ended, "That was too fast; I'm teaching guaguancó, not giribilla."[7]

What is the meaning of a dance form that is losing its dance? The motivation for giribilla is not the same as that of its rumba predecessors. Danced seduction, play, commentary on life, and friendly competition apparently are not relevant; the vacunao is eliminated. The purpose of rumba forms is to dance with the music, creating elaborations of the rumba step. Apparently, when giribilla is heard the music dominates as it does in jazz music. Giribilla is to rumba what bebop is within the jazz idiom; the music is so complex and fast that the dancers give way to listening. In this way, giribilla denies the sensuality that usually accompanies rumba, but it embraces sensuality of a different sort, more abstract and perhaps less emotional. The future will tell how rumba develops in this fast, primarily musical variation.

The other contemporary development of rumba, batarumba, is a combination of three separate dance traditions: rumba, Yoruba, and son-derived casino (see chapter 2). Batarumba combines Yoruba religious chants, rhythms, and gestures with rumba guaguancó and casino. It is an entirely different kind of rumba. Unlike giribilla, batarumba is a development of rumba that accentuates dancing and incorporates rhythms that are not usually associated with rumba.

Often, dancing partners hold hands and waists in European-American style and perform passing and turning figures that developed originally in son. Batarumba is close to son in many ways, and from the dancers' point of view they could be interchangeable (compare rumba and son clave in music example 1). The argument for placing batarumba within the son complex emphasizes body orientation and positioning. In batarumba, the dancers most often position themselves in straight, upright posture, that is, in typical ballroom fashion, and go to a forward tilt of the back, found in rumba, only on occasion. Male and female orientation in batarumba is unlike the more African stance of traditional rumba, where partners rarely or barely touch. African principles alternate with European-American principles in both the music making and dance construction of batarumba. Also, batarumba is an example of the cross fertilization within rumba, the interpenetration of popular material, popular social forms that infiltrate and influence one another.

In batarumba the typical and representative feeling of rumba is restructured. There is a different power in the combined drums and traditions

Rumba

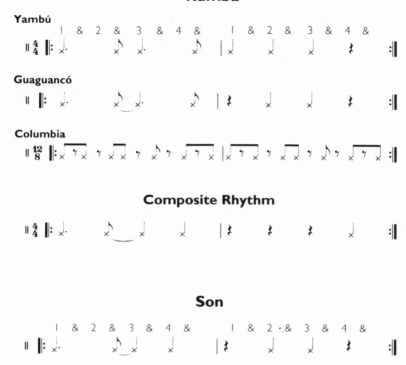

Claves, music example 1.

that is dynamic and Afrocentric. There is excitement in the Eurocentric partnering, slick turns, fast-changing designs. The sensuality and allusions to sexuality within the character of rumba are deemphasized in batarumba; the rules of rumba dancing are pushed to their extremes, almost violated, in combining rumba and casino. The most fundamental rule of Cuban music/dance, however, is that the clave holds it together (like the clavicle of the human skeleton), and the clave is that of rumba.

Rumba dancers may choose to utilize the movements for any orisha, for example; participate in the sensuous danced courting of guaguancó; relish in the passing and turns of partner dancing from son-derived casino; or, more commonly, alternate between all three. The results are a rich, thick texture of rhythms, a driving thrust in the passing, turning, continuous interweaving of dancers, and dynamic change. The music is accompaniment to the dancing and vice versa. Simultaneously there is dance independence and improvisation as well as musical independence and improvisation.

Rumba has been a mélange of popular and traditional elements throughout its history. Both religious material and popular material from the streets were mixed in rumba standards, as in the lyrics of rumba. Through this latest elaboration of rhythms, gestures, positioning of the dancing couple, and upright body orientation, rumba embraces the dance that most Cubans can and do dance, casino, and in doing so, rumba has the potential to be embraced by more Cubans. The feeling of batarumba is different from other types of rumba, yet it has not been rejected by rumberos who are quick to guard the authenticity of rumba. Perhaps the feeling batarumba evokes is the same sense of a collective community that is found historically in spontaneous rumba, and thus batarumba mediates potentially clashing traditions.

RUMBA MOVEMENT

What accumulates in minor gestures, facial expressions, and postures in rumba is an overall picture suggesting an air of deliberation and conscientiousness, an elegance for women and a kind of grandeur for men. Certainly an allusion to pride, strength, courage, arrogance, and bravado is found in the male attitude and body orientation while dancing rumba. Women use control subtly and create an air of restraint, soft sensuousness, and, at different times, both seriousness and playfulness. These qualities are similar to expressed male qualities, but they vary in the hierarchy of possible attitudes between the male and the female; deliberateness is secondary in the female attitude while dancing but is primary in the attitude assumed by males.

In rumba, the body combines a more elongated "Spanish" and more flexed "African" structural orientation to etch a Cuban creole concept of proper body orientation. Straight back, with a slight forward tilt, shoulders raised with elbow activation, and head alternately rotating from side to side create the male stance of rumba (especially for columbia). Female postures paralleled the social position of women; body orientation became standard in low level, not just slightly but deeply bent downward, yet alert, flexed, or ready to move. Females hold their skirt edges often, perhaps in imitation of courtly practices copied by the Spanish folk and later by women of color. Females watch, discover, respond, and initiate occasionally, according to their own strategies.

The vacunao, the heavy emphasis on hip movement, and undulation display African elements of movement (see Thompson, 1974:1-46). The lifted chest and the intricate foot movements for males may relate more closely to Spanish dance elements. The pelvic area is revered in many African contexts because it contains the reproductive organs and body parts that have important effects on the person, the couple, and hence the extended family, the group, the community, and the nation (Primus, 1969:1-13).

Space

The space for rumba is a closed, usually semicircular area with the parameters marked off by onlookers. The space is contained, often tight, and is delineated nonverbally through the kinesthetic response of the dancers, mostly encircling each other in a clockwise or counterclockwise direction or sometimes traveling a diagonal, zigzag, or straight path. The couples who dance do not follow any particular floor pattern; the floor design is improvisational, relying on the steps and appropriate responsorial movement.

At the same time, the dance space is only the focal point of a Rumba which takes place either in an outdoor environment or a theater that has an open and flexible setting. The openness of an outdoor, public event contrasts with the enclosed circular space for dancing. Spectators often press inward and diminish the dance space considerably. Spatial dimensions shift with the number of people watching and the demand to focus carefully on the dancers and musicians.

Time

Before the Revolution, the usual time for Rumba was on Saturday evenings. The dance was performed more or less spontaneously and lasted for several hours over several days. But these days, spontaneous Rumba rarely occurs. The time for a rumba performance is more limited; it continues to be performed on Saturdays, but it is prepared, not spontaneous, and lasts approximately three hours. Although other days are used for performances (Sundays in Old Havana, for example), performance time has changed from primarily nights to afternoons. Prepared Rumba in the cities of Matanzas and Havana generally occurs twice a month. In the provinces, it occurs at least once a year, during each province's Culture Week or when traveling traditional groups give performances. At the national level, prepared Rumba occurs annually at the Rumba Festival for one to two weeks in October.

The duration of a prepared Rumba may be extended up to ten hours if a spontaneous extension takes place; I refer to this as prepared spontane-

ous Rumba. It occurs only occasionally, but as more of the general population learns rumba, it probably will increase as a part of parties, celebrations,
and holidays.

In the prepared or spontaneous Rumba event, time may be augmented
or diminished by several variables: the improvisation of singers, the creativity of dancers, audience participation, technologcial production limita-
tions, the availability of rum or beer, the heat, fights that break out, visiting
rumberos who join the performance, rain, and so on.

Another rumba time frame is found within the music/dance complex
itself. The song portion preceding the dance portion divides the time
frame of each rumba. Dancing stimulates the repetition of the chorus and
thereby the dance section may continue to unfold, build, or develop. Only
one rule guides the performance time: the song and instrumentation precede the dance, so that there is a separation between the nondance portion
and the dance portion of a given rumba. Among nonprofessionals, rumba
is generally performed first within a Rumba event while other dances generally follow afterward.[8] Professionals sometimes reverse the order on
Rumba Saturday in order to make rumba the culminating focus of the performance.

Energy

The energy level of rumba can be ascertained by the awareness of body
position, orientation of both male and female in rumba, and qualitative assessment of movement intention and dancer concentration. The male
dancer holds his back very straight with a forward tilt and with shoulders
raised slightly. The head retains a raised position and alternates between
side right and side left. The elbows are raised extremely to moderately high
in middle range. In the arm movements, men often fling their arms in a
direct outward flick and hold them at a given spot. Arm movement is from
side to forward, in an arc. The tiny, tight, rapid steps (*pisaos*) the male
dancer executes are elaborations of a walk on tiptoes that crosses each foot
rapidly and narrowly. The energy needed to maintain such positioning is
restrained, with recurring bursts of percussive pulses often ending in soft,
sustained arm movements.

In guaguancó, males display staccato elements with quick and heavy accents. The vacunao is the best example of this, but also arm movements jab
and punch the air attempting to distract and trick the female. Males lift the
chest and upper torso high and keep them rather stationary in comparison
with the lower torso. There is a great deal of movement in males' lower
bodies, with rapid foot gestures, traveling patterns, and virtuoso flexibility.

Even though much of the time the chest is lifted, at times the chest is also included in arm movements and lunges forward or side.

In columbia, men are focused. Their concentration appears inward and they alternate between direct and indirect, large and small, percussive and vibratory movements. They rise to releve only to sink or fall and spring back up again. They use a releve in plie and accent the second or third beats of a measure with isolated body parts. Some men use a full body vibration; more commonly, a half body vibration lowers the body from place high or anatomical position to forward tilt at angles between forty-five and ninety degrees. They usually travel in a circular path, as the space is curved toward the drums, even when there is no audience to delineate the dance space. There is very limited aerial work, even among the younger generation. A few jumps using a handkerchief as a rope or a jumping descent into a split are the noticeable few aerial steps.

With rhythm changes, the middle back initiates a kind of abandon, seen in examples of columbia danced with knives. While this feat must be practiced to avoid cutting the entire side of the face and all the muscles and nerves therein, when it is properly executed there is a sense of abandon. The head alternates quickly from side to side, the knives alternate in a plunge on each side of the neck or waist or under the leg.

Female movements suggest two contrasting moods. One is ever diligent, serious, concentrated, and controlled; the other is daring, playful, sometimes aggressive, but always controlled. The female dancer has a straight back with a slight forward tilt also. She uses swing energy, i.e., bound to flow, but laterally and from forward to back in as much simultaneous execution as is possible. Female energy is percussive when she escapes the vacunao by the swift slap toward her lower abdomen and groin area. Her head is held high and her focus is on the male dancer as he travels around her in the dance space. Her arms fling to an indefinite point, when not holding her skirt edges, and her shoulders rotate in a forward direction as a result of the arm roll carrying the skirt. Undulation of the spine is almost constant: her torso can be divided into upper and lower sections and moves in forward to back swing energy. Her rib cage lifts with the undulation and alternates from side to side. Her knees are flexed and shift softly from side to side accommodating the polyrhythms above the feet. Undulating movement in this case is with swing energy accommodating the rhythm, sometimes on the accented beat, often in syncopated counter-rhythm to the expected accent. The lower torso participates in the undulation by means of hip flexion and extension. The flexion becomes a characteristic part of the exit pattern at the close of the dance.

Females use small, quick undulations or percussive, successive movements punctuated with vibratory shoulder movement. They stay in low level as they maintain hip flexion and forward high chest carriage. Females in guaguancó are hesitant and tighter than in yambú. They are not as free and use more bound energy as they are in anticipation constantly. They swing more than males also and continue arm movement, probably in order to prepare a defensive action against the vacunao. Their movements are more percussive, but light and often freeze and are held immobile at the vacunao.

The three forms of rumba thus necessitate a great deal of implosive energy which, after deliberately pulling or collapsing inward, resolves outward. In yambú, dancers are reserved, males more than females. Both the male's and female's feet repeat a touch, step, touch, step pattern that is not quite percussive, but surely not sustained. Both male and female dancers lower and twist in a sustained energy quality. At times, the feet stay still and stabilize twists in the body as the torso lowers and the arms raise or lower. In the professional version, observers can almost see emotional energy between the performers in the highly stylized projection of feeling.

Symbolic religious movements can occur in rumba also. In columbia, floor (ground) work is rare, so it is curious and noticeable when rumba dancers fall to the floor in a ritual salutation for the deities of Yoruba descent. The salutation to the drums or to a dancer (in guaguancó) is a fall forward followed by touching the earth or kissing a person on both cheeks. The direct fall may alternate the entire body to each side or simply stay still momentarily with arms at the side and palms facing upward to mark a classic spirtual salutation in the Yoruba religion. This is decidedly different from the vast array of upright movements found in columbia or the intense couple concentration in guaguancó. Also, females make the symbolic gestures of particular deities, in yambú especially. They use sustained arm lifts which descend along the body's side, touching and marking female curves (the sign of Ochun, a Yoruba deity) or percussive arm "dives" from forward diagonal high into the pelvis (the sign of Chango bringing energy of lightning into the body).

Male movement aims at sporadic drama; male concentration is extremely high. Female movement is cautious and continuous; female concentration is sustained, but not noticeably overt.

The labanotation (see appendix) clearly shows that rumba movement relates to specific dance steps found in other parts of the Caribbean and Afro-America.[9] The knee clapping in plie on half toe causes the knees to rotate from out to parallel position on each beat. This is seen in the "funky chicken" of the 1960s in the United States and in *banda* over centuries in

Haiti (Emery, 1972; Dunham, 1947; Yarborough, 1958; Daniel, 1980). The notation also shows a close relationship between rumba and the *samba* of Brazil (see Mariani, 1986) and points to the Kongo-Angolan heritage in Cuban dance (see also Kubik, 1979). The notation shows a spatial emphasis on circular paths and a full display of polyrhythms within the body that characterize the dance.

THE STRUCTURE OF RUMBA MUSIC

Cuban musicologists and others agree that the antecedents of rumba are found in the transformation of African and Spanish musics, which were woven together in Cuba (Carpentier, 1946 [1979]:31-36, 106-18, 231-42; León, 1984a:151-65; Urfé, n.d.:9-16; Ortiz, 1951 [1985]:432-433). Today rumba drums are commonly called *congas* because of their barrel-shaped antecedents in Kongo-Angolan beginnings, called Congolese or Bantu in Cuba. The major parts played on the drums and the instrumentation of rumba, although different, relate to West Central Africa, particularly to rhythms from Palo, the religion of Kongolese or Bantu descendants in Cuba and other "Bantu" dances, such as *palo, yuka*, and *garabato*. Yuka and makuta are the existing antecedent dances of rumba. Yuka, for example, utilizes the *caja*, the *mula*, and the *cachimbo*, three Kongolese drums, and the *guagua*, or *guácara*, the wooden box played with sticks, an instrumentation that parallels that of rumba musical structure.

The rhythms of rumba, particularly of columbia, have a relationship to the rhythms of a dance called *baile de palo*, which is characterized by a fast, energetic, and brisk style of dancing. In another dance from this tradition, garabato, dancers use long sticks from a guava tree (*lungowa*) to accentuate another layer of polyrhythms among the instruments. These thickly textured rhythms find expression in the fast-paced, highly rhythmic columbia.

Carabalí influence from the Calabar River region in southeastern Nigeria in West Africa is found in columbia as well (Alén, 1987a:10; Urfé, 1948:176-78; Michael Spiro, personal communications, 1986, 1988; Lachatánere, 1961). Gestures from Abakuá dancing can be seen in the highly gestural displays of male solo dancing in columbia to augment and emphasize rumba rhythms taken from the same musical tradition.

SOUND AND INSTRUMENTATION

Historically, space affected the sound of rumba music; the street corners, a patio within an enclosed housing compound, or even within a room inside a house encouraged particular sounds. Some of the most revered rumba were called box rumba, for their subtle poignancy. Two boxes were used, one pitched high and one low. Boxes, as well as the sides of wardrobes, closets, or drawers turned upside down were used to make drumming sounds and to accompany poetic improvisations.

From time to time (and throughout the Caribbean), laws had been passed prohibiting the use of real drums because the colonists' fears of slave insurrections (Herskovits, 1941:138; Knight, 1978:128-29; Moreau de St.-Méry, 1796; Bremer, 1832). The colonists believed that drumming attracted crowds and incited rebellion. Therefore enslaved Africans substituted boxes to satisfy their need to make music and dance and in order to communicate. Boxes and crates were often dismantled, sanded, and rebuilt without cracks to improve the sound. Later, discarded boxes that had been used for imported salted cod or candles were preferred for their wood's special resonance (Char Carbonero, 1982:118; León 1984a:154-55). Succeeding generations of Afro-Cubans retained the use of boxes as additions to real drums, but also as substitutes for the sounds of spoons, pans, and the surfaces of doors used as instruments long ago.

The music of contemporary rumba includes other instruments beyond drums, as well as a specific song style that precedes the dancing. The claves, or wooden sticks, begin the rumba. As noted earlier, clave rhythm is basic to much of Cuban music; it feels metronomic and fixed, yet frequently it is used to accelerate the pulse and it can vary its patterns. The claves set the tempo and the mood of the rumba; they usually signal the type of rumba to be danced, as in music example 1.

The claves are answered in specific patterns by the largest and lowest-pitched drum or box used as a drum, followed by the midrange drum, then the highest-pitched drum. The drums are named according to their function or according to the register in which they are played. The deepest-pitched drum may be called the *conga, tumbador, hembra* or female, or *salidor* or opener.[10] This drum is usually the first drum to sound and anchors the drum ensemble in pitch and in an *ostinato* or repeated pattern. The drum of the middle register is called *segundo* or the second, *macho* or male, *seis-por-ocho* (six by eight, possibly referring to six-eight rhythm), or *tres-dos* (three-two), possibly referring to counter-rhythms or three against two.[11] Usually the second drum to sound, it carries a rhythmic contrast to the claves and the conga. The *quinto* is the highest-pitched drum; its name refers to the general and very relative interval of a fifth over the standard tone of the lowest-sounding drum. The highest-pitched drum is the most improvisational of the drum trio. Although there is a great deal of improvisation, elaboration, and creativity within each drum's pattern, the function of the quinto is to improvise. Each drum part creates a tension or pull in the rhythmic feeling with respect to other drum parts.

In addition to the drum trio and the claves, two other types of percussive instruments are included in the standard or "classic" rumba ensemble: the *madruga* or shaker and the *cáscara* or *catá*, which is a cylindrical or bamboo instrument that is played with sticks (Alén 1987b:4). Shakers are a part of many Cuban musical forms: *maracas* in popular social music, *chekerés* or *güiros* in Santería or in Abakuá music. Shakers are also important in Cuban Kongo-Angolan music such as *nkembi* (León, 1984a:71, 156), and the two largest drums of the yuka dance (the caja and the mula) are struck on the sides with sticks, as is the caja or cascara of the rumba percussion battery.

In rumba, shakers are often used on the wrists of the drummers (*muñecas*, wrist shakers), but the madruga is the tin or metallic shaker that keeps a steady basic pulse in the rhythmic texture. In early rumba ensembles, one musician would beat rhythmic patterns on the sides of the drums with sticks (Alén, 1987a:4); this was called the cáscara (shell, rind or husk). Later, an instrument was created for this purpose from a hollowed piece of wood or large bamboo. The cylindrical instrument was named catá, which may simply be onomatopoeia of the two strong beats that sound as the instrument is played with two sticks.[12]

CREOLIZATION IN MUSIC

Cuban rumberos have reversed one of the main characteristics of many African drumming styles. Often in African musics, segmented rhythmic parts in lower registers carry the melodic or vocal interest. In rumba, concentration and musical or rhythmic interest shift to the upper registers. This is a characteristic of European musical interpretation and points to the syncretic nature of creole art forms. In much of African religious music, clearly in Afro-Cuban religious music, improvisation over a steady beat or pattern occurs predominantly in the lowest-pitched drums (León, 1984a:45-46; Ortiz, 1950 [1985]; Alén, 1987b:5; Michael Spiro, personal communication, 1988). Within rumba, Cuban drums demonstrate African polyrhythmic concepts and European timbre placement by using the quinto or highest voice as the major improviser.

RHYTHMS

The composite rhythms of the percussion ensemble have identifiable motifs and use the same names as the types of dances in the rumba complex: yambú, guaguancó, and columbia (see music examples 2, 3, and 4 to compare rhythmic differences). The drums play fixed parts generally, especially the conga and segundo; however, depending on who is playing, there can be a high degree of elaboration and decoration in both the rhythmic and melodic lines. (Drums do make melodies.) The quinto is the most liberal, with elaboration generally. Of the three types of rumba, columbia is the most demanding if one is to maintain its fast, dynamic feeling, a complex rhythmic structure with the claves and quinto in 4/4 and the other drums in 6/8 and with all drums augmenting their parts with improvisational, decorative, and highly syncopated patterns (Tomas Jimeno, per-

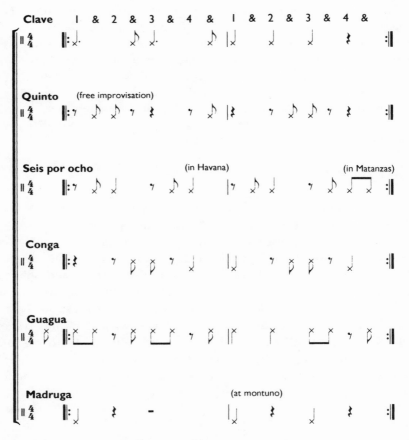

Yambú, music example 2, a typical but skeletal musical pattern. Indication of intervals is approximate.

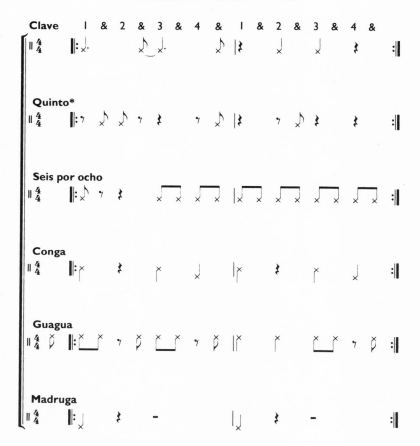

Guaguancó, music example 3, a typical basic
pattern of Titi and Chachá of Matanzas.

sonal communication, 1987; Augustín Díaz, personal communication,
1987; Sandi García, personal communications, 1986-87; Jesús Alfonso, personal communication, 1988; Michael Spiro, personal communication,
1987).[13] Guaguancó is the rumba rhythm that was used by large rumba
choruses at the end of the nineteenth century (see Alén, 1987b:11-12; Urfé,
1948:185-88, and n.d.:12-13; León, 1984a:160-65). It has also been used and
elaborated upon as a base for contemporary bands and electronic music in
the twentieth century in orchestras led by Mario Bausa and Tito Puente in
the United States and in Cuban orchestras such as Los Van Van, Irekere,
and Dan Den.

In batarumba, rhythms are fully complex. This musical style has been

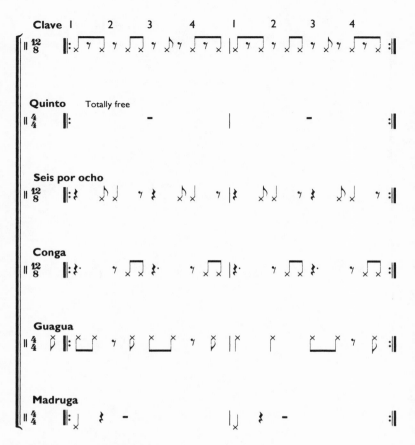

Columbia, music example 4.

popularized by a traditional rumba group from Matanzas since the 1980s, Pedro Tapanes and Francisco Zamora of Afro-Cuba (cf. Andy Gonzalez in Boggs, 1992:295). The clave used as the base of batarumba is rumba clave, which classifies the dance as rumba and not son. These two clave rhythms are not very different, however. In fact, there is only the difference in placement of one beat: son clave has a beat on the count of four and rumba clave has a beat on the "and" of count four (cf. guaguancó and son clave in music example 1).

The rhythms are managed through interpenetration of the traditional rumba drum trio and the batá drum trio (from Santeria). Most often the drummers combine the two drum "families" for a richly textured, exciting sound.[14]

Rumba Dance and Song Structure

Section I: Music
    Diana or *Lalaleo*   vocalizing
    Inspiración   duet, set verses
    Estrofa   solo, improvised

Section II: Music and Dance
    Estribillo   responsorial refrain; dancing:
                              yambú, guaguancó, columbia,
                              batarumba, etc.
    El fin   drum ending

SONG STYLE

The song style of rumba is a combination of improvisation and fixed antiphonal response between a soloist and a chorus (see the rumba dance and song structure chart). The lead singer begins the *diana,* or introductory song phrase. This diana is a melodic fragment of syllables, often called the *lalaleo* (or *llorao* in columbia), which is passionately or playfully sung. It establishes the key of the song and the basis for the two- and three-part harmony that follows: Ana-Na-Na-Ana, Ana-Na-Na-Ana; Eh-Ah-Ae-Ae-Ea; and Ayi-Ya-Ya-Yayi-Ay-yai-yai. The syllables may not have been meaningless. Many African languages have tonal meanings and onomatopoeia, and it is possible that the meanings have been lost over time in Cuba.[15] The lalaleo or diana uses vocalizing and changes in timbre to draw attention to the song's lyrics. The audience's attention focuses on a set section which gives the reason for the rumba song or the Rumba event.

The verse is called a *décima* or *estrofa* but has little relationship to the classic décima form, the ten-line stanza of Spanish literature. Some sample lyrics will show the approximation of décima form (those translated by persons other than me are noted); some were published in the National Folkloric Company's brochure as well-known rumbas while others were taken from standard rumba programs.

Here is one called "Yambu Matancero."

        Yambú, yambú, yambú
        Caballero
        Éste es mi yambú
        Imaliano

Yambú, yambú, yambú
Caballero
Venid a oir mi yambú
Imaliano
Yambú, yambú, yambú
Caballero
Éste es mi yambú
Imaliano.

It is about yambú, the rumba type, and the poet, Nancy Morejín, says simply: "(Hey) man, this is my yambú, Amaliano (usual wording); come listen
to my yambú."

Leguleya No
(Guaguancó matancero de Julian Mesa)

Leguleya no
yo no quiero discusión
quiero cumplir mi promesa
poqque yo soy IYABO
no me puedo incomodar,
no me puedo lloviznar,
no me pueden dar las doce
del día ni de la noche,
poqque yo soy IYABO,
y si llego a delinquil
lo malo lo sufro yo.
O KAMABO
Mi padrino me dió la letra,
O KAMABO
Mi padrino me dió la letra,

Coro:
O KAMABO
mi padrino me dió la letra,
O KAMABO

This example is about a Lucumí initiate (Yoruba, Santeria devotee)
who wants to keep his vows. He does not want to disturb anything or
to make anyone cry. He is not allowed to have sweets from morning to
night. If he is late, he will suffer evil, O KAMABO (Lucumí). His godfather
has given him the letters, i.e., he has received instructions from Ifa divination.

The next example is an homage to one of the most famous rumberos,
Malanga of Unión de Reyes in Matanzas Province. The author feels a voice
calling him which tells of Malanga's death. The town of Unión de Reyes
cries for its great rumbero. People come sprinkling flowers from Havana to
Morón. Unión de Reyes cries because Malanga has died.

A Malanga (columbia)

Solista:
>Siento una vo que me dice
>Areniyeo
>Siento una vo que me llama
>Malanga murió
>Siento una vo que me dice
>Areniyeo
>Siento una vo que me llama
>Malanga murió
>Malanga murió
>Unión de Reye llora
>a su timbero mayo.
>que vino regando flore
>desde la 'Bana a Moron
>Que vino regando flore
>desde la 'Bana a Moron.
>Unión de Reye llora
>poqque Malanga murió
>poqque Malanga murió
>poqque Malanga murió

Coro:
>Unión de Reye llora
>poqque Malanga murió.

Solista:
>Poqque Malanga murió
>Poqque Malanga murió.

Coro:
>Unión de Reye llora
>poqque Malanga murió.

In the following song, the singer says, "Listen, a guaguancó from Matanzas! It's calling me to enjoy a good party. Make it typical and pleasurable. The earth trembles when they drum a good rumba in Matanzas."

Guaguancó Matancero

Oye, oye! Oye, oye! el guaguancó
>matancero.
Me 'ta llamando para gozar un buen
>rumbón.
Dale tipo y savoroso.
Tiembla la tierra, la tierra tiembla.
Cuando en Matanzas se toca un rumbón,
La tierra tiembla.

In rumba songs, the singer comments on life, love, politics, the current ambiance, brotherhood. The following songs were some of the first composed when Los Muñequitos, one of the most famous and revered rumba groups, first formed their ensemble. These songs have become standards in rumba literature.

Yo Cantaré para Tí, Niña

I'm gonna sing, I'm gonna sing for you baby. I'm gonna sing. This is the latest. This is the latest of the Munequitos. I bet you haven't kept up with the Saturday comics! Little Orphan Annie, Jeff is calling for Mutt. His buttons are popping off his shirt so much that it's making food for the chickens. Vanity Fair, Bohemia, She magazines. Wow! it's so good that I still get chills. I was looking for Casper the ghost, Dick Tracy is coming to investigate. The male frog said to the female frog on the edge of the river, "Don't be so lazy, cover me, I'm cold." (Translation: J. Gomez)

Chorus: Llámala nadie, emi llámala seboda (Arará chant for Chango).

I Bring a Story to the People

Long life to the drums! (Original song before the Revolution said the drums stopped and were negative, as was rumba.) Now the people are happy and long live the drums. The kid goes to school. Let's read. I'm Cuban and I love Cuba and I die for my flag. I dedicate the guaguancó from Matanzas region (to this audience). Havana is the leader as the blessed Capital. There you can find everything that you need, from a fine, hot flirtatious babe who can turn you on, to the highest authority in the country. Education of the people is the first thing you have to learn. It is the youth who are in charge of defending the interest of this nation. (Translation: J. Gomez)

Chorus: Omaoma, okeoke (Yoruba chant).

El Marino

My friend, you told me one day that the Marino barrio would end. The comparsa or group from the Marina district wouldn't be heard any more. What confusion! The Marina has had its day to sound on the street and to delight all the rumberos on that day. (Translation: J. Gomez)

Chorus: Oh, how good the Marino barrio is!

Odie arere, odei arere, Olofi aberícula omi orisha Olofi, Olofi aberícula omi orisha Olofi. Okeke y mu agua orereleo.

The first time I registered in a new crowd of Santeria folk, I could say that it didn't cost so much: one duck for Yemaya, to pay for the rights to Oya, four roosters and doves. Look and see if there is a Toequin del pinar (a Cuban bird).

Chorus: Odie arere, odie arere. Olofi aberícula omi orisha Olofi, Olofi aberícula omi orisha Olofi. Okeke y mu agua orereleo.

Obaisere Chango woro. Rumba is calling me, Congo maye. (Translation: J. Gomez)

La Jerigonsa (Nonsense; Gollito's song)

Listen first so that later you can say it like I say it. If you don't understand this jerigonsa, it's a new rhythm I've invented. My rhythm has "Spanish soul" and things from Cuba and no one can say it like I say it! I like shredded coconut dessert.

Chorus: If you play, I'll go crazy.
Soloist: But how delicious the food (cosube)!
Chorus: You know that very well.
Soloist: Happiness touches me, fills me.
Chorus: That gives you empathy or feeling.
(Translation: J. Gomez)

Little Chinese Man

What are you selling? I don't sell pumpkins, I bring Guines potatoes, cabbages, new sweet potatoes, ripe plantains.

Chorus: What are you selling?
Soloist: I don't sell pumpkin.
Chorus: Engoma (Congolese, Palo word meaning to talk. (Translation: J. Gomez).

Xiomara (Saldiguera's song)

We can hear it from the corner—a very special Rumba party. The Rumba is bathing the street with its spring brightness. The night is coming and nocturnal mysteries (also). The justice of my soul reflects in my thoughts. I have happiness in my soul because I kissed you last night to the *son* of your gaze. I gave you my love. But why do you have to give up, why, in this new love, should history repeat itself? Why Xiomara, why Xiomara, why Xiomara?

Chorus: How I pity Xiomara!

Soloist: Why are you like that? Listen very carefully, Xiomara. If you are sorry for loving me as much as I love you, you will never understand how much I love you. You should never forget how much I adore you. Now that everything is finished, you see yourself without a friend, without a love. I, myself, like everyone else, wish that one day I would have money, friends and love. Love has forgotten me and my friends are traitors. My friends! My love!

Chorus: What a pity Xiomara! How I pity Xiomara! How I pity Xiomara! (Translation: J. Gomez)

The following rumba was broadcast in the United States on national television (NBC, February 18, 1988):

Mr. Reagan

Chorus: Oh, Mr. Reagan where are your brains? With Grenada, you've sunk low.[16]

Contemporary programs alternate songs of homage to rumberos, patriotic fervor, love, street hollers, Yoruba and Kongo-Angolan chants, religious and nonsense situations. Commentary on Cuban politics is scanty.

When the rumba "breaks loose" (*rumba rompe*), the singer is joined by other singers who repeat the refrain (*estribillo*), most often in intervals of a third or three-part harmony, sometimes with no other musical accompaniment—even without percussion (e.g., arrangements of songs by Muñequitos and Tataguines). The lead singer continues to improvise verses and in responsorial style; the chorus answers with a repeated refrain. Others may become lead singers with improvisational songs that challenge the previous singer and begin a new topic. The song continues until all who demonstrate ability for the musical commentary are finished and then the chorus responds with the repeated refrain. The closing of rumba comes when the lead singer signals the chorus for the last singing of the refrain and the drummers perform a standardized rhythmic ending or coda-like break.

At the end of last century, rumba choruses appeared often in parades and concerts; their performances excluded the danced portion of rumba (León, 1984a:154, 160-64; Alén, 1987b:10-11; Urfé, 1948:183, and n.d.:10, 12-13). These groups usually practiced and performed around Christmas time. They also competed with groups from other areas within the city. Havana, Matanzas, Trinidad, and Sancti Spíritus provinces had popular coros de rumba and claves or choral societies, e.g., El Ronco, El Paso Franco, Los Jesuistas, Los Dichosos, Los Columbianos, Las Delicias Jardineras, La Tuya, La Hoja de Guayaba, Coro de Clave, Perdon de Negros Curros, Cabildo Lucumí, Bando Azul (Arará cabildo), Los Congos de Angunga. Often these groups or associations used more than one hundred voices. They would decorate rehearsal spaces and raise money to support their activities. They were led by a *decimista* who could improvise songs, a *censor* who checked lyrics of composed songs from the literary point of view, a *clarina* who identified the group with her clear and powerful (female) voice, and a *tonista* who began all songs and kept everyone on pitch. Smaller choruses (from twelve to thirty voices) still perform today as part of Rumba Saturday and neighborhood cultural house activities. They are accompanied by percussion, a small drum, water jug, little harps, or a pair of claves (León, 1984a:163).

Personnel

To perform a complete rumba today, at least five people are needed: a claves player-singer, two drummers, and two dancers. The usual rumba grouping, however, would include three singers, three drummers, one claves player, one madruga player, one catá player, one cajón player, and two dancers, or approximately twelve people. In this way, rumba is a group form and even includes the general public, bystanders, nonmusicians, or other participants who watch, comment, and evaluate the movement and music. There is much to experience: the song of the commenting soloist, the innovation within the drum ensemble and from the dancers, and the creativity between the musicians and dancers.

PERFORMANCE PRACTICES

My focus now shifts to rumba's ambiance, the way rumba appears and the way it is executed. First it is necessary to differentiate between professional, traditional, and public rumba dancing and to elaborate further on spontaneous, prepared, and prepared spontaneous Rumba events.

THE MINISTRY OF CULTURE AND RUMBA

Rumba performance is influenced indelibly by the Cuban Ministry of Culture. Like all other dances (and performing arts in all of the provinces of Cuba), rumba is organized under this ministry. The ministry directs professional dance through national company organizations and through professional training schools; it directs amateur dance through *casas de cultura*, neighborhood cultural houses, or centers.

Each center's requests for performances of particular groups are reconciled with the ministry's program to inform and educate the Cuban public regarding all the arts. The local ministry office secures performances, provides access to performing spaces, and encourages a schedule of dance instruction for children and amateur adults. Professional trained teachers from the *enseñanza artística*, professional art school, are used in neighborhood culture centers, but also in primary schools, nursery schools, and day care centers, to promote and cultivate an appreciation of dance.

> El instructor de arte, promotor y organizador de la actividad cultural masiva, es un elemento fundamental de las Casas de la Cultura. En su labor, el instructor no sólo forma y orienta a los aficionados al arte, sino que apoya activamente la educación estética de los niños y jóvenes, contribuye a la formación de un público cada vez más crítico y exigente, desarrolla el gusto estético del pueblo y colabora en el rescate de nuestras tradiciones culturales. (The art instructor, promoter and organizer

of cultural activity of the masses, is a fundamental element of neighborhood cultural centers. In his or her labor, the instructor not only molds
and orients amateurs in the arts, but also actively supports the aesthetic
education of children and teenagers, contributes to the formation of a
more and more critical and exacting public, develops an aesthetic taste
within that public and collaborates in the redemption of our cultural
traditions.) (Back cover of all dance guide textbooks, Ministry of Culture, 1979, 1982)[17]

PROFESSIONAL PERFORMANCE

The most frequent setting of rumba today is in prearranged performances by professionals, i.e., in secular rituals. The rumba performance ac-
crues the main characteristics of ritual, that is, separation of rumba time,
specialists, and space; transition to the marginal time of heightened, affec-
tive expression; and incorporation—the consequent responses, intensification, or transformation as a result of the rumba experience (Van Gennep,
1909 [1960]; also Kealiinohomoku, 1976:115, 234).

By *professionals*, Cubans mean performers who earn their living by
dancing, who perform regularly as dance specialists, and who have been
formally trained. All workers are professional in Cuba because all workers,
including dancers, earn their living by working in their areas of expertise.
The Cuban government supports the arts by paying specialists (in dance,
music, theater, or plastic arts) to work daily at their discipline. Professional
dancers are paid for minimally six hours per day, five or six days per week
(every other Saturday is a work day) and to perform an additional eight to
twenty four hours approximately, spread out over one month. They create,
rehearse, train, and maintain performance level.

Cuban dance professionals include those who perform as soloists and
members of dance choruses on the hotel circuit as well. These professionals are responsible for extravaganza and theatrical dance performances as
opposed to concert performance. When rumba begins, the dancing is executed with absolute command of the steps and sequences and the songs
are sung in perfect a cappella harmony. The announcer acts as host, nar-
rates historical information, and announces different dance/music. The
public is invited to join in at specified times or, on some occasions, people
will anticipate their invitation and join the performance spontaneously.
Usually, however, most members of the public pay for their entrance, sit in
positioned chairs facing the stage, or stand and watch the event.

Normally in professional settings, one version of rumba is performed
and then the public is invited to attempt that particular type of rumba.
Sometimes a bottle is placed at center stage and a professional dances

around the bottle, executing virtuoso steps without knocking it over (this particular rumba is called *mañunga*). The audience is then challenged to try. The public comes forth dancing and demonstrating how difficult it really is to dance well and not kick the bottle over. At other times, a professional dancing couple will stop in the middle of demonstrating and the female will choose a man from the audience and the male will choose a woman to continue the dance. The audience's attention and involvement increases, as do evaluations of each succeeding couple. Sometimes, several couples will come to the center while the professional couple is demonstrating. This allows many age groups and people with different levels of skill to dance together.

There are three professional folkloric companies in Cuba: Conjunto Folklórico Nacional in Havana and Folklórico de Oriente and Cutumba in Santiago de Cuba. Conjunto Nacional represents the national heritage in dance and presents a very strict, conservative, yet thoroughly dynamic style. It gives a performance of rumba every other Saturday (except during the four to eight weeks per year when the company travels).

Folklórico de Oriente presents rumba and other folkloric traditions also, but leans toward contemporary stylization of traditional forms. Often this company displays modern dance technique and dramatic choreographic concepts. It stretches the boundaries slightly beyond the artistic direction of the National Company, yet it stays within the tradition. Oriente style is heavily influenced by the young graduates of the national training school and several adventurous choreographers. The company represents the reality of traditional culture as a dynamic, constantly changing phenomenon.

Cutumba formed as an outgrowth of Folklórico de Oriente and also presents rumba; however, Cutumba's presentations are mainly representative of the style and traditions found in the eastern provinces, particularly Haitian-Cuban forms. The style focuses mainly on Haitian elements and regional variations of body orientation and performance dynamics. (Cutumba and Folklórico de Oriente emphasize the Caribbean culture of which Cuba is a part and not the international view which is represented by Havana's company.)[18] These differing emphases result in variation and compound Cuban styles.

All three professional companies are needed to serve the Ministry of Culture's educational objectives throughout the island. In these companies, the goals are to present folkloric materials from specific geographic regions; to identify specific Spanish, African, and Haitian segments of Cuban heritage; to entertain, inform, and reeducate the Cuban public; and to familiarize an international audience with the whole of Cuban culture.

These companies teach an appreciation of dance forms and project a vivid impression of Cuba's people. The performances engage foreigners, instill pride in Cubans, and spread knowledge of cultural values, attitudes, history, and traditional dance/music complexes.

All three professional companies perform rumba as part of their cultural and entertainment goals. The national company, however, emphasizes rumba more than the others by designating two Saturdays each month as Rumba Saturday and by replicating the original Rumba concept of a festive gathering. Nevertheless, these are prepared, not spontaneous, versions of Rumba.

The rumba dancing that is found in hotels and tourist establishments is also professionally prepared performance.[19] The caliber of dancing is very high and the performers are well rehearsed. Extravaganza dancing is modeled on the National Folkloric Company but is administered by its own organization, such as Artes Escénicas. In this kind of performance, there are momentary excerpts of rumba within a few songs or sometimes whole choreographies based on rumba.[20] Ornate costumes and elaborate sets are used to create the mood of a patio, and modern instrumentation follows traditional guidelines to introduce the singers and dancers.

If graduating dancers are not successful in auditions for the national ballet, folkloric or modern dance companies, they often find employment in theatrical extravaganzas (see the dance organization chart in chapter 3). The shows create an entirely professional atmosphere, although amateur groups that aspire to become professional appear with professional dancers from time to time. For example, Raíces Profundas began as an amateur company at the Habana Libre Hotel. It was organized under the direction of Juan de Diós, a prominent dancer from Conjunto Folklórico Nacional.

TRADITIONAL PERFORMANCE

In Cuba, "traditional" dancers are specialists in folkloric dance traditions, such as Yoruba, Palo, Kongo-Angolan, Arará, rumba, son, and comparsa. The Ministry of Culture classifies these groups as traditional, *aficionados*, or amateurs—a special category of amateurs. (Some company members have employment besides dance; however, many do not have part-time employment; they practice and perform as representatives of Cuban folklore.) Most important, it is the traditional performers who establish the norms and criteria for judging what is proper and appropriate in a specific tradition of folklore. They are the core of the traditional form and especially in rumba: Los Muñequitos de Matanzas, Afro-Cuba, Obbatola, Portales de Cárdenas, Abury Okán.

By "core" of tradition, I mean the source of living tradition. The artists and groups are often studied by professional dancers from the national companies and dance schools and by diligent directors of bona fide amateur groups. Foreign dancers observe traditional dancers intently in order to maintain traditional performance practices. Members of traditional groups in effect represent generations of experts in rumba singing, drumming, and dancing. Very often, whole families are in a group, or one family may be spread among two or three traditional rumba groups by the Ministry of Culture.

Some traditional performances have no microphones and look like spontaneous events with rumberos playing on the street corner. There is a tremendous amount of spontaneity even though traditional performances, like professional performances, can be well-planned and prepared. During traditional performances, younger groups precede or alternate with older, well-established groups. Older performers watch and listen carefully, and on occasion they switch off instruments with teenagers (i.e., "jam," "get down," in this case, "play") and instruct in this manner. There is always a critique of drumming, vocal timbre, and feeling or sentiment within the song. The criticism is usually friendly but can become acerbic in dressing rooms or on bus transports after performances. Occasionally new arrangements of songs are made. Once, in a traditional group performance, an Abakuá (secret society) dance was performed as a rumba and at another time, an Angolan song (brought back by Cuban soldiers/performers) was restructured and integrated into a rumba.

Traditional rumba ends with the setting of the sun or, if there is little audience involvement, after four or five songs. On days when the crowd is small, family members dance and sing and encourage the wee ones (two or three years old) to perform in public. On rare occasions, traditional performance continues all night.

PUBLIC PERFORMANCE

All others who perform rumba are considered bona fide amateurs, people who love to dance, sing, or drum rumba but are not members of either professional or traditional ensembles. These performers are designated in this book as amateurs, *el pueblo*, or public performers, and in Cuba would be classified as aficionados. It is not unusual for work organizations to have amateur dance groups. Most university campuses have amateur performing groups that practice routinely, give annual and semiannual concerts, and include rumba in their programming. There are amateur dance groups consisting of medical students, hotel workers, chemists, construc-

Rumba, in a solar with cajones, Santo Suarez,
Havana, 1992. Photo by Samuel Fernandez.

tion workers, and hospital workers, for example. Those who are experi-
menting with novel projects involving movement and those who did not
qualify for the national school tracking system but who love dance and
dance training often practice as conscientiously as professional dancers.
They perform periodically for the public as independent groups of interested dancers.

Aficionado groups also participate in performances during the Rumba
Festival, which is held for two weeks during the year, usually in October.
The festival places aficionado public dancers with traditional and professional artists. It includes a series of performances as well as lectures by specialists. Traditional rumba performers travel throughout the country during the festival, giving performances in parks and plazas to stadium-size
crowds. The best quinto player is selected, the best traditional and amateur
groups are announced, and all dancers show off new trends and fads which
they have incorporated into the rumba complex.

Rumba is taught to the general public in casas de cultura, where classes are offered that educate and reeducate the public. Other folkloric dances from all parts of the world are taught as well. On most of these occasions, traditional or amateur groups play the musical form and sing the inventive songs, but the untrained public dances. On other occasions, the general public will gather in homes spontaneously, for various festive celebrations, and dance rumba interspersed between contemporary casino dancing.

In night clubs, disk jockeys with records are the norm, although live bands do appear on occasion. Rumba is performed only occasionally, as in the performances of Los Van Van, Irekere, Ritmo Oriental, and Dan Den (some of the most popular musical ensembles in Cuba when I was there). The most popular dance in this setting is casino, recently *casino de la rueda,* an elaborate circle dance made with four couples and a leader who calls out changes or formations (a kind of Latin square dance in a circle); however, sometimes casino is interrupted with a short section of rumba, to everyone's delight.

When the public is not directed to dance rumba but is inspired to dance, it is an amazing sight. A real participatory event develops as fat and skinny, unskilled and somewhat skilled, old and young execute the rhythmic fun of rumba. People clap the rhythm of the claves, sing with the chorus, laugh and shout encouragement to the dancers. The dancers often dance as individuals, not trying to create a uniform choreography but a pleasurable, motion-filled nonverbal game.

There are many variations from traditional style when the public dances. Often people who have been drinking will come forward first, sometimes at inappropriate times, as during the introductory musical section. Most of their movements display basic, "classic" rumba. The typical vibrating shoulders of professionals are exchanged in public versions for an alternation of shoulders pressing forward. These often inebriated caballeros execute hip circles and vacunao gestures, not so modestly. They laugh suggestively in the knowing limelight of the moment.

Sometimes older women, usually well over sixty years old, come forward alone. They dance subtly, energetically, and often with virtuosity. The crowd cheers them on rather than laughing them off, as they do when inebriated soloists dance.

At other times, young men, seventeen to twenty-five years old, take the center space with amazing displays of movement and obvious skill. They dance columbia mostly and receive applause for their intricacies and rhythmic interchange with the quinto player. They integrate small movement motifs into long, unusual, and unique sequences. The sequences multiply to form visualized streams of consciousness, visualized thought progressions within movement threads that connect sequences and deliver a new whole. On these occasions, the quinto drummer does not know the form or style of the dancer and much depends on the kinesthetic feeling (sensitivity to movement) and improvisational techniques of both musician and dancer. When dancers display their talents in dynamic, stunning, or deceptively wondrous ways, the audience applauds and cries out, and often the dancer comes to the drums and salutes the drummers.

The public dancers are serious; machismo is at the fore. Men are advancing on women while their peers and neighbors are watching. All errors will be ridiculed for days on the streets. Women do not want to be "taken" in public by the vacunao. Consequently, everyone displays altertness, personal strength, knowledge of each rumba form. Sometimes there is a burlesque, and a woman or a man throws herself or himself aggressively at his or her partner. Men respond by fanning themselves or giving the aggressive female to a compadre. Women, of course, have more occasion to respond to the advances of men and roll their eyes, wag their fingers, or stand still with their hands on their hips. There are times when couples dance in a straightforward fashion instead of the cautious, suspended drama of the professional prepared performance; in this case, the audience witnesses a "real" chase between a woman and a man who elude and evade each other in artful dance and pantomime. Overall, few people dance compared to the numbers who watch, but no one seems to mind, because most are still participating.

DIFFERENCES IN PERFORMANCE PRACTICE

The differences between professional and traditional groups are that most designated professional folkloric dancers have trained in dance schools, while traditional group members have not, and most traditional dance groups do not generally project an image of theatrical sophistication. Without the prestige of professional categorization and the accompanying governmental support services (costumes, sets, backstage personnel), traditional groups cannot project an equal image of professionalism and cannot maintain all the accoutrements of theater performance. Many, if not most, traditional groups give quite professional performances and perform with professional companies.

Traditional groups are considerably smaller in scale than professional companies and usually have few or simple costumes. Usually twelve to twenty musicians and dancers comprise traditional groups, compared with fifty to ninety professionals in an elaborately costumed company.

Traditional renditions of rumba dancing rely on the interchange between music and dance, between the movements of the dancing couple, between the kinesthetic play of dancers and musicians. Their rumba concentrates primarily on feelings, as there are few accoutrements to complement what is going on musically or in terms of gestures. This is not to say that the renditions of professionals lack interchange; rather, professional companies use many theatrical elements to enhance the feelings within the music/dance. The performance practice is simply different. Traditional groups are more basic, professional companies more elaborate.

There is a significant difference between both kinds of performers in terms of stage presence, as when beginning or ending a piece. Professional performers begin as soon as they can be seen by any audience member and keep projecting the dance until the audience cannot see any part of their body. Traditional dance performers begin simply when the song portion of rumba ends and the responsorial section acts as a push and, to some extent, regardless of placement on stage, body position, or ensemble readiness. Endings for traditional performance are determined by the song, instrumental cadence, or movement dynamic and not by a concern for the audience or presentation values. One group obviously builds a sense of climax or drama that culminates in a precise ending; the other has precision, but beginning and ending precisely is not a major concern. It does not follow, on the other hand, that traditional groups are undisciplined or careless about presentation. In both kinds of groups, the singers are usually masterful in their vocal style and wit; in both, the dancing couples are spectacular; in both, the musicianship is astounding.

There is a major difference between professional, traditional, and amateur performance in terms of space. Mainly, traditional performance is on cobblestone, dirt, or irregularly paved streets, while professional performance more often has the distinct advantage of a smooth surface to dance on. This spatial consideration imposes constraints on balance, design, and virtuosity for both traditional and amateur performers. Therefore it is especially wondrous and even more impressive to witness traditional expertise and to realize that despite all difficulties, these performers are often the smoothest and most agile of all.

Performance practice differs also in terms of content. Both kinds of performers project rumba ideals, attitudes, and values and produce incredible virtuosity and exciting entertainment. Traditional groups, however, very rarely execute rumba del tiempo de España, the rumba with narratives and pantomimed characterization. This places the burden of preservation, of safeguarding the knowledge of rumba del tiempo de España, on professional performers.

On the other hand, traditional groups create the mixtures that originally spawned rumba. As public performers do also, traditional performance practice displays interacting or mixed traditions. For example, rumba is a secular dance and accordingly is not usually discussed in terms of religion. It is clear from the dance or movement perspective, however, that there is some kind of relationship between the orishas (the spiritual forces of the Yoruba religion) and the rumba dance in traditional performance.

For example, among some traditional rumba groups, the female dancer dances rumba foot patterns and simultaneously makes the symbolic gestures of the orishas with her arm movement pattern. Also the lyrics of many rumba songs use chants taken directly from Yoruba and Palo ceremonies (as seen in the lyrics above). When questioned about the meaning of incorporation of other dance complexes into rumba, and a religious style in particular, one dancer in Matanzas said that "sometimes, the dance is like Ochun, and I like Ochun to dance with him [my partner]. Sometimes I am talking to Ochun or Chango." Another in Havana said, "This is the rumba of today when I call Chango to the rumba."

Folklórico Nacional dancers are not allowed to put any of the orisha movements into their versions of rumba. They must execute each dance as a separate historical entity in order to guard and protect the established representations of Cuban folkloric traditions. It is true that they have tremendous dance vocabularies and advanced improvisational skills and are revered for their knowledge and performance practice of orisha dances. Additionally, many have a specialty in rumba for which they are recognized: Mario (columbia), Ramirez (guaguancó), Domingo (columbia), Nieves Fresneda and Margarita Ugarte (yambú and guaguancó), Librada Quesada (muñeca or rumba de los viejos, as well as columbia and practically all Cuban dances), Johannes García (guaguancó), Analuísa (guaguancó), Leonardo (columbia), Villa (yambú), Chique (cuchillos, or columbia with knives), Nancy (guaguancó), Lourdes Tamayo (yambú, bañista), Eunesio (botella, guaguancó), Rido Mendez (papalote and caballo [rumbas del tiempo de España]), and Mirta (yambú). However, by virtue of their membership in the national company, the license to elaborate or create stylization that might mix dance traditions is not available to them.

Within the public sphere, among traditional groups and amateur dancers, this is not the case. Nonprofessional public performers take bits and pieces of popular, secular and religious material to formulate rumba songs and movements. That dance motifs from orisha dancing are incorporated into rumba dancing suggests a contradiction between ideals and the reality of practice. (See chapter 5 on secularization.)

Rumba Performance

Type of Performer	Type of Performance	
	Participates in	Initiates
Professional	Prepared	Prepared
Traditional	Prepared (*rumba profesional*)	Prepared
	Prepared spontaneous (*rumba extendida*)	Prepared spontaneous
	Spontaneous (*rumba de cajón o tradicional*)	Spontaneous
Public	Prepared Prepared spontaneous Spontaneous	Spontaneous Prepared spontaneous

SPONTANEOUS AND PREPARED RUMBA

SPONTANEOUS RUMBA

Spontaneous Rumba defies rules. Also called *Rumba tradicional* and *Rumba de cajón*, spontaneous Rumba is people-initiated as opposed to institution-initiated (see the Rumba performance chart). It is not focused on a prepared program but occurs as a result of feelings whenever people desire to make it happen; they make a party with all sorts of things, in fact, whatever is at hand. Spontaneous Rumba refers also to the first Rumbas that were subject to the slave codes after 1842, which prohibited the use of drums after daylight hours. During this type of Rumba, there is not differentiation between professional, traditional, amateur, or general public dancers. With more people in the general population that are learning to dance and sing rumba in casas de cultura, it is quite possible that more spontaneous rumba will occur.

When it occurs, it follows a very dynamic course; its intensity is not constant. Levels of excitement, concentration, and involvement increase and decrease; it is the presence and power of the singing, drumming, songs, and dances in combination that initiate a shift in either direction. From descriptions of spontaneous events and ritual-intensity charts, one can get an idea of the shift in numbers of people who become totally involved with rumba dance/music (public display), and the character or quality of their involvement (ritual intensity) can be determined (see Sweet, 1976; Cole, 1975; Cashion, 1984; Snyder, 1988).

For many Cubans, straight rum with no ice is the welcomed stimulant that shifts the ambiance from hot muggy evening with fatigue to enchanting starlit night with gossip, political discussions, performance evaluations, personal whispered conversations, and ultimately joyous or melancholic rumba. Neighbors hear the activity and add chairs in front of their doors, which also open into the shared patio. Clotheslines are often the ceiling decorations and broken cement, with lumps and gullies, or hard-packed earth become the dance floor. A tape recorder or a radio in a window may be used for music at first. Food is usually in abundance as friends share ingredients for huge mounds of rice mixed with beans (*congrí*) and, of course, the favored specialty, barbecued pork (*lechón*). Gradually people use the sides of walls, table tops, drawers, a couple of spoons, and the slightly muffled resonance of *cajones* announces that rumba has begun. There is singing all through the night. The dancing usually includes casino, bolero, sometimes conga and rumba.

A spontaneous Rumba occurred in Matanzas when a couple arrived from Havana around nine o'clock one Saturday morning. The couple was merely visiting close friends in Matanzas for the first time in months, maybe a year; perhaps it was the couple's first retreat from work, family, and duties in quite a while. Immediately, chairs, tablecloths, and ice were gathered and a high degree of excitement prevailed among the dozen animated people who gathered. Drinks were served and radios were turned up full blast. Furniture was rearranged and cooking began for the all-day, all-night, and next-day festivities. By midmorning there was a decline of excitement as two women were cooking a huge fish and pork and preparing a rare hot sauce and salads. (Most Cubans prefer foods that are not spicy hot.) Two children were sent to shop for whatever was available, and later, four women left to find something special to prepare. This day, avocados, tomatoes, and cucumbers made a salad as accompaniment to the homemade rum that was served. Six men were seated, drinking, laughing, and talking.

By noon the heat inside and the effects of the rum caused the men to go outdoors to cool off in the shade on the communal patio. Radio music was playing from somewhere inside one of the homes, and one of the men started to dance, at first alone, then with a female partner. After a time, about six couples were dancing casino in the extraordinary midday heat of May. There was increased involvement, excitement, activity. When the radio played a rumba, everyone let one couple dance in the patio center; one man loudly challenged a woman to the guaguancó. Joking began over the style and proficiency of both dancers, but the heat and total exhaustion of the dancers caused people to saunter off, and involvement and activity diminished. That seemed to end the rumba dancing, and this part of the Rumba event. People went indoors to eat, probably to avoid the sun, and to rest from the previous excitement.

The intensity of the Rumba declined; however, the Rumba was not over. The honored couple received more visitors, perhaps a dozen other people came in and out, greeting the visitors and making plans to come back or to contribute to the preparing of foods. By two o'clock, everyone had showered for the customary second time that day and was dressing for the prepared Rumba in the town center.

Spontaneous Rumba does not require a presentation or show; however, on this occasion there was a prepared Rumba already scheduled. It was a coincidence that the visitors arrived on a day when the hosts were scheduled to work as rumberos.

At this performance, the excitement was great; performers were enthusiastic about their presentation, giving the entire ambiance a high degree of excitation and pleasure. A large crowd of sixty or more people remained around the rumba group, although many people drifted back and forth; the crowd swelled to about eighty persons on occasion. Those who encircled the performers were exceptionally interactive. After the presentation of several prepared rumbas, the honored couple danced together and then the Rumba soared higher. The woman was given to two other compadres, who tried to conquer her by both faking and making vacunaos. This was an unusual occurrence, since most men rarely let their partners dance with another male during one song, especially women that they are married to or care a great deal for. The crowd became very vocal, attentive, and active. A local woman (untrained public) danced with two of the male performers that day. One left her abruptly as she publicly challenged him in a raucous manner while the crowd cheered them all on.

At dusk, people dispersed, only to gather again at another home patio space. Women brought ingredients to share and huge plates of prepared foods. Men helped move furniture around, set up tables and chairs, went looking for cases of beer or good quality rum, served drinks and socialized. Children played with adults, wandering from home to home on the patio; they practiced dancing and frolicked with other children. Serious discussions were minimal, but not absent; people talked of Fidel Castro's latest report or evaluated the musicians and dancers at the earlier performance. The mood was festive and lively, with a good deal of excitement, though not as much as there had been during the dancing and singing of rumba earlier.

By late evening (around ten or later), a small group was singing in harmony, using tabletops and the walls of the house as drums and a couple of spoons as claves. The song lyrics were descriptive of the wonderful time the day had been and the nostalgia for remembered festive times of the past. Gradually the tempo shifted and dancing with real drums in addition to the cajón organization began. There was no set circle around a drum battery, and people danced as couples, freely, sometimes observing the rules of rumba, sometimes ignoring them to dance improvisationally.

The performer/host requested that videos of the day's performance be shown to all. Everyone gathered inside around a television and critiqued all participants. This encouraged some drummers to dance, since, on this rare occasion, the music was taped. People watched the television and ridiculed the dancing musicians (who were not half bad as dancers). The event ended when most were asleep and the honored couple left for their bus trip home. Other participants slept for a few hours and then began the morning rituals of bathing, shopping, and cleaning. There was little excitement, although much activity, and few people gathered together.

I experienced another event that may have been spontaneous Rumba on Teachers' Day in Havana in December 1985. It was the last day of classes for the semester, and dance students of the national dance academy, Cubanacán, prepared choreographies based on their recent studies. Dance studies were presented that involved spacing, design, and dramatic problems, but these shifted to short satires based on student relations with teachers, bus drivers, and other school personnel, an end of the semester celebration. This comedy was followed by claves and drums announcing a rumba. Perhaps this rumba was planned, perhaps not. Students began to invite guests and teachers to dance, sing, and drum rumba. The atmosphere quickly deepened with gaiety and laughter. As time progressed, everyone joined in the contagious excitement, which continued until it was time to take the buses for home. There was an abrupt end to the excitation that had peaked as quickly as rumba had emerged in the program.

PREPARED RUMBA

Prepared Rumba, *Rumba profesional,* is a performance, a show, a concert or tourist art where selection of songs, dancers, musicians, drummers, and an order of program are prearranged. Prepared rumba can be performed by either professional companies or traditional groups.

PREPARED SPONTANEOUS RUMBA

Prepared spontaneous Rumba occurs as a result of the feelings generated by the prepared Rumba itself or due to lively, joyous events that extend the prepared Rumba event. Prepared spontaneous Rumba, *Rumba extendida* (see Turner and Turner, 1978:243-55), refers to the kind of Rumba, generally instigated by traditional performance, that occurs after a prepared program as a result of the ambiance and spontaneous desires of participants. It involves an extension of time and occasionally a change of space. It is performed by traditional companies sometimes with professionals and the public or by the public, including all types of categories. For example, on one occasion the prepared program of several traditional groups had been completed, but the public and the group members continued singing and dancing well beyond the usual time. Despite the darkness, people were still found dancing and singing, not willing or ready to disperse. This extended the event and comprised traditional performers and the public. On other occasions, people choose to honor a person or an event, like a birthday, with a continued festive time after a prepared Rumba.

The prepared section always precedes the extension. Usually it takes place in a plaza or some public place and the extension continues either in the same place or in another location. There is no order or requisite style of dances. If no rumba is performed during the extension section, this would still constitute a prepared spontaneous Rumba event. A party or rumbón without rumba dancing or song, however, would be hard to imagine among Afro-Cubans. Spontaneous Rumba has always been intermittently performed.

PUBLIC DISPLAY AND INTENSITY

A Rumba event is an example of secular ritual, structured play apart from routine activities in a distinct space and time that promotes varying degrees of intensity and transformation. It has particular formulaic patterns that accumulate with increased tension, activity, suspense, drama, and emotion. Within one rumba, dance, song, and drumming can create a heightened state, and one rumba can demonstrate its own set of ritualized behaviors. When several rumbas are performed in succession, as in a Rumba event, increased excitement and transformation usually occur. Of course it is possible that a series of rumba can be performed and no response of exhilaration, hyperactivity, or heightened expression occurs. This would suggest that either the performers were not proficient or another kind of tension inhibited the usual route of excitation among performers and constrained the normal responses among spectator/ participants. "Success" or "failure" in ritual activity is not the determining factor of a ritual, but that the activities proceed from phase to phase is.[21]

Some Rumba events are lively, more vital or exciting than others. Within Rumba, many rumbas are performed and each has its qualitative effect on the whole. Each rumba performance manifests it own shape and ambiance; however, each contributes to a ritual of intensification. In this secular ritual, the consequence, if not the objective, is a transformed state of being, from dancer, singer, drummer, or spectator to rumbero, a person who is enthralled by and dedicated to rumba performance.

Even though in most cases today the Rumba event is initiated by the Ministry of Culture's programming, the structural form of rumba dancing and Rumba events creates certain feelings and sensibilities. The structural form stimulates emotions and initiates aesthetic responses. The entire event, including many nonaesthetic activities, creates a shape that becomes characteristic. Likewise, each dancer or musician gives the event an indication of emotion which can be interpreted in terms of interest and involvement or disinterest and uninvolvement. Between the emotional display of participants and the overall capacity of the songs to attract, the drumming to stimulate, and the dancing to arouse, ritual intensity can be outlined.

Charts of ritual intensity attempt to trace perceived levels of accumulated excitation and activity that surround, accompany, and contribute to a Rumba event and a rumba performance. Each of the five charts presented here (A-E) represents a particular Rumba that I experienced, but all of the charts are models of the fundamental structure of numerous variations that can occur.

Prepared performances reach a climax within a generally predictable time limit (see chart A) or end owing to an unexpected situation (chart B). Some prepared Rumbas begin to taper to their normal closure, but because of the energy that ignites the senses of performers or spectator/participants, the rumba is extended, either in the same space (professional Rumba, chart C) or in another space (traditional Rumba, chart D).

In totally spontaneous Rumba (chart E), there is a decided difference. The initial swelling of the number of participants (public display) and the degree of excitation (ritual intensity), due to the greeting and rejoicing phase of rumba, finds the very beginning of spontaneous Rumba at an exceedingly high pitch, near climax level. This is followed by a decrease in the number of participants and a decline of ritual intensity as participants prepare foods, invite others, dress for the occasion, and so forth. Numbers of participants build up again and generally maintain a full level at this phase for the duration of the Rumba event. The total numbers may never exceed thirty actual participants, but the same thirty people are not always present; people leave and enter or reenter. This is historic rumba, spontaneous rumba, Rumba tradicional or de cajón.

More specifically, the prepared Rumba chart (A) shows that within the

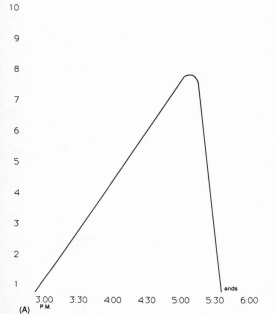

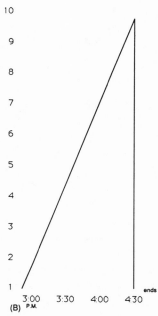

A. Chart of a prepared Rumba, showing perceived ritual intensity.

B. Chart of an interrupted prepared Rumba, showing perceived ritual intensity.

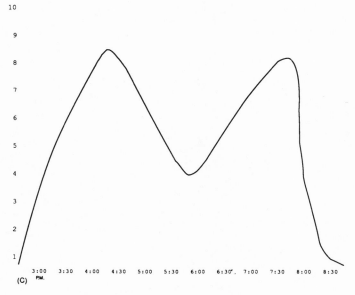

C. Chart of a prepared spontaneous Rumba, a professional Rumba, showing perceived ritual intensity.

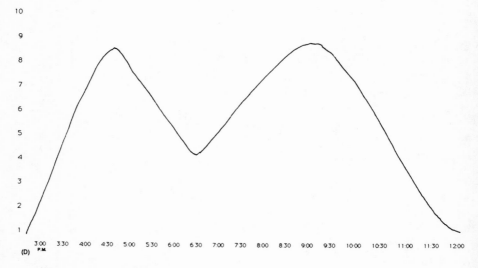

D. Chart of a prepared spontaneous Rumba, a
traditional Rumba, showing perceived ritual intensity.

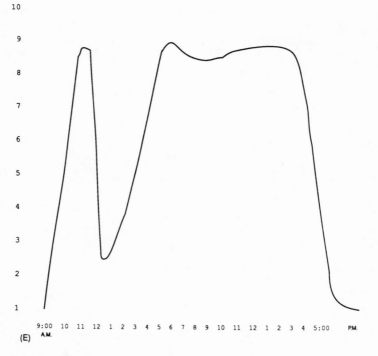

E. Chart of a totally spontaneous Rumba, a
traditional Rumba, showing perceived ritual
intensity.

three hours of performance a gradual excitation accumulates and subsides. The number of spectator/participants increases; the force and dynamics of each song/dance increases by tempo mainly, but also because of lyrics that become less neutral and because of dancing that creates more interest, through increased richness of texture and excitation. Stimulants are a part of the increase in emotional content and, as the examples have demonstrated, often provoke people to play or tease, sometimes to fight.

Nonetheless, the vast majority of rumba performances are relaxed, pleasurable affairs. In one sense, the performance is similar to any other very good concert performance that has been planned with an audience in mind. The program for rumba allows people to get comfortable with a slow yambú or with an old well-known standard from the guaguancó literature. Then it gets down, enlivening the pace with literally faster rumba and more demonstrative virtuosity in both the music and the dance. It ends with everyone wanting, but perhaps not receiving, more, so that there is a sense of reaching, longing, or pleasurable incompleteness.

Within one rumba the same pattern surfaces. The diana is the call to get comfortable and relax, and the madruga actually pushes the pace as the dancing begins. The final layering of single voices to chorus, one instrument (the claves) to five, and then competitive, suspense-filled, tension-building multisensory and multivocalic movement fulfill the pattern.

Emotional states heighten or diminish in intensity and generate or inhibit public display. The movements and their consequent stimulation generate arousal states that bind participants temporarily and increase the intensity of the event. In prepared Rumba, the peak of entertainment and excitement is followed by a relatively sharp decrease in intensity as groups usually perform a song that is known to be their trademark or ending song, which effectively announces that the rumba is over. Some people begin to leave at the beginning of this rumba, but all promptly clear the space, usually in about ten minutes of the drum ending.

Ritual intensity rises and falls more often according to public display of technique and sensual content. Movement itself stimulates kinesthetic responses. Percussion in relatively low pitches, with repeated, almost hypnotic patterns draws participants into an aesthetic realm. Smells of bodies, foods, and drinks stimulate participants. Breathing, squeals, and other noises of effort and response (beyond music) stimulate reponses (Meyer, 1956; Needham, 1978; Wilson, 1981; Feld, 1982). Both open-air and tightly packed spaces facilitate involvement and display. Combinations of sensory elements cause one Rumba event to differ from another, but also create similar effects among performers and spectators and between performers and spectators.

What the charts cannot show is the change of space as ritual intensity increases. When Rumba events begin, they are in relatively open spaces, even when they are in a small patio or one room of a house. As the Rumba continues, more people crowd into the space and people push forward to witness or involve themselves with the rumba spectacle. The actual space for performance becomes diminished as expression is augmented and intensity is heightened. Spatial intensity is therefore measured with a gradual decline in the diameter of the circular space.

The force of the event is amply demonstrated among those who know and love this particular dance/music complex. However, it is amply proved by the response from those who know nothing of its rules or regulations as well. People often sit still and watch, but most describe the experience of a total rumba performance with animated gestures, superlative verbal expressions, and visible excitement. Spectators are impressed with the response of those who understand its rules and participate, but also, they are often compelled by the rumba, or a series of rumba songs, to join in and dance particularly, or to sing with the chorus. It is probably harder for someone to respond by joining in the instrumental section, but everyone has a body and can respond kinesthetically and imitatively to movement.

It is probably true that some people do not like rumba and that others get tired or bored with rumba from time to time. These spectators leave early or leave and return, and that contributes to the variation in public display during a Rumba event.

Intensity increases with outstanding virtuosity among dancers and musicians, with eloquent or particularly humorous improvisation from the singer, and with more people who actively participate or concentrate deeply, that is, with hyperactivity and focused concentration. Intensity can decrease with fatigue, with cultural codes that signify closure (the closing trademark song, sloppy or imprecise musicianship, inept technique, ineffective expression, drunkenness, physical disruptions, ignorance or prejudice among spectators), or with sudden natural interruptions, such as rain.

What is most notable is that with all kinds of Rumba and rumba performance, dynamic energy is generated. This energy can remain among performers only, but in rumba performance it often crosses the audience/performer boundary and, even within a culturally unconditioned spectator group, it can induce pleasurable feelings and behavioral expressions. Judith Hanna reminds us that "emotions that occur during the course of everyday social life differ from emotions that occur when one is an observer of others in social interaction" (1984:188; and see 181-93 for statistical data on audience and performer responses to staged theatrical dance). Even though dance is not lanugage and has few universal meanings, rumba creates a situation in which cultural boundaries are blurred and cross-cultural experiences are embodied and felt. What the charts show is that in both short and long durations of time, in small and crowded or large and spacious surroundings, the energy flow of rumba dancing and the Rumba event retains the same configuration: a surge of energy, an increase of potential power.

This chapter has detailed the structure of the rumba complex, focusing on the appearance of African-inspired and European-influenced movements that produced three main types of rumbas. It has sketched musical concepts, instrumentation, and song styles of African and Spanish heritage that culminated in the creole form, rumba. It has also focused on rumba performance and how performance practices vary.

Rumba has a variety of settings, including prepared performances, spontaneous or originally developed festive affairs, and a combination of the two. It is generally performed within a prepared formula for foreign tourists or for relaxing Cubans, and it is seen by the general Cuban public during culture weeks and Rumba festivals in the provinces.

When the spontaneous type occurs, it is a participant-initiated consequence of good feelings and a desire to celebrate joyfully. In Rumba and in the rumba complex, the effects of an aesthetic experience that is grounded in secular ritual are seen. The important elements of the rite are the joining of artistic systems in order to create spontaneously, that is, the rich elaboration of improvisation; the interchange between performers and spectators that transforms spectators into participants; and most important, the generation of a sense of belonging to a group of rumba enthusiasts.

SYMBOLIC ASPECTS OF RUMBA

RESTAGING MEANING

Maurice Bloch describes the persuasive power of art and ritual, including dance, and points to its "illocutionary force," the force that makes dance appear believable, undoubtable, unquestionable (1974:51-81). Dance is not like everyday communication, which is declarative but challengeable as well; it is definite owing to its illocutionary force, even when it portrays tentativeness. The illocutionary force in rumba is its repeated framing of powerful, authoritative images. These images are visual and kinesthetic assertions made with specific elements and channeled in multisensory ways (see Royce, 1977:197-209). The Cuban government facilitates its objectives with regard to national development when rumba is presented. By means of certain visual impressions, rumba ignites particular feelings and conveys special meanings. It is manipulated to foster and augment the efforts of the state, which have both domestic and international consequences.

It is not surprising that a popular dance form would be used in the national and international interests of Cuba. Both intentionally and unintentionally, dance promotes ethnic and national identity through the bodies of its performers. It engages and influences spectators, and, in national demonstrations or holidays, it rivets an image onto the mind, in this case, a Cuban image. Through a conscious process, rumba is used to define, embody, and assert images of national and international identity.

As noted in earlier chapters, within the world dance community, Cuba is well-regarded for its array of professional ballet, modern, and folkloric dance. In music history and among ethnomusicologists, Cuba is known as a site of musical creation, as exemplified in danza, danzonete, and danzón in the nineteenth century and mambo and chachachá in the twentieth century, not to mention many noted Cuban symphonic composers and popular artists. I have also remarked on the influence of Cuban dance/music traditions in film and recording industries of the international arts market during the first half of this century. With a reputation such as this and with an international demand for "exotic" Caribbean tourism in recent times, it is not hard to see how Cuban dance might be suggested for use in garnering domestic attention and fostering international prestige.

The Cuban Ministry of Culture could have chosen Danza Nacional as its distinctive and "exotic" dance medium in response to international interest in Cuba. The National Company has a world-class reputation and incorporates Afro-Cuban motor behavior into modern dance technique; therefore, it is distinctly Cuban and has the potential to represent government objectives. But Cuban danza also represents an "American" or North American indigenous art and for this reason did not emerge as a prime facilitator for a national image from the Cuban dance community.

The administrators of Cuba's folkloric dance companies could have chosen the Cuban variants of Yoruba, Arará, and Kongolese dances with their hypnotic and sensual charge. These dances generate excitement and identification from Cuba's historical roots. Yet these dance traditions, for which Cuba has a particular reputation in the Americas, did not surface as primary factors in representing Cuba at both national and international levels.

Cubans themselves, by dancing and thereby emphasizing their own choices, could have exalted the *jíbaro*, or peasant worker, and could have identified with their Spanish heritage as well, by selecting zapateo as the authentic, most popular, or most representative image for a national dance portrait. Or either of the two dances that are performed by the vast majority of Cubans could have become national images: conga and casino. They are more easily executed by the general population.

But it was rumba that emerged as the key form that has been used to express national identity and that has promoted public ritual. Rumba is politicized by such use and, as a result, becomes entwined in political, economic, social, and religious arenas. The aesthetic system thereby interfaces with nonaesthetic systems.

In Cuban-Marxist terms, art symbolizes the productive basis of society (Farris, 1979). Rumba therefore was selected over other Cuban dances because it gets closest to the member of Cuban society who is most venerated ideologically, the worker. Enslaved and free black workers have contributed much to the history of Cuba, in sugar, tobacco, and coffee production during the colonial period, in liberation struggles when the newly freed slaves of Manuel de Cespedes, for example, joined force with creole and Spanish settlers against Spain. In more contemporary times, Cubans have identified with black rural sugarcane workers of the past as they assisted the Revolution of 1959. All Cubans are considered workers in efforts toward social reform, the challenge to capitalism and imperialism, and the development of Cuba as an independent nation. Cuban scholars and poets, such as José Martí, Fernando Ortiz, Nicholas Guillen, Nancy Morejín, and Samuel Feijo, have acknowledged the contribution of *los humildes, los jíbaros, los negros pobres, los trabajadores*. These are the focused groups of rumba lore.

Rumba emphasizes the fundamental essence of human social activity that is necessary for production—sex and congeniality within the community; it resonates as a life symbol. Rumba's style and organization of energy focuses on sensual qualities that analytically reference sexual activity. Whether in home patios or in larger theaters, intimate spaces are filled with compact sensory stimuli. Layers of sound, colors, shapes, lights, smells, bodies, traffic, the sea, the sun, foods, drinks, even garbage—all bombard the senses as multiple stimuli accumulate. Relationships of performers and the interacting of spectator/participants, audience, or onlookers are expressed and idealized in the dancing couple.

The sixth sense is stimulated to intuit the vacunao, the expression of the relationship between performers. Time is suspended. For the moment, work is over; play is at hand. Relaxation and release are the content of the moment, the space, and the event. These contingencies are announced emphatically by the dance and the dance event and, for the period of dancing, these assumptions are not challenged. In fact, the interconnecting parts of the symbol (music, costume, setting, movement) jointly seduce the spectator/participant and often the performers as well, and create an image of Cuba that is compelling.

Interestingly, the shift in meaning that so often accompanies the conscious manipulation of aesthetic material does not obtain in the case of rumba. In Rumba, the loss of meaning associated with traditional art that has been politicized or commoditized has not yet occurred. Unlike the case of the Basque Alarde, for example (Greenwood, 1977:129-138), which saw a decline of involvement in a traditional festival owing to commoditization and tourism and then a resurgence of interest, (Greenwood, 1989:180-85), cultural meaning in Rumba is sustained because of the *communitas* it produces and because of the medium of dance. Unlike the disappearance and reappearance with loss of meaning of men's houses and woodcarvings of the Asmat in New Guinea (Rockefeller, 1968; cf. Schneebaum, 1975), Rumba in Cuba is a thriving and developing form.

DEVELOPMENT AND DIFFUSION OF CULTURAL VALUES

Development is paramount in Cuban concerns, and it influences all aspects of social and cultural life, including dance. Development in Cuba is the story of the Revolution and the ongoing, ever-present struggle for equality and social justice (James, 1938 [1963]; Fanon, 1963; Frank, 1969; Freire, 1970 [1982]; Reed and Walker, 1976; Cole, 1980; Hintzen, 1982; Lewis, 1983; Berreman, 1979; Thomas, 1988; and for discussions of Cuba from varying perspectives see Mesa-Lago, 1971; Bonachea and Valdés, 1972; Bonachea and San Martin, 1974; Szulc, 1986; Black, 1988; Smith, 1988; Leo Grande, 1988; Moore, 1989; Torres Rivera, 1993). To implement the objectives of the Revolution or to develop contemporary Cuban society, symbols have been organized beyond traditional usage or original artistic (choreographic) intent. Cultural expressions become didactic symbols when they are associated with the nation. The initial images that rumba projects and the apparent values that are emphasized throughout the Rumba event become symbols that inform, educate, and are capable of causing change. The use of rumba to gather and maintain commitment to values is simply part of the thorough thinking and dedication to a more egalitarian society that exists at the core of Cuban ideology.

Ideals surrounding such social values are publicized in separate but often connected systems. National goals and objectives are articulated in proclamations by Fidel Castro, the Communist party, and various institutes and commissions within the ministerial organization. For example, the party platform for 1976 states (quoted in Hernandez, 1980:110):

> La sociedad socialista exige un arte y una literatura que, a la vez que proporcionen el disfrute estético, contribuyan a elevar el nivel cultural del pueblo. Debe lograrse el establecimiento de un clima altamente creador que impulse el progreso del arte y de la literatura como aspiración legítima de las masas trabajadoras. El arte y la literatura promoverán los más altos valores humanos, enriquecerán la vida de nuestro pueblo y participarán activamente en la formación de la personalidad comunista. . . . Con el triunfo de la Revolución se abrieron nuevas vías para el desarrollo cultural del pueblo. En el capitalismo la mayoría de los artistas, totalmente desamparados social y económicamente, estaban marginados o sólo eran aceptados para deleíte de la élite burguesa. Cientos de talentos se frustraron al sucumbir ante el ambiente hostil que los rodeaba. . . . Los escasos centros de difusión cultural sólo satisfacían

a minorías privilegiadas. . . . Las ciudades del interior, abandonadas, no ofrecían el menor vestigio de vida cultural. (The socialist society demands an art and literature which, at the same time that it offers aesthetic enjoyment, contributes to elevate the cultural level of the people. It should succeed in the establishment of a highly creative climate which forces the progress of art and literature as legitimate aspirations of the working masses. Art and literature will advance the highest human values, enrich the lives of our people and will participate actively in the formation of a Communist personality. . . . With the triumph of the Revolution, the way is open for the cultural development of the people. Under capitalism, the majority of artists, who had been totally disenfranchised socially and economically, were marginal or were only accepted for the delight of the bourgeoisie. Hundreds of talents were frustrated as they surrendered to the hostile climate which surrounded them. . . . The limited centers of cultural diffusion would only satisfy the privileged minority. . . . The abandoned cities of the rural areas were not offered the smallest vestige of cultural life.)

The objectives that most affect dance and are central to contemporary Cuban society as well are domestic social equality and international self-determination. If all Cubans are to share equitably in the solidarity of the Cuban nation, particularly dark-skinned traditional or folkloric artists, inclusion of members of the former lower class becomes important, if not crucial. The Ministry of Culture projects its interests into provincial, municipal, neighborhood, or district administration. For dance, this means that the Ministry of Culture organizes artists and their presentation of cultural symbols in neighborhood culture houses (see chapters 3 and 4 and the back covers of dance textbooks).

Investigation of Cuban dance organization shows professional and amateur units, theater management, and a significant international unit (see the dance organization in Cuba chart under Ministry of Culture). This indicates a recognition of the international consequences of the arts at the ministerial level of government. It highlights domestic development of dance programming and the interest in utilizing, or at least managing, artistic products of the Ministry of Culture in accordance with national goals. Analysis of programming and choreographic content has shown the use of rumba as a vehicle for identification with the Cuban worker and for light- and dark-skinned solidarity. In international arenas, analysis shows that rumba is used as a symbol for the goals of the Revolution, of a sovereign, egalitarian nation thriving though struggling.

Beyond politicization and the education system, other social systems are activated by ministry programming. With dancers positioned in every sector of the population and within arenas of international exchange as well, dance becomes enmeshed in economic activites. Dance opportunities have been publicized and dance forms have been metamorphosed to fit into the international arts market, that is, commoditization has taken place. Additionally, in the presentation of religious material that has been removed from its original religious context and placed in the context of Rumba Saturdays, the ministry in effect permits and supports a secularizing process. From the ministerial point of view, programming supports national heritage in which religious dance plays an important role. This kind of programming, however, demonstrates a form of secularization and Rumba is the instrument used to affect such a process.

Finally, the communication and transportation systems ensure the proliferation of preferred values. The government through the Ministry of Culture at provincial levels supports a systematized information flow, albeit through slow and labored channels, by bus, Jeep, and truck. The values within rumba are brought to rural and urban districts throughout the island through rumba performances. Technology transports rumba intermittently by means of cultural programming on the two television stations and multiple radio stations. Both intentionally and unintentionally, rumba has been drawn into politicization, commoditization, and secularization processes, all of which demonstrate the symbolic aspects of rumba. The following discusses such processes separately.

POLITICIZATION

NATIONAL IDENTITY

Rumba represents an ideal which the Revolution embodied: equality with the working masses and an identity with its Afro-Latin heritage (see, for example, Guevara in Deutschmann, 1987; Castro, 1968, 1984b, 1985c; Cole, 1980; Randall, 1981; Reed and Walker, 1976; Mandela, 1991). As noted, rumba has long been equated with workers, beginning with the slave, free black, mulatto, and white workers of the nineteenth century. Although rumba was considered African, Afro-Cuban, *baja cultura* (low culture), obscene, or too sexual by some Cubans before the Revolution, it has been aligned with notions of dignity, recognition, equality, and inspiration since then. In striving for social equality, the government has attempted to unify elements of the historically hierarchical social system. Rumba openly reveals the Revolution's legal reality of nondiscrimination contrasted with historical cultural biases that deemphasized common ancestry with blacks and denigrated equal association between Cubans of African and non-African descent (see Martinez-Alier, 1974:1-20, 71-75).

It is a difficult task to reformulate cultural values to conform to new categories and to include expressions of a previously lower class. The national prominence of rumba has contributed to and continues to fortify efforts toward social equality in Cuba. Rumba assists in moderating cultural behavior and social ideology. It fosters reeducation and the practice of sociopolitical principles (cf. Christopher, 1979, on ballet as a national symbol in China).

The repeated display of rumba signifies the desire of the Cuban government to publicize its affinity with the working masses as well as its African heritage from Spain through Moorish contact and its African heritage from West and Central Africa through the Atlantic slave trade. This recognition in turn conveys the government's antiracist ideals and objectives, not only to foreigners but also to the nation as a whole.

Acknowledgment of historical connections between African heritage and lower-class status in the presentation of rumba also identifies the national government with the working masses more than with an elite or aristocracy, which could be symbolized in ballet, for example. It emphasizes socialist values of egalitarianism and sharing. Not only are these ideas and objectives presented; they also bombard the senses of viewers as nonverbal lessons from government-sponsored agencies. Rumba (and dance in general) is an immediate and powerful mode of communication by means of multisensory channels of vision, kinesthetics, and sound. These and other cognitive channels are simultaneously stimulated in dance performance and have the capacity to send vivid and lasting impressions (Royce, 1977; Hanna, 1979; Blacking, 1973; Bloch, 1974).

Rumba has changed from a people-initiated, recreational dance form into a primarily government-initiated, politicized activity for multiple diplomatic and public relations occasions. The Folklórico Nacional performs for most visitors, diplomats, and tourists (as well as for fellow Cubans in regular bimonthly performances), specifically at Rumba Saturday or as an integral part of season concerts in national theaters throughout the island. Rumba appears as part of the regular program. Even groups of scholars or laborers, such as the international volunteers for the sugarcane harvests, *la brigada*, participate in collateral activities of their meetings, which include private performances, rehearsals, or theater performances involving rumba. During the annual visual arts festival (*Bienal*) in November, the International Film Festival in December, and the annual festivals of electroacoustic, jazz, and popular music, participation of two hundred to eight hundred or more international visitors is generated. These events serve as opportunities to present carefully constructed images of what Cubans wish the world to envision when someone thinks of Cuba. What is displayed in rumba is contradictory at the analytical level but central in portraying Cuba as a Spanish- and African-derived culture, a congenial and vivacious people, and, among small nations, a thoroughly organized society.

Rumba communicates these aspects of Cuban culture in multiple ways simultaneously, that is, rumba is multivocalic (Royce, 1977:197-209). In accomplishing multiple tasks at the same time, rumba's power accumulates. Its effect becomes stronger because its messages are reinforced or underscored. By means of dance, Cuba's official message is reiterated. As discussed in chapter 4, the language of the songs, the generalized song form, and vocal style point to Spanish history. The details of rumba costuming are evidence of Spanish heritage as well: long, wide, ornately layered dresses with long shawls for women and tight pants, ruffled shirts with vests, hats, and scarves for men. Simultaneously, rumba alludes to African heritage by its call and response patterns, body orientation, polyrhythms in music and in the body, torso-generated movement, body part isolation, etc. The dance is executed predominantly by dark-skinned Cubans, although it can display a full spectrum of white, brown, and black performers. These dancers visually and nonverbally convey the dualism within Cuban identity. They confirm an African affinity in Cuba which offsets a commonly held image within the Caribbean, that of "Spanish" Cuba, the "white" Caribbean island. Rumba, which traditionally and visually represented one segment of the Cuban population, has been augmented to symbolize the nation as a whole, historically, ethnically, and aesthetically.

POLITICAL REALITY OF RUMBA AND DANCE

A "classic" performance of rumba by Los Muñequitos de Matanzas while the group was in Havana for Sábado de la rumba reveals how the dance and the dancers are actually regarded and evaluated. Cuban or foreign diplomats living in Havana would probably go to see Los Muñequitos as part of official duties and as one small part of social activity in diplomatic circles. They have probably seen and heard the group live and via radio and television many, many times. They view rumba as an entertaining folk dance.

The bureaucrat, the civil servant, and the university student are aware of the importance of Los Muñequitos also, but depending on personal interest and preference, these Cubans rarely go to see rumba unless it is included as part of other local cultural activities. For these Cubans, rumba is important to their education or to their political-social status more than their voluntary social life.

Campesinos may see rumba on television or as it is performed in provincial festivities a few times a year; however, they display particular interest in Los Muñequitos' performances. For these workers, a visit from Los Muñequitos generally signifies party time. Rural workers usually enjoy Mexican music and casino-style dancing rather than rumba. There are some rural workers, however, who not only come as spectators but actively dance as participants in rumba's center circle. They lead an improvised song or even alternate with a drummer.

Conversely, it is rare to see a representative of the Ministry of Culture's administrative level, for example, in attendance at local performances given by Los Muñequitos or other rumberos. Sound technicians and occasionally receptionists or secretaries come to see a performance, but division heads, assistants to provincial directors, and directors themselves are only seen at provincial events, at Culture Week activities, for example, that might include rumba but do not emphasize it. In Havana, often when Los Muñequitos are scheduled to perform, officials who are present at the beginning leave before the performance ends, stating their status obligations behaviorally as well as their personal evaluations.

Despite the popularity of rumba among professional dancers and within ministry programming, light-skinned or white Cubans do not attend rumba performances very often (Daniel, 1991:1-10). The light-skinned or white audience of Sábado de la rumba are generally foreign visitors and tourists. The light-skinned Cubans who attend with any frequency or regularity are those whose childhood and younger years involved living in an area particularly important for rumba, such as the Simpson District in Matanzas or the Regla District in Havana. It is more often white-collar workers who appear at rumba performances, not the masses of Cubans, either light- or dark-skinned, who are supposed to embody the more enlightened and changed values of the Revolution.

Participation in terms of skin color is important if the ideology of the Revolution is to be achieved and if Cuba's Afro-Latin identity is to be believed. It is striking that discrimination and prejudice, the festering relatives of racism, interrupt national egalitarian efforts and affect national identity. Rumba, the representative dance of the lower class, is a symbolic but political attempt to affirm the equality Cuba represents internationally. Rumba performance symbolizes, on one hand, the unity and solidarity of equality and, on the other hand, the rupture and tension of inequality. Cuba's identity lies somewhere in the gap between the apparent and the analytical levels.

WOMEN'S EQUALITY AND MACHISMO

The display of rumba also includes a dominant male image as demonstrated in choreographic analysis. The notions of accommodation and sub-servience to men which reside deep within Cuban culture are maintained in the rumba dance and event, although Cubans are more aware of elements denoting women's liberation and equality (see Stone, 1981).

More women are working outside the home than ever before. Child care is available as part of government-sponsored programs, and fathers receive paternity leaves and incidental, family-associated absences to assist in child care duties. Since 1965, child care centers, *círculos*, have been constructed and professionally staffed for the care of infants (from forty-five days old) and for the education of young children up to six years old. These círculos allow mothers to enter the work force more easily than before the Revolution. Additionally, jobs which were previously considered inappropriate for women were opened for female workers in 1968, and even more important, women receive equal pay for their labor. It is quite common to see women as supervisors and administrative heads of factories, dance companies, or ministry organizations.

It could be argued that because of these social advancements, rumba offers one place where the display of machismo is socially tolerated. Rather, machismo is deeply embedded and far more resilient than a fad or social current. Rumba displays a slice of the private sphere of Cuban society which often, if not overwhelmingly, demonstrates domestic inequality (Rosaldo and Lamphere, 1974).

Cuban poet Milagros Gonzalez has written a poem (undated) that expresses reality for contemporary Cuban women and echoes reality for women elsewhere. The poem (purchased by Barnard College's Women's Center, translated by Margaret Randall, and printed in Randall, 1981:18-20) includes these lines:

First Dialogue

> . . . Where are you: manspirit of my time,
> every afternoon home from work become exactly
> that fountain of rude stares
> reproaching me the quick lunch, pile of
> unwashed clothes, handkerchiefs not perfectly
> ironed. This daily existence. . . .
> What difference to you that the children
> make their beds, pick up their shoes and help
> me dry the dishes if you study for your next
> class in the most comfortable chair we have
> and keep your fear in shadow, almost hidden so
> no one will discover that "macho" at the base
> of your spine!
> . . . Learn then to heat your food while I
> study, put your diplomas away, . . . Because

Revolution is more than I want,
more than Party member, more than Congress,
Assembly,
                    REVOLUTION
is also we who make and do who plow
with you, who pencil, who trench. . . .
Comrade, when the day breaks, you'll have
risen finally, TO THE HIGHEST HUMAN PLANE.

Machismo is at the root of many social values in Cuba, as it is the root elsewhere. While this poem was written sometime before 1981 (the date of Randall's volume), it activates memories of the experiences of women I knew and witnessed between 1985 and 1990 (see Daniel, 1990b). This type of inequality is not easily revealed in Cuban social interactions but shows up only over long periods of familiar, intimate, home relationships. Contemporary Cubans are products of both *machista* and revolutionary culture; they exhibit both machista and revolutionary concepts and values, but in differing domains. While the official public domain coerces Cubans to display the institutional precepts and behaviors of the Revolution, Cubans are also privy to and influenced by the attitudes and biases of their private sphere.

Women's reality, which is reflected in rumba in terms of spatial relations within the dance and in rules for who dances and how one dances, is an enduring dependency. Its base is found in a fundamental machista attitude within Cuban culture. Rumba reflects this reality as it simultaneously projects the national identity for which it was originally politicized. Women are only strong and able to exercise some power defensively, as in their ability to deflect male attempts at domination. Change is in the making, but it has not permeated the whole.

To be macho or *guapo* is to be a man and to assert manhood, and guapo is symbolized in the costumes that are used most often in rumba. These are stylizations that echo early Spaniards of African descent, such as *los negros curros de Manglar* (Ortiz, 1926 [1986], 1984). They lived in Havana in the eighteenth and early nineteenth centuries and were known for their independent, scandalous, and irreverent life-style, their characteristic dress and their particular speech patterns. Their traits are associated with the behavior of streetwise men of the taverns, bars, ports, and marinas, and their manner in Cuban folklore is the epitome of macho.

Manhood, associated with males seeking and protecting females, is at the center of Cuban cultural values. Men strategize to have or to appear to have power over women. They compete with other men for women, to possess, control, or own women or to be admired by them. The government and the Federation of Cuban Women (FMC, Federación de Mujeres Cubanas) have made deliberate efforts to sensitize and reeducate Cubans with regard to gender equality, but the preservation of male self-worth continues to be linked with male superiority. The human need for a sense of well-being and security directs both men and women toward affection, love, sex, freedom, and spontaneity, and Cuban men seek these things from women generally. Their attitudes and actual efforts, however, point to fears that men cannot or will not secure these desires and needs. Their fears provoke behavior that results in domineering and inequitable relations with women (see Schlegel, 1977; Slocum, 1975; Rosaldo and Lamphere, 1974; Mernissi, 1975; hooks, 1990; Trinh, 1989).

Most often in Cuba, male behavior is a display of strength, leadership, and control over women and children, which is considered proper and appropriate protection. Women's protection serves as a cover for men's need to control situations and to gain self-worth or security. Dance reflects those values and affirms them indirectly by providing visible evidence of male protection and respect for females. In genteel mannerisms of respect, cordiality, and admiration, male rumba dancers assert themselves as strong, benevolent protectors of women as wives or prospective wives primarily. Men are assured their usual position: in charge, superior to women.

Machismo abounds in motor behavior patterns walking down streets and within daily social relations inside homes. In Cuba, physical touching is exceedingly common, from greeting acquaintances with kisses on either side of the face to fondling in public parks. Despite the genuine affection which is displayed in physical touching and despite the postcard scene of loving couples of all ages carrying out normal routines in daily life, elements of male dominance are pervasive.

Whenever couples step outside the home, men hold women around their waists, around their shoulders, or, most commonly, by their hands. On buses or at public events, it is not unusual for men to sit on women's laps. Most important, women rarely go out alone despite the absence of rape or large-scale robbery. Cuba is one of the safest societes in Latin America, and Havana is one of the safest large urban areas in the Americas. It seems hardly necessary to bodily protect women, yet male dominance is revealed prominently in these examples of public behavior.

Not only is a sense of machismo communicated to females; it is also strongly communicated between men. Men communicate to other men by means of physically shielding women who are in their company. When men place their arms fully across both sides of the woman's shoulders, women are thereby protected from possible (and probable) comments, from supposed physical abuse, and from presumed ever-lurking eyes. Harsh unwritten rules speak of discomfort, insult, rudeness, and possible anger should a woman greet a man while talking to another. Indeed it is serious or dangerous (depending on the individuals involved) for a woman to linger in conversation with one man while she is talking or walking with another. The male's sense of pride and self-worth are affronted, and he may demand respect as the man the woman is with and as a man in general. While this behavior is not openly valued, it is often probable.

Cuban machismo is reflected in rumba and the Rumba event through two possible images in male performance, one protective, the other opportunistic; both emphasize male dominance. One is concerned with a romantic Latin male who dances sensuously and protects his female partner or mate. The other is a controlling figure who conquers his partner's vulnerability and possesses her. Both images enjoy a positive audience response to the ritualized chase of the sexes. The preferred and most apparent image is where the male displays charm, strength, and concern and where women are protected. Most women and those men who are sensitized and committed to women's liberation from machismo see this successful, romantic image but fail to acknowledge the simultaneous inequality therein. This image is used in terms of politicization, since it emphasizes women's equality in the public sphere. The domineering qualities of this image are considered secondary, almost hidden, but they present glimpses of the machista behavior from Cuban private spheres.

The private sphere includes the fathers, uncles, and grandfathers who control household members, as they have historically, within the home. Women still confont fears of loneliness and self-doubt, and many refuse to seek assistance from the FMC but remain in unhealthy, dependent relationships and in a domineering, oppressive atmosphere. The younger generation that has grown up in the Revolution and its values have fewer spokespersons for male chauvinism; however, they have lived within the private sphere of Cuban homes with the same fathers and grandfathers who control their mothers and sisters and who model for them and their brothers. Dual sets of values become their reference frame. The existence and the ongoing activity of the Cuban Federation for Woman are proof that problems exist as everywhere. Rumba epitomizes the values that are most embodied but attempts to reconcile behavior from both the public and private domains.

COMMODITIZATION: METAMORPHOSIS OF RUMBA

Expressive culture is often created for one purpose and used for another. Dance has been practiced as part of cultural tradition and as recreation and has been evaluated as artistic, as "art by destination." Yet it has also been discovered among other items in an art market elsewhere, "art by metamorphosis" (Maquet, 1971:3-10, and 1986). Maquet refers to these phenomena respectively, but he is primarily concerned with visual and plastic arts and the destination he implies is the European-American art network of galleries, studios, and museums. I use his analogy to refer both to the transition of rumba from one arena to another and to the transformation of its character. As rumba and the Rumba event are analyzed in their national showcase, what began as the redemption of cultural dance traditions appears as a commodity and the nexus among foreign consumers in an international art market. In this manner, dance, an aesthetic system, interacts with the economic arena of Cuban social relations.

Cuban dance forms are manipulated as are other cultural resources in order to generate foreign exchange. Cuba, however, has not had tremendous resources for dance because Cuban resources have been earmarked for development, mainly for health and education. Most available monies have been used to feed and house the Cuban people, to provide electricity and gas, to buy medicines and medical technology, to build and maintain medical and educational facilities, to improve rural housing and transportation throughout the island, and to maintain Cuba's military forces for self-defense and for the defense of liberation movements elsewhere. A deliberate effort has been made to spread resources in an equitable manner among the total population, rural and urban. The results have been significantly successful considering Cuba's isolation through the United States embargo and the Soviet Union's diminished support, and most recently, by the demise of the Soviet Union.

The first successes were exhibited in soaring literacy rates and improved health care through declines in infant mortality rates (see Feinsilver, 1989, on "health tourism"). The financial implication of this growth, however, is a decline in or strain upon foreign exchange. The embargo imposed by the United States (February 3, 1962) and the later neglect of the Soviet Union due to its own domestic turmoil have forced Cuba to maximize its efforts to acquire foreign currencies. These are needed to buy foodstuffs, supplies, and technology (Williams, 1970; Levine, 1983; Erisman, 1985; Szulc, 1986; Zimbalist, 1987).

Ordinarily, diplomatic stores (*diplotiendas*) provide access to needed foreign exchange as well as protection against outflows of foreign currency. They sell a range of foods, household supplies, and luxury items, such as cigarettes, cosmetics, perfumes, clothing, and quality textiles. These stores sell at prices that do no reflect tariffs; to most foreigners the prices are comparatively low. They buy believing they are making a deal; and many buy in bulk as a result of numerous demands, often from local Cubans who do not share this access.

Nearly all the hotels and restaurants require foreigners to pay in foreign dollars, even if they have previously exchanged their dollars into pesos, the Cuban currency. Until 1990, tourists would change money at banks or on the street (black market) only to find that they could not spend Cuban pesos except for small, financially insignificant purchases. Living and spending in U.S. dollars or foreign currencies have been made compulsory for foreigners, but this appears inexpensive to the foreign visitor and continues Cuba's advantage.

As a result of economic transactions surrounding visits to and attendance at dance/music events, Cuba receives needed foreign currency and dance/music enthusiasts have their bargain also. Rumba Saturday and the enticing array of folkloric dance forms presented by the Folklórico Nacional have provided benefits to Cuba in terms of prestige and status, but also, perhaps unexpectedly, in terms of foreign exchange. Cuba has used its national dance forms as one means of economic support by attracting students of dance and music, specialized tourists, for study and entertainment. While being entertained, learning cultural aspects of the exotic Caribbean, and glimpsing behind the U.S. political-economic screen over Cuba, consumers of dance impact the Cuban treasury. This impact is small, but acts like economic vitamins from the aesthetic system, with small, steady, nutritional supplements for a healthy whole (Daniel, 1990a).

In this way, dance is metamorphosed as a commodity and becomes "commoditized" (Graburn, 1984:27; Appadurai, 1986; Cohen, 1988:381), one of the most appealing and softest-selling pitches of Cuba's "good deals." Something needed or wanted by those with adequate or abundant foreign exchange is simultaneously in great supply among the Cuban people. The supply of Cuban dance/music has been rationed and shared in relation to demand and the going price, and Cuban dance organizations are encouraging more students and visitors.

Originally the aim was not profit, marketing, or exporting Cuban music/dance, but over time there has been an awareness of potential foreign exchange. Otherwise the company directors would stress touring and performance only. By including dance instruction and performance workshops, dance organizations can assist national economic efforts, even if only in a small way, and at the same time further organizational and artistic goals. An investment in dancers and dancers' needs (good cloth, cosmetics, paints, scenery, instruments, sound systems) pays off in dividends of foreign exchange and, when handled properly, yields prestige in good public relations and international publicity. Cuba maximizes opportunities for foreign exchange and for prestige as "symbolic capital" (Bourdieu, 1977:177, 180).

Each professional company of Havana has instituted a program of international dance/music workshops; such programs ultimately buy and sell ballet, modern, and folkloric dance training and performance. The ballet had foreign dance students for many years before the Revolution. The folkloric company has had international dance and music workshops since 1983; some years it has had two a year (the major one is in June or July and the additional one is in January). The modern dance company has had international workshops since January 1989, when it inaugurated its first workshop in celebration of its thirtieth anniversary and that of the Revolution. It was rumored in 1990 that Folklórico de Oriente, the company in Santiago de Cuba, was initiating its own workshop season as well.

What has happened is a response to the excitement Rumba events cause. It is an attempt to accommodate large numbers of interested students and tourists with the prospect of accumulated foreign exchange. While dance companies receive prestige and status for artistic recognition of such international events, they also have the possibility of generating financial security for their organization. As an organization acquires more financial support from both earned income and ministry budgets, it can improve the quality of production. As a result, practically all students are accepted, regardless of ability or level of proficiency.[1]

There are multiple consequences to the packaging, publicizing, and distribution of rumba, that is, the commoditization of rumba. The consequences are seen not only in terms of change in the dance and music structure but also in terms of the society and the performers. "Symbolic capital" is exchanged among rumberos, foreign students, tourists, and dance companies within ministerial organization, as well as among nations.

For the nation, rumba commoditization assists politicization. It provides the framing of Cuba's national image, international publicity, and preservation of cultural traditions. International workshops advertise Cuban historical traditions, perpetuate Cuba's contemporary international image, and augment Cuba's efforts to accumulate foreign exchange. The nation receives funds directly (real and symbolic capital) from workshop and festival participation of students, and indirectly the nation profits from stimulation of related industries that manufacture instruments, produce recordings and tapes, and sell workshop souvenirs, such as tee shirts, skirts, and scarves.

For the artists and administrators, commoditization of rumba provides regular employment opportunities, avenues for company development, and access to professionally related items as well as rare products; but, more important, it provides an ambiance for creativity. International workshops ensure employment for both professional and amateur musicians and dancers. The cultural educational calendar is augmented with workshop engagements and offers multiple settings for Cuban music/dance. Many Cuban artists are included as performance obligations exceed the national companies' possibilities. Amateur and other professional artists gain steady employment in hotels and resorts for the growing numbers of students and special visitors. Also, artists gain access to items that are limited, if ever available, in Cuban stores, such as high-quality blank tapes and long-lasting batteries. Cuban artists often receive tape and video recorders as expressions of thanks for the artistic experience shared with students and fellow professional artists. Performance response includes the possibility of access to rare items from diplotiendas.

By far the major effect of commoditization on administrators is the opportunity to accumulate foreign capital to use in developing organizationally, to improve technical equipment, acquire needed supplies, and maintain facilities requisite for production as well as for teaching.

The most important effect of commoditization on artists as artists is aesthetic nourishment. Commoditization of rumba provides this service to Cuban artists particularly. Historically, musicians and dancers have been involved in sharing their music/dance, or "jamming," through both spontaneous and planned performance events. During workshops and during rumba performances especially, important jamming occurs. These times provide aesthetic nourishment, opportunities that permit an exchange with different artistic conceptualizations, contemporary trends, and novel ideas, as well as Cuban reaction to and development of innovation, both among individual artists and within groups.

Artistic creativity is also stimulated inadvertently. Because students do not usually know the unwritten rules thoroughly, they are often indulged when they mistakenly cross boundaries. These mishaps and the responding behavior that attempts to make the foreigner feel safe and free from embarrassment allow Cuban spontaneity and improvisation to flow. These seemingly unimportant occurrences impact creativity. For example, when the traditional form of rumba in Rumba Saturday is interrupted with student or tourist involvement, the rumba of today can appear, irrespective of official rules to the contrary. The "now" rumba and thus the organic process of traditional folklore are accessed with new innovations and intratraditional mixing (for example, Yoruba steps in rumba).

The consequence of commoditization for students involves aesthetic, cultural, and spiritual nourishment. First, students receive specialization in traditions they not only admire but also treasure. They treasure instruction because of the isolated position of Cuba and the difficulties that must be overcome in order to study there. Students receive training from master musicians and master dancers, and some perfect their own virtuosity. Most enter into a magical world of liminality, a world of betwixt and between, where they are freed from ordinary tensions and are indulged in their speciality, a near-ecstatic experience for lovers or professionals of Cuban rumba. Intensity in the courses, intimacy with rumba idols, and immediacy of context in the Cuban environment produce an out-of-this-world, meaningful, and profound impression. Non-Cuban artists gain knowledge of new forms, close affinity with important and revered artists, and deeper understanding of the Cuban aesthetic. Most students are consequently transformed by the experience. Some divert their research energies totally toward Cuban traditions; others start ensembles on their return and perform Cuban dance/music. Still others prepare to ritually repeat the experience annually as a periodic artistic supplement to their lives (see Graburn, 1984:27, 1989:21-33).

The effects of rumba commoditization on the dance/music itself can be described as restructuring of form and content, conservation of culture, dispersion to new groups, and intratraditional synthesis (see the effects of rumba commoditization chart). In the workshop setting and in tourist environments as well, rumba form is miniaturized to conform to classroom time or foreigners' concentration time. It is crystallized for student consumption. Performance contains important elements, yet it becomes compact by the elimination of others. Creativity is limited within the restructuring of an improvisational form.

Although many songs have repeatable lyrics and music, as well as consistent dance motifs, rumba's ultimate expression is the spontaneous inspiration from a singer, the unpredictable invented movements of a particular dancer, the unrehearsed interactions among musicians or between musicians and dancers. This necessarily involves mixing of elements and differing traditions when students perform. These elements are de-emphasized in workshop presentations that promote rumba in a set time and space and contain a set, fully choreographed formula. The tendency toward set choreography changes rumba content and Rumba structure. Additionally, the commoditization of rumba has had a secularizing effect on Cuban religious traditions that are often performed in the same setting with rumba.

The commoditization of rumba in international workshops stimulates research of rumba musical and choreographic materials in efforts to conserve and continue historical culture. In terms of research and conservation, rumba commoditization has stimulated the maintenance and promo-

---

Effects of Rumba Commoditization

For Cuba
- Framing of international image as a unique island nation
- Economic vitamins: increased foreign exchange, development of hotel and related manufacturing industries

For the Hosts (Dancers, Musicians, Arts Administrators)
- Employment
- Aesthetic nourishment: spontaneity, jamming, creativity
- Access to professional items: tapes, recorders, batteries, foreign musics
- Access to nonprofessional items: rum, jeans, pullovers, cosmetics
- Development of arts organization structure
- Development of production capacity: technical equipment improvements, supplies, maintenance of facilities

For the Guests (Foreign Visitors, International Students)
- Aesthetic nourishment: specialization, research, virtuosity
- Spiritual nourishment: liminal experience, indulgence in preferences
- Cultural nourishment: knowledge of rarely viewed society and culture

For the Products (Dance/Music)
- Form miniaturization
- Secularization
- Cultural preservation: protection of traditions, popularity, diffusion
- Cultural conservation: aesthetic vitamins for vitality and aliveness, intratraditional synthesis

---

tion of older artists and large rumba choral groups. Additionally, white or light-skinned informants who have been particularly involved in rumba have been identified and their impact as well as other aspects of rumba are beginning to be assessed by major investigators, including Rogelio Martinez-Furé, Alberto Pedro, Olavo Alén, and Israel Moliner.

The problem with rumba conservation, as with that of other performed artistic forms, is conservation of vitality. There is a qualitative difference between conservation and preservation, although both are concerned with saving, guarding, and protecting (as others have noted elsewhere). Preservation simply assures the lasting image or artifact, usually framed behind a glass or within long corridors of museums. Conservation assures the lasting image as well, but *with* (hence *con*) something. Conservation of dance/music involves preservation of the sounds and lyrics on records, tapes, and compact discs and video documentation of several performed versions of the dancers and musicians, along with the unencumbered creative process of input of music/dance makers themselves; thus artistic and documentary control are shared with performers. In this manner, the traditions are guarded and allowed to grow organically at the same time.

In the case of rumba, conservation involves its holistic reality and vital essence. Most often, artistic forms lose their wondrous qualities when they are situated in routinized venues or, as in the case of rumba, when it is situated in a prepared rather than spontaneous environment. While rumba has so far eluded "performance death," or the loss of its wondrous vitality, it is still important to encourage those mechanisms that keep traditions alive and well. Spontaneity and change are conservation keys; thus innovations should be noted and, if accepted over time, analyzed and encouraged.

Rumba commoditization has encouraged the spread of rumba to previously uninterested and rejected groups, namely to European-American or white drummers and to female drummers as well. Drumming proficiency is increasing among many populations, and rumba instruction in Cuban workshops has been a great impetus. While many European, Asian, and European-American percussionists have been more interested in trap drumming or timpani, an increase in those interested in hand drumming, rumba style, can be seen. Additionally, females who have been restricted from playing drums, either for religious reasons or because of gender biases, are now appearing in significant numbers as rumba drummers (Carole Steele and Nurudafina Piliabena are examples).

Lastly, commoditization of rumba has affected its organic development. As noted, rumba evolved from a combination of songs, religious chants, street hollers, and sung poetry, a mixture of contemporary and historic materials. The spontaneous moments of artistic interchange, jamming, or artistic nourishment that occur in workshop events stimulate artistic discovery and creativity and continue to produce new variants of rumba, such as batarumba.

Programs incorporating performance and instruction can grow and supply Cuba with at least a portion of its needed foreign exchange. Further growth depends on confidence and efficiency established in the programs offered so far. Foreign students must adapt to Cuban teaching methods and small-nation living conditions in return for the excitement of learning the beginnings of traditional dance/music forms and experiencing the powerful dynamics contained therein. If this condition is met, dance, and particularly rumba, will continue to be a viable commodity. When students have successful and pleasant learning experiences in rumba, they contribute to the marketing process and further advertise Cuba's offerings to future foreign students. Such programs can be encouraged, limited, or eliminated depending on the extent of foreign contact and subsequent foreign exchange Cuba is interested in nurturing and securing.

SECULARIZATION AND RUMBA

Some might analyze orisha movements in rumba as the secularization of highly powerful religious dancing. Others may see it as sanctification, the process of making rumba special or holy by means of expressive behavior from a religious context. The mixture may, however, confirm that the original purpose of rumba was liberation and protest through music/ dance (Martinez-Furé in Chao Carbonero and Lamerán, 1982:114). It may demonstrate religious persistence within a contemporary social order that is basically atheistic and generally antireligious. It may be a minuscule but public display of faith from a spiritual world view. All possibilities depend on the answers to questions that are most avoided in Cuba at this time.

In any case, dance movement and dance symbols have been taken from the realm of Afro-Cuban religions and placed in the secular settings of Rumba performance; on occasion, traditional and public dancers perform the gestures of the religious deities while dancing rumba. The mixing of "secular" and "sacred" gestures in rumba accommodates the creative impulse and perhaps a desire for embellishment in social dance, but this mixing also establishes equanimity from the ideological standpoint. For national leaders, ministry officials, and arts administrators, the staging of religious forms apart from their original environment in secular, tourist or commercial atmospheres decreases the awe of religious activity and increases the dramatic quality of secular activity.

There is little separation between what some would call the sacred and the secular in many Afro-Cuban contexts. The particular mixture of sacred and secular in rumba affirms Afro-Cuban notions regarding spirituality. As Jahn succinctly explains, "On the basis of African philosophy there can be no strict separation of sacred and profane" (1961:83-86). And a Cuban informant in Havana told me that "whenever the black man sings or dances or drums, he is involved with his orishas; it is a private relationship and no one else knows at a given moment if there is a relationship with the orishas or not. Even when you see a black man sitting by himself, he very easily could be communicating or in relationship with the orishas." In dancing rumba, Cubans sing songs considered religious, such as "Ave Maria," and use gestures for deities in order to enrich the artistic present. With the addition of recognizable gestures from orisha dancing, rumba has the potential to stimulate more powerful responses. Rumba with orisha gestures appears strengthened, and it has additional sensory power. Dancers are more animated with the additions, and audiences who understand the gestures are more activated.

Most Cubans agree that there is a separation between rumba and the dances of the orishas, but many informants also say that orishas can request that a Rumba be performed. And a *santero*, or priest, can organize a Rumba (if a petitioner has requested a favor or a particular blessing and in return has promised a fiesta or party for the orisha who is believed responsible for granting the favor or request). In this context, the Rumba is commonly called *bembé*. The orishas are invoked to play and dance with devotees in Rumba-like bembés.

Furthermore, there are *rumbitas*, rhythms and songs for the orisha (Ortiz, 1951 [1985]:460; León, 1984a:47-48). Rumbitas are used in religious contexts but are not accompanied by other sacred phenomena, such as sacred batá drums and possession trance. They are used to bid each orisha goodbye at the conclusion of ceremonies.[2]

Interestingly, some very learned master drummers, who are both master bata players and master rumberos, acknowledge a long association between rumba music and music of the orishas. They sing Santería chants with Yoruba words and explain how these fit into rumba clave and how they are used quite frequently, in fact with some regularity, in the programs of most traditional rumba groups (see chapter 4 on rumba songs).[3]

Despite these connections, the reason most Cubans say there is no relationship between rumba and orisha music/dance is that historically the two traditions have been categorized separately and Cubans have heard years of repeated rhetoric about separate arenas. One traditional dancer told me that she has given something of her own creation to rumba by injecting movement motifs of the orishas into traditional rumba dancing. She also said that there is no relationship between orisha dancing and rumba, that they are separate entities. Yet she has been singing, dancing, and demonstrating rumba with orisha gestures for the Cuban public since 1972. It is easy to understand, therefore, how traditional rumba has been imitated and perhaps standardized by the public.

It is common now to see young dancers from the public, as well as elders, who inject orisha movements into rumba. It is also possible that traditional performers have imitated the public style of intermixing dance traditions. Regardless of which group initiated the mixture, when one considers how many and how often traditional groups have performed throughout the country since the Revolution (casa de cultura after casa de cultura, town after town, province after province), it is easy to imagine the influence of traditional performers on public performance practice, through Los Muñequitos, Afro-Cuba, Obbatola, Aburý Okán, and other groups.

From the movement perspective, it is almost impossible to completely separate the dances of the orishas from rumba. They appear at times to be variants of a singular foot pattern. In the sacred sphere of Yoruba dance, the traveling foot pattern of secular rumba is discernible. In rumba, the orisha gestures and their passing step occur (see the labanotation example in the appendix).

In prepared Rumba, professional dancers may not infuse other traditions' gestured movements in rumba; however, the professional programming of the Rumba event places rumba as an umbrella over fragmented excerpts from religious ritual, thus implying secularization. In an analytical sense, traditional performers are physically and artistically balancing the secularization that is suggested in prepared professional performances of religious traditions by sacralizing rumba with orisha gestures and traveling steps.

Bourdieu has suggested that without consciously knowing it, participants behave according to cultural presumptions, and this situation may be an example of his "habitus" (Bourdieu, 1984:169-75). Certainly traditional dancers are not consciously attempting a religious coup in a Cuban society that has begun to lift the rigid restrictions and prohibitions against all religious practices. However, there is an acceptance and now a conscious development of religious gestures in secular presentation among traditional groups. Batarumba has resulted; it expressly reaches instrumentally for a religious and secular combination. Its choreography routinely intertwines secular rumba and casino with religious orisha dancing. While this development has been seen as innovation, it can also be interpreted as cultural resistance, religious resilience, or adaptive strategy. Since slavery, Africans in the Americas have kept alive remnants, slices, and whole categories of belief and knowledge in their bodies, to be demonstrated publicly within or through whatever confines the power structure permitted (see, for example, Herskovits, 1941; Bascom, 1950; Cabrera, 1954 [1983], 1979 [1986]; Verger, 1957; Métraux, 1959; Bastide, 1978; Walker, 1972; Nettleford, 1985; Rabineau, 1980; Mason, 1985; Murphy, 1988; Bolívar, 1990).

Dancing for the orishas is ritualistic, and rumberos begin to effect a similar transition state as they perform. The orishas never appear, however; no trance possession occurs, and perhaps this is evidence that to date a sanctification process is incomplete in rumba. But orisha-inspired rumba performances are spreading, both by repeated performances of traditional groups and by organic, creative innovations within the structure of the rumba complex.

The most striking observations remain: that motifs from religious dancing can be recognized in rumba, and rumba foot patterns are discerned in bembé dancing; and that Rumba events, particularly Sábado de la rumba, continue to secularize Afro-Cuban religious dancing by placing historically religious dances within Rumba.

RUMBA AS STRUCTURED COMMUNITAS

As a result of both its organic development and its manipulation within socio-politico-economic processes, the Rumba event can be explained in summary by means of "structured and existential *communitas*." Victor and Edith Turner (1978) have discussed how a commonness of feeling, i.e., "communitas," is generated from an assembled "throng of similars" and how it can be preeminent despite disunity and heterogeneity of ethnicities, classes, or cultures. When all the rumba and Rumba data are taken into account, the consequence or resulting behavior indicates that Rumba speaks to and of feelings of communitas. Furthermore, the analysis shows that there is an earnest attempt by the Cuban ministry to generate such feelings by means of social and aesthetic behavior. The feelings imply, symbolize, and sustain ideas that Cubans have about themselves and want to inculcate from generation to generation, but also, they imply universal resonances which apparently engage other culturally different peoples.

Turner and Turner (1978:252-54) describe two forms of communitas. Spontaneous, existential communitas attends solely to improvisation, unprepared, or voluntary behavior, the opposite of social structure, i.e., spontaneous Rumba in this case. Turner describes the other form as ideological communitas, the "blueprint" of remembered attributes of the communitas experience which is used for the reformation of society (1969:132), i.e., prepared Rumba in this case. When the Rumba event is placed in such a conceptual framework, it transports to the present exciting, pleasurable feelings of sensuality, spontaneity, fun, and freedom, which rumba is capable of producing. Within a communitas blueprint, Rumba models how dance/music can be employed effectively by the nation.

Most Cubans participate in Rumba kinesthetically and aurally, i.e., they are stimulated by watching movement and are engrossed by means of the movement's affect. They are aroused or sensitized by the rhythmic sounds of drums, soloist, and chorus. They understand the lyrics and any double entendres within. They are drawn to a festival atmosphere with a captivating chase of a beautiful dancing woman. Light-skinned or white Cubans, despite the fact that they do not go to Rumba often, see and hear it as part of the accumulating folklore, literature, and ideology of the Revolution. Cubans (black, brown, and white) share the ideal of rumba as the epitome of sensuality and sexual attraction. They are attracted to a setting where males are publicly affirmed as exciting, sexual, and important figures. Attraction and seduction are heightened by hypnotic rhythms, and sensuous allusions; time and tensions are suspended. In other words, the Rumba event generates and accumulates multiple sensory stimuli which urge individuals and encourage groups to cross into the aesthetic realm of ultrasensitivity. The liminal world of "betwixt and between" (Van Gennep, 1909 [1960]), so characteristic of the aesthetic mode, transforms spectators into participants and transports them to the zone of communitas.

Simultaneously, however, as the data have revealed, new values, ideas, and considerations are equally tapped and promoted. Reeducation accompanies familiar images of sensuousness: a previously degraded dance is officially encouraged instead of ridiculed, dark or black Cubans are singled out to demonstrate behavior which should be imitated rather than light or white models of behavior; and from time to time, females publicly challenge males in virtuosity and skill. Such new values are promoted subtly, but repeatedly thus, emphatically throughout the island.

The majority of Cubans (in Cuba) have involved themselves intensely with the revolution and its notions of change, and the Rumba event is a behavioral challenge. For those who become involved, the discrepancies of the real world are postponed in the moment of the dance and Rumba becomes a liminal world unto itself. It is the liminal world of Rumba that coincides with socialist, egalitarian ideology.

This chapter has reviewed various processes that operate on rumba dance/music and on Rumba, the event. It discusses and demonstrates how rumba affects other aspects of society beyond the aesthetic system. It also shows the ambiguities of multivocality, i.e., when the same data yield different, even contradictory understandings within the overpowering illocutionary force of communitas. Rumba in the political arena conveys contradictions between alleged equality and the reality of practice in terms of color and racial discrimination and with regard to gender biases. Rumba in the economic arena conveys the ability of a dance form to assist the economic system in incremental, but steady deposits of real and symbolic capital. Rumba in the religious arena places the dance and the event in conflict, i.e., when rumba dancing is viewed with religious gestures, sanctification of rumba is suggested; when the Rumba event is viewed as the encompassing agent that includes religious materials, secularization obtains.

The symbolic level of dance analysis displays the interconnections of an aesthetic system to other arenas of social life. It shows what dance can do—how it can display values, relate concerns, or reiterate messages. It also shows how unintentional voices are relayed as well as intentional ones and it suggests how such information might be used. When the accentuation of dance is woven into belief, as in religious ritual and ceremonial presentation, excitement, richness, and intensity are augmented exponentially and multiple spheres of understanding are accessed and recorded (see Brandon, Hall, Mulira, and Thompson in Holloway, 1990).

SOCIAL AND AESTHETIC CHANGE IN CUBA

ORGANIC CHANGE IN DANCE

Because dance involves the body as the tool of the art as well as the art product itself and because the body is part of a constantly shifting process of physical change, each performance of dance, each enactment of special movement, is subjet to minuscule, incremental, or drastic change. While artistic directors, choreographers, and dancers at all levels of proficiency may strive to retain specific movements, replicate designs and an organization, or recreate feelings, the dance is constantly influenced, reinterpreted, and reformulated. As performers continuously embroider, emphasize, miniaturize, augment, crystallize, or spontaneously create nuances and embellishments, even while dancing within set sequences, slight changes occur that eventually develop and shape the dance as a whole. The dance product changes in the eyes of viewers, who have different understandings depending on their historical backgrounds, contemporary trends, and the immediate environment of the performance. Change, as a result, is a significant part of tradition, but it is a constant in dance.

Traditional dance is not static, therefore, but part of a dynamic process. This process is an ongoing one of selection, presentation, elimination, augmentation, and manipulation. Specific esteemed elements of movement, which are recognized within a given group from a given location and which characterize a style, complex, or tradition, are identified and given social value. In many ways, traditional dancers and performers of other traditional arts must work carefully to safeguard a particular style or form of the past. Aesthetic preferences and dance qualities evolve slowly (although sometimes "traditions" are not so old; see Hobsbawn and Ranger, 1983, and Horner, 1990, chap. 1). They are selected from many available cultural items; they come into being as "traditional dance," both through the molding of separate aesthetic elements into a structured form and through the incorporation of gradual change. Immediate or severe change is seen and felt as a violation of consensus, precepts, or rules. Traditional dance defines, traces, captures, projects, and enlivens a particular set of images and symbolizes ideas and attitudes that are culturally understood and generally agreed upon.

Cuban traditional dances negotiate delicately between the prescribed repetition of set music/dance sequences and necessary, natural, organic change. Cuban dance traditions that are performed daily as part of professional company rehearsals display the peculiar play between the unchanging and the changes of tradition. Cuban dancers and dance administrators limit and channel movement because of organic tendencies to vary and change. Daily repetition of esteemed dance patterns safeguards the dance structures but places the content, substance, or essence of dance in jeopardy of performance death.

Without change, performance can become deadly, dry, lacking in excitement. Lifelessness in dancing or music making often occurs when the performance is separated from the original purpose of the tradition. (Consequently, for the musical theater dancer, lifelessness due to repetition is not so serious a problem, since the dance purpose is intimately involved in its repeated performance.) If the dance is routinized by repeated practice away from its significant context, its vitality can dissolve; performance death can occur.

Professional Cuban dance companies alternate the performance of dance traditions to present dynamic entertainment and didactic artistry; however, they are still subject to the dangers of routinization and performance death. Even the use of informantes—the living archives of traditional dance—cannot always ignite the vivifying essence of dance in its original setting, nor always sustain freshness and vitality in performance (Martinez-Furé, 1986). While musicians and dancers remain the experiential librarians of varying traditions, it should be remembered that it is through their ever-changing bodies that scores are stored. Efforts to conserve dance traditions must acknowledge and incorporate change as an organic and vital component of dance.

CHANGE IN RUMBA

As with other ethnic dance material, that is, dance that is connected in important ways to national or ethnic identity, such as the Mexican hat dance, Hawaiian hula, and Haitian Vodun dances, rumba's African and Spanish movement sequences connect powerful physicality and aesthetic stimulation to feelings regarding the Cuban nation and its people. Like other African-derived dance traditions, rumba incorporates other arts (music, drama, storytelling) and makes reference to aspects of social life within movement (see Primus, 1969; Wilson, 1981; and Nketia, 1965). The "consummate vitality" of African sculpture, according to Robert Farris Thompson (1974:1-48), and the "dynamism" of Surinamese carving, according to Sally and Richard Price (1980:166-87), are compounded and accentuated when applied to dance performance. Thompson identifies the characteristics that shape African performance, including its "get-down" quality, coolness, swing, flexibility, and ephebism. The Prices refer to performance among the Surinamers of African descent in terms of spontaneous expressions that are enculturated early and result in dynamic essence. Rumba has the same force or surge of physical energy. Its dynamism, or consummate vitality, is embodied in performers through the exertion of specified movement and is kinesthetically transferred to viewers. The physical demand on the body culminates in fatigue, but the body is deeply relaxed as a result of such a demand in dancing. The aesthetic force of rumba in combination with the physical release of tension govern its potency. Rumba focuses a multiplicity of stimulating elements; it overlaps phrasing and moments of emphasis and thereby creates suspension and dynamic interest within physical action. Such physical power and illocutionary force are the reasons for the continuity of Cuban rumba despite its mixed messages and political-economic appropriation.

Although few Cubans dance rumba well and those who do tend to be black or dark-skinned Cubans, rumba generates particular interest and draws special attention: it is treated like no other dance in Cuba. No other dance is accorded a one–two week festival in its honor. No other dance punctuates the calendar of events in casas de cultura programming. No other dance form within balletic, modern, or folkloric styles is exposed as much to international visitors. It is used strategically to display Cuban culture and to promote deep, fundamental change in values. Within non-Cuban contexts, it portrays a new Cuba in an artistic manner and encourages gradual change.

Rumba could be designated the Cuban national dance of the twentieth century, yet it competes with conga and son (see chapter 2 and Evleshin, 1989). Of the three dances, conga is most easily performed by all ages and both sexes; thus it can be argued that conga is more communal. It is a group dance; everyone dances at the same time. Rumba, on the other hand, is the dance of a single couple or male soloist, dancing alone most of the time. Rumba is communal performance, while conga is communal participation. Even though conga is easier and more communal, rumba has received more official support.

Neither was the most popular, social, and historic dance, son (which continues as salsa in current North American terminology and as casino in contemporary Cuba), appropriated as the national dance of the twentieth century (Orozco, 1984:382-85). In light of its tremendous popularity as the most performed social or popular dance in Cuba, it is conceivable that most Cubans would select casino as the national dance. Apparently casino lacks something seminal to national objectives, as conga does also.

Rumba's prominence apparently was based on criteria other than ease, popularity, and communal participation. In a structured form, within specific spaces, and at particular times, rumba fulfills strategic goals. Analysis points to the fact that Cuban society has a preference for performance within a mass as opposed to mass performance. Rather than the mass participation of casino or the unstructured abandon in conga, rumba gives prepared culture to the masses; it provides education and values. Rather than a focus on the individualistic passing, turning, and designing of patterns in casino or a focus on the improvisational and unstructured activity of conga, rumba has emerged as a dance structure that coincides with socialist perspectives, a cultural symbol of social relations.

Meaning in rumba has varied consequences in terms of the dance and its performers. In the dance, there is a search for the vacunao, for possession of the female and community prestige. Dancers work at the search through the call and response acknowledged between dancers and drummers and through the exchange of movements between dancers (exchange of vibrating shoulder motifs, the series of responsorial actions in vacunao, turns, fake vacunaos, implosive holds). The meanings of rumba are not only possession of the female or winning the competition between males or between drummer and dancer but also prestige and status among rumberos, Cubans, and foreigners (see Graburn, 1976:49-51).

A more problematic meaning of rumba manipulation and appropriation, which is shared by other Cuban artists, is concern for artistic freedom, a parallel issue with routinization of performances but now in terms of performers. The dark-skinned or black rumbero still sings of liberation and is concerned with social dignity and personal artistic self-worth; however, where is artistic freedom in rumba as it is officially and most frequently presented? In Cuba there are few presentations of new ideas, new performance modes, or new creative dances and, until very recently, little social criticism. Artistic freedom is limited—that which would permit rumba to develop in the spontaneity of the moment and would be congruent with its original form. How will rumberos receive artistic stimulation to invent or fashion something new other than redundant prescribed messages, if rumba is always prepared? Routinization develops technique but stifles, if not suffocates, creativity in all artists.

Regard for artists entails more than providing a means for their personal welfare and performance or maintenance of techniques and performance technologies. It encompasses an ambiance of artistic freedom that generates creativity and requires attention to their notions of self-worth and dignity. Such an environment permits and encourages experimentation, growth, and acceptance or rejection of all sorts of ideas. In a striking manner, Sally Ness uses the image of a basketball that is held loosely but possessively as she analyzes *sinulog* dance and Filipino society in terms of looseness within a possessive relationship. She states that "basketball is a game about possession and control. However, its most important object, the ball itself, cannot be clutched firmly. It has to be released continually from any possessor's grasp" (1992:124). Cuban artists, particularly rumberos, need and deserve such a loose hold.

Rumberos represent not only Afro-Cubans but also fellow Cuban artists in the development of creativity and artistic freedom. Rumba signals a need for rectification of injustice to artists, certainly to rumberos and folkloric dancers. In this manner, rumba echoes human universals and basic aesthetic needs (Langer, 1953; Blacking, 1973; Hanna, 1979; Lewis, 1984).

Although artists were hesitant to discuss this point with me in 1986 and 1987, an article by Coco Fusco in the *Nation* suggests that conditions are changing:

> In contrast to tense moments in the past, when the official response was to redouble control, the current interest in and tacit approval of the younger generation are signs of the foresight and sensitivity of many in power. . . . Stylistically heterogeneous, this generation of artists has an unabashed interest in information about art outside Cuba. What unifies them even more than their artwork is their strong opposition to any reductive or repressive definition of revolutionary culture. (1988:399)

CHANGE IN CUBA

Although dance is not a specific priority within national objectives, it assists Cuba's commitment to self-determination, social equality, and collective solidarity as a small, independent nation. In Cuba, dance and all forms of expressive culture are used to support socialist ideology and egalitarian behavior. Within domestic organization and the international arena as well, national ideology emphasizes values that rectify historical hierarchy and dance can express such changes.

Cuban artists and expressive culture are exciting and powerful aids to political struggle and economic development. Throughout Cuba, the arts are celebrated; ample and active participation of the public in close dialogue with artists (painters, sculptors, and writers as well as dancers and choreographers) has been encouraged as part of governmental directives specific to the arts. Artists are a vital component of education programs via the casa de cultura system. In other words, the artistic community has been accessible to national efforts that inform the public of contemporary events, increase awareness, and develop consciousness of national goals. Through performance of national dance traditions, the construction of a new value base has been underlined; the use of the arts has been developed as a means of educating and reeducating the public toward government objectives and as a means of indoctrinating new values.

What rumba dance/music does irrespective of what people say or believe and irrespective of what the government intends is revealed both in the social currents and conditions of contemporary Cuba and in the dancing body, that is, in changing values and attitudes. A reformation is in process: of economic, political, and social circumstances on one hand and of sentiment, attitudes, ideology, and values on the other. By means of a well-established dance and the important sentiments and feelings that are generated within, around, and because of it, the gap between ideals and reality is perceivable and change can be initiated.

Rumba is well-established, identifiable, and successful over other dance forms in evoking elevated feelings that are necessary for symbols of national consequence. Rumba has emerged in postrevolutionary Cuba by means of three sociopolitical processes: politicization, commoditization, and secularization. Through the examination of Rumba within these differing milieux, a model that investigates social change is established; rumba becomes an indicator or a test of change in Cuba.

While there are artistic reasons for promoting rumba (it makes a great finale, it can involve audience participation, it contains play, interest, and suspense), other reasons have instigated the special position of rumba in contemporary Cuba. One current comes from the top, within the Ministry of Culture and from arts administrators. As discussed, the ministry broadly organizes and outlines cultural activities toward the goals of the Revolution. Fidel Castro's framework for the arts has been the mission of the ministry, given succinctly in June 1961: "Inside the Revolution, everything; against it, nothing" (Matas, 1971:432-36). By means of financial, organizational, and ideological support, the ministry and arts administrators have been instrumental in the promotion of rumba and have determined its prominence among dance professionals and within the public.

Apart from the forceful persuasion of governmental support at the top, another current comes from the bottom, among sincere folkloric performers and the public at large. Folkloric dancers and musicians have enjoyed the new elevated status of folklore and have been eager to integrate the goals of the Revolution into their artistic lives. Dancers have put material into their choreographies and dance events that have been ignored previously and material that they consider relevant to their future. In 1980, Teresa Gonzalez and Rogelio Martinez-Furé received consensus among company members in the *asamblea* to support Rumba Saturday as a peak event. Folkloric and artistic contribution to contemporary Cuban history was validated and, from the bottom up, artists were instrumental in the emergence of rumba as a nationally promoted dance. The enthusiastic support of the public was important as well, and as a result of Cuba's cultural education programs, the general public accepted and echoed the elevation of rumba officially.

A third current of national concern comes from the international dance community (see Graburn, 1984:393, and 1986). The aesthetic power of rumba is that which mesmerizes the international dance community. Even though international dancers do not share the exact meanings of rumba with Cubans, they become involved through the reputation of rumba and are affected by the experience of rumba, the dance/music complex and Rumba, the dance event. International students and artists have seen and heard rumba as it has been promoted and professionalized lately, but also they have experienced Rumba throughout the world. Rumba Saturday's success did not go unnoticed.

Within Cuba before the Revolution, rumba had been widespread, spontaneous, and popular among dark-skinned or black Cubans. Rumba was not taken from these Cubans; they were not paid to perform a meaningless symbol. Instead the government paid Cubans within one segment of the population, who formerly danced rumba frequently yet intermittently, to perform it more frequently for the entire nation. There is little resentment from those who formerly enjoyed rumba because rumba is still accessible to them—even more than before. Now it is prepared more frequently than ever and is showing small signs of growth in terms of popularity beyond the Afro-Cuban segment of society.

The larger segment of the population, which did not share the dancing, has been slow to take on new and previously lower-class values (cf., on the crisis of meaning, Hintzen, 1978:1-47). But the larger sector is learning how to dance rumba through its youth. Young persons of all colors are learning rumba in schools and casas de cultura all over Cuba. These young dancers and dance teachers participate in Rumba from time to time and teach the dance form to others. They are the white or lighter-skinned Cubans who join in the competition of columbia or who know how to deflect the vacunao in guaguancó. While there is still reluctance, the force of multivocalic rumba that has official support and ideological references yields its important position and demonstrates its potential.

Clifford Geertz (1973) says that art is interpretive, a story that participants tell themselves about themselves. In this case, rumba announces the class equality that the Revolution has sought to implement by featuring the former lower-class representatives; rumba is no longer confined to the barrio but is representative of the nation in community centers and theaters. Its illocutionary force projects and persuades its audience as well as its performers, so that the images, messages, or statements presented are usually unquestionable and inarguable and cannot be rejected. Rumba's overiding statements are concerned with social equality, national identity, and communitas.

The data presented show evidence of promotion, manipulation, and appropriation of rumba in order to elevate and conserve it as a cultural symbol. Professionalization of the form through dance company organization and proliferation of dance performances through casas de cultura organization have institutionalized rumba throughout the country. Meanings previously associated solely with the choreography are transformed to national interests and international demands. Racial and gender stratification that are discovered with analysis are subordinated under current issues of Cuban identity and women's liberation. Stimulated by national interests and international demands (including tourist demands and dance specialists' interests), the symbols within rumba are immersed in a reformation process. Rumba is the nexus of sensuality, solidarity, attraction, unity, and well-being, and ultimately it expresses the essence of postrevolutionary Cuba and its efforts toward egalitarian organization.

TOWARD CHANGE

When people experience bodily the dynamics of a dance/music event as it builds climactic segments and speeds toward a rhythmic and harmonic apex, they also experience sensations of well-being, pleasure, joy, fun, sex, spontaneity, tension, opposition, musicality, or simply human physicality. Cubans and non-Cubans associate pleasurable feelings and sentiments with Rumba, and Rumba is capable of transforming their reality.

Among rumberos, social interconnectedness increases, diverse world views are meshed if not suspended, and differing degrees of social stratification unite in the liminal world created by the Rumba event. Rumba dancing provides what the Turners call "the structured, highly valued *route* [my emphasis] to a liminal world where the ideal is felt to be real, where the tainted social persona may be cleansed and renewed" (1978:30). Cubans and non-Cubans repeatedly acquaint themselves with the equality and social justice that the Rumba event suggests and primarily promotes. Equanimity is real, experienced bodily, in the liminal world of Rumba, and its extension into the social world seems possible. Rumba persists by means of its power to generate communitas and because of the fundamental, dynamic, and contagious nature of dance.

The occurrence, popularity, and understanding of Rumba are increasing and ever thriving among rumberos, Afro-Cubans, and international art market patrons; these attributes also are increasing gradually within the general Cuban population. There is continuity of meaning in the communitas no matter how the form changes or the timing shifts. Whether the form is yambú, guaguancó, columbia, or batarumba, Rumba means heightened sensitivity and communal fun. When the speed increases or decreases or when the duration is expanded or reduced, Rumba still focuses mainly on attraction, seduction, competition, and play. Even when the space changes from barrio to theater, the potential to generate communitas is intrinsic and ever present.

The intrinsic quality associated with communitas is within the nature and essence of dance. Not only does the eye or the ear bring excitation and ultimately understanding, but the entire human body, with all of its sensory receivers, does so too. The many sensory channels of dance mediate multiple meanings simultaneously. Meanings come from its origins in the nineteenth-century Cuban experience: a dance of lower-class Afro-Cubans expressing male and female attractiveness in rhythmic form. Simultaneously, other meanings are imposed from the social conditions of twentieth century Cuba: a dance of all Cubans expressing egalitarian goals. All meanings are embodied in the dance and are exposed fully only by means of detailed analysis.

The Cuban Ministry of Culture and folkloric *empresas* change the time and space of Rumba, but they count on the intensification of energy in rumba as the ultimate expression of communitas. The formal setting is transcended and often even unconcerned, disinterested, detached attitudes of musicians, dancers, or spectators are transformed and involved. Rumberos transform themselves and others as they create a sustained stream of pleasurable feelings or an explosion of pure emotion.

Organizers in postrevolutionary Cuba seek ways to develop a new orientation from the hierarchical past, ways that encourage communal interest and collective involvement. Educators and managers of the arts attempt to attach the consistent and repeatable dance/music elements of Rumba to egalitarian meanings. Dance, and Rumba in particular, afford the exceptional possibility of a nexus between communitas and ideology, between feelings and goals. To the extent that white or mulatto Cubans participate in Rumba fully and enthusiastically with black or darker-skinned Cubans, that women dance columbia and dance less defensively in guaguancó, that Rumba Saturdays in Cuba and rumba workshops elsewhere generate foreign currency and prestige, that Rumba continues to embrace religious dance material, the complex process of changing values in Cuba can be identified and measured.

Rumba analysis reveals the contrasts and contradictions that exist in contemporary Cuban society. Rumba articulates social conditions: it illustrates socialist ideals as well as social control, machismo as well as women's liberation, sociological race as well as national identity. Rumba performance mediates contradictory issues: spontaneity, freedom, sensuality, and, simultaneously, structured form and set order. Cubans must evaluate all that rumba does and weigh the benefits to determine if it is sufficiently and effectively strategic as it now operates within Cuban society.

Rumba can and does assist ideology, but it can do more. Rumba has a potential for change that is intrinsically present. The potential is the communitas that it is capable of generating: a combination of dance–music elements that encourages a liminal state and consequent equanimous feelings. This potential makes rumba essential, not simply in reflecting social change but also in effecting social change.

Even though it is exceedingly difficult to change values and attitudes, it is not impossible. Rumba, in its prepared form, ignites communitas, but in its extended, spontaneous forms it sustains and maintains communitas even more. The encouragement of spontaneous Rumba events and the proliferation of spontaneity in prepared and extended Rumba would permit the organic development of a fundamental Cuban expression and would allow the resultant communitas to grow, to increase in intensity and in scale. More Cubans would potentially be susceptible to its liminal world of equality and equanimity and more Cubans and non-Cubans might be subject to attitude and value change. The organic emergence or resur-

gence of batarumba offers the possibility of more significant rumba performance and thus an increase in the efficacy of rumba as a national symbol.

A RUMBA PORTRAIT FOR THE FUTURE

The Rumba that is awaited is the congregational fiesta of Cuba and the
United States. The clave has been sounded since independence came to
the Americas—the insistent, persistent, resistant call of the people, the
clave of Americans who speak Navajo, Cherokee, and Seminole languages,
Spanish, French, Patois, Papimiento, Taketake, English, Dutch, German,
Chinese, Japanese, Korean, Vietnamese, Arabic, Hebrew, Farcsi. Their
rhythm is rumba clave since they dance to a syncopated rhythm, suspend-
ing the "and" of beat four and tending to vibrate their shoulders adeptly,
often on that beat alone. Cuba's conga has voiced its decorated ostinato in
concepts of solidarity and sovereignty, followed by the seis por ocho of diplomatic maneuvers over three decades in order to generate equality as a
founding principle of their social organization and of global relations. Castro's indefatigable efforts to fight against the inhumane principle of profit,
the enunciating brass capitalist call around the world, have been heard as
the virtuoso, improvisational quinto that smacks harshly and irregularly but
ingeniously and with the ultimate of philosophic integrity. A small chorus
in the United States has held a solitary madruga pulse as a democratic refrain, "liberty, freedom, equality," for the rhythmic preparation of new
U.S. leadership. The guagua is the quick, busy, fleeting, but interested
voice of young Cubans in Cuba who want the values of their homeland and
relatives, but who also want experiences and discoveries afar. Their voice in
the polyrhythmic layering, "ahora, rectificación," gives the rumba gas to
progress and intensify on both sides. The displaced Cubans from south
Florida and northern New Jersey to San Francisco are eligible estrofa singers who are daily creating verses of longing for their childhood homes and
families, real *congrí nativo*, and radical change. The main personages, the
Cuban and United States government officials, are the long-awaited
rumberos. The rumba circle is prepared; why don't they dance the rumba
of respect and interdependency together? It is only through cooperation
that we will experience a less unfair and more equitable world.

In light of this study's conclusions, dance reveals its potency. It is because rumba is multivocalic, multisensory, multilayered, dynamic, lively,
and full of spirit that it is able to effect all its meanings. More specialized
neuropsychological data may give a tangible form to the route of rumba's

communitas and articulate the elements that form its essense or determine which combinations permit a heightened, humane state to emerge.

Dance, as part of an aesthetic system, offers intangible but indelible results. The non-native may not share the same meaning of the dances with native performers, but with willingness to be aware and especially to dance, cultural understandings become more evident. In dancing rumba, Cubans and groups of unrelated, culturally plural people are drawn together in their distinctiveness.

I hope that Cubans will continue to conserve their folkloric dance forms and document and publish the resulting analyses.[1] I hope that the information contained here will be of assistance in that effort as an outside perspective on rumba and that this study has communicated the concern I have for rumba, Cuban dance, and Cuba. I expect that the essence of rumba will resonate within its diverse audiences and that the communitas it generates will facilitate substantial change, hopefully from inequality to equality.

Appendix:
Labanotation

LABANOTATION KEY

Dynamics

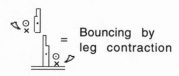

⟨≡
⟨≡ = Bouncing by change of center of weight
•

= Bouncing by leg contraction

∿ = Tension

⌠- = Effort symbol: Slash

⦙ = Vibration

◣ = accent with sound

◺ = accent

◺ = resilient

Timing

▮ = 4 squares =

Yambu = 106-116
Guaguanco = 132-144
Columbia = 152-160

Variations

= Lowered from forward middle by one third

= One third toward

= Halfway point between place high and forward high

= Center of gravity pelvis lowering

= Leg action: half support and half gesture

= hand sliding along chest

= Repeat as quickly as possible

Objects

• = man   ↓ = woman

= man's pants

= woman's skirt

= scarf of woman, worn around neck

BASIC RUMBA STEP PATTERN FOR WOMAN

**HIPS SWAY IN RESPONSE TO STEPS. KNEES
ARE ALWAYS SLIGHTLY BENT, NEVER LOCKED.**

2

1

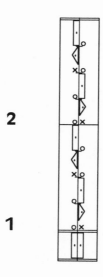

Yambu

This example shows the "knee claps", one of the basic men's steps in Rumba, which also historically resonates in Haitian Banda and the "funky chicken" in the U.S.

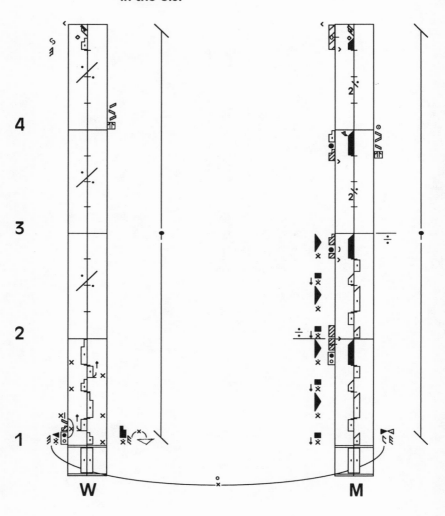

W

M

Yambu, cont.

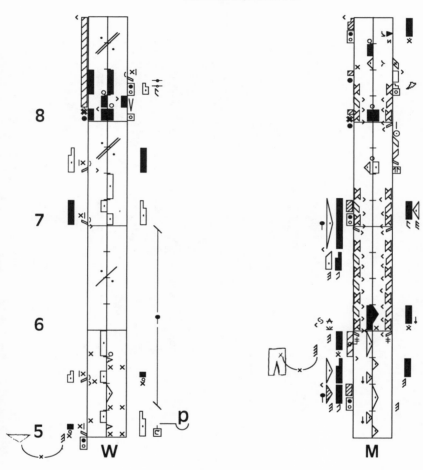

Yambu, cont.

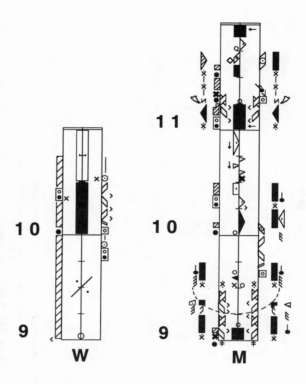

Yambu

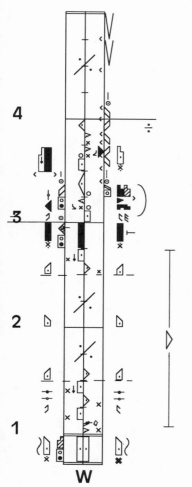

W

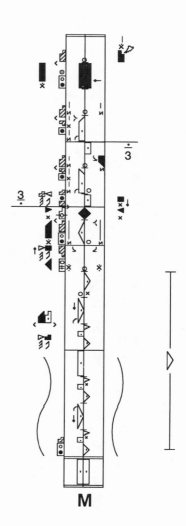

M

Yambu

These movements are
characteristic of Rumba, but
the arm gestures in
measures 3-4 are frequently
found in the dances of the
Orishas, in this case Ochun.

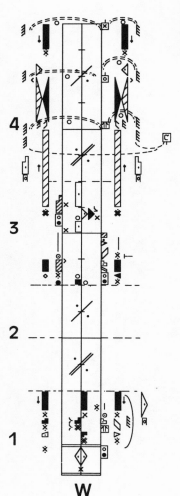

W

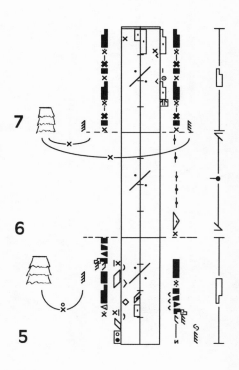

Yambu

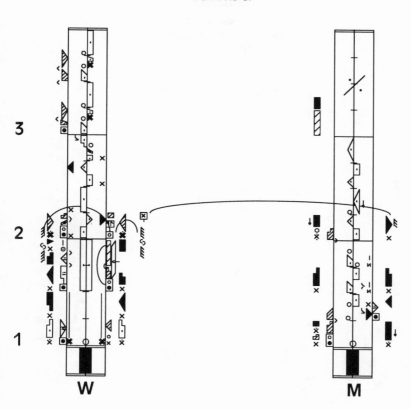

W

M

Guaguanco

The first 4 measures show the ritual salutation for initiated devotees of the Yoruba religion. He uses the salutation to possibly distract from his vacunao, shown in measure 6.

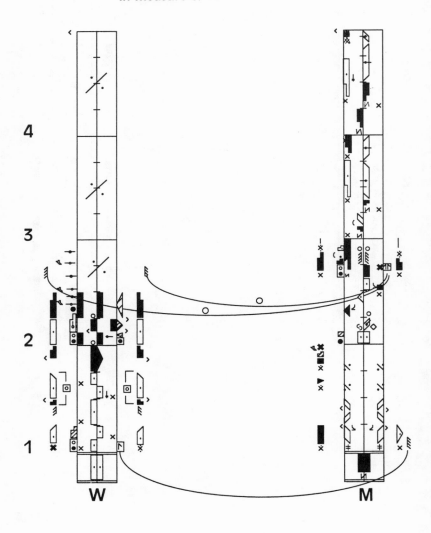

W   M

Guaguanco, con't.

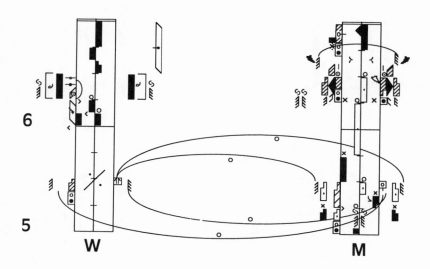

6

5

W   M

Guaguanco

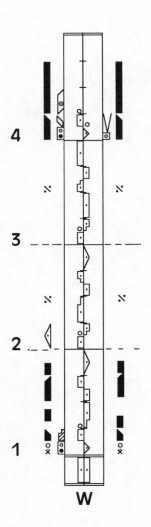

W

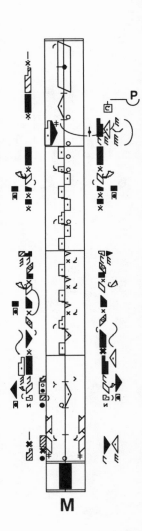

M

Guaguanco

These examples show the
woman's expression of defense
against the vacunao.

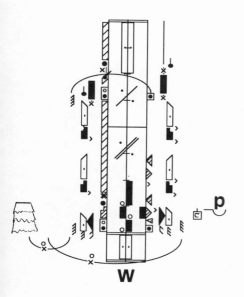

W

p

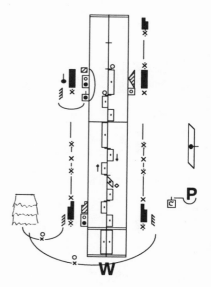

W

P

Guaguanco

2

1

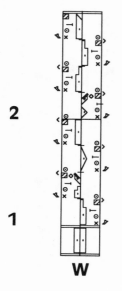

W

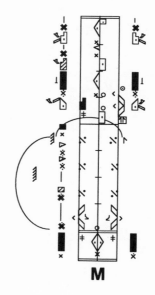

M

Columbia

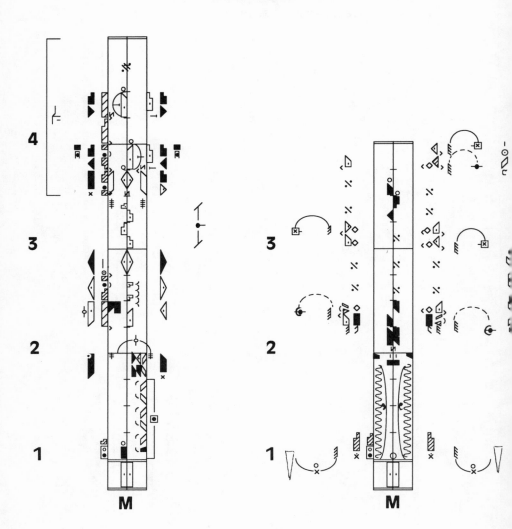

Columbia

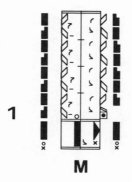

M

Columbia

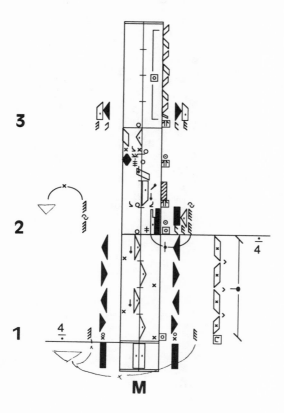

M

Columbia

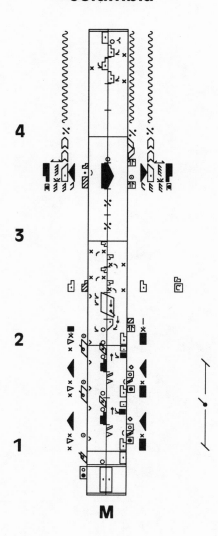

M

Notes

1. INTRODUCTION: PORTRAITS OF A DANCE

1. At the time of the Revolution, many community members who were recognized and acknowledged experts of major dance traditions were hired as pivotal company members. These singers, drummers, and dancers were placed in each section of the National Folkloric Dance Company's classes as special teachers, or *informantes*. They taught and demonstrated the appropriate stylization of dance steps, movement sequences, and correct musical structures of each dance tradition. Often they worked directly with choreographers to mount a dance tradition as it was altered for theater productions in prepared choreographies. They worked with dancers who had not grown up in the traditional religious ambiance of the dances and who were less acquainted with the gigantic lore from which these dances came. The role of informante did not end with the establishment of a repertory and the solidification of national folkloric companies. Informantes function today in each professional company as active teachers, working with a second teacher. The second teacher is responsible for technique, the perfection of that which the informantes embody and demonstrate. One teacher teaches from a physical perspective, the other from a more cultural perspective. The cultural view stresses the feeling and significance of folklore within the movement. Informantes are "living libraries," according to Rogelio Martinez-Furé (personal communication, October 1986), who educate artistic directors, managers, and performing professionals regarding the guidelines and goals of varied dance traditions. Informantes within the national company have also set standards for other companies regarding the representation of Cuban dance and music culture. They are the guardians of folkloric dance and music traditions.

2. Whether drummer or dancer initiates the movement is questionable and probably varies between the two. Generally, musicians say that they play to the dancers' feet and dancers say they dance to, elaborate on, or contrast with the drummers' riffs (short rhythmic and tonal musical ideas).

3. *Rumba* has been transferred to video and is distributed through the Center for Cuban Studies in New York. It documents the special significance of rumba found throughout Cuba by Cuban investigators.

4. I refer to *mambo* and *salsa* from the North American perspective, in this case. Mambo is a popular Cuban dance creation of the 1940s. In Cuba, it has a specific movement sequence; it has a different movement sequence in the United States and elsewhere, as it was popularized internationally. (The popularized dance version would be called a variant of *son* or salsa among Cuban dance and music specialists.) Salsa is a type of son that has been indelibly developed by Puerto Ricans in New York City (see Boggs, 1992; Roberts, 1979). What is important to note here is that differentiated Cuban dances influenced other parts of the world and are often confused with or labeled as rumba. (See chap. 2 for dance definitions.)

5. Susan Cashion, Dance Coordinator of Stanford University, told me of rumba performance in March 1985. She told me to look for it when I first went to Cuba in December of that year. Curiously, however, in 1982, in Suriname at the Festival of Black Arts in the African Diaspora Conference, I had participated in a multinational spontaneous dance event that overflowed from the theatrical stage out to the streets and I danced next to the Cuban contingent, which I am now sure was dancing Cuban rumba. I did not connect that spontaneous dancing, among Surinamers, Jamaicans, Brazilians, Cubans, and African Americans, with a particular name, but Urdilio Urfé, musicologist from the Cuban contingent, encouraged me at that time to come to Cuba to study popular forms.

6. Acknowledgment is given to Judy Van Zile, editor of *Dance Research Journal*, who suggested using this distinction in a short article I wrote on this research (Daniel, 1991:1-10).

7. Rogelio Martinez-Furé suggests that *mba*, the root of the word *rumba*, now refers to dance and is found throughout the Caribbean and Latin America. According to him, it represents similar festive dance events and has similar accents in the dancing, e.g., on flirtation, chase of the female, or bumping the pelvis area. Another connection to a related form, *rumba flamenco*, takes its name from the Cuban traditional dance as it was brought to Spain in the nineteenth century; however, the Afro-Cuban dance itself is not part of flamenco categories. What Cuban rumba complex and Spanish flamenco complex share is a name, language in the song, attention to rhythm, lifted arms, and particularized skirt work, most of which is very general.

8. *Creole* refers to the mixture and interpenetration of African and European legacies that created new, independent, unique cultural and structural forms in the Americas. Creole forms in Cuba are not African, Spanish, or African-Spanish (from the Moors in Spain), but are definitely Cuban creations, *creaciones netamente cubanas*.

9. There is conjecture on the ethnic group or groups responsible for transporting rumba's African antecedents. Ortiz's statement concerning the Ganga has not been challenged so far, but more recent detailed findings from research in Angola by Cuban ethnologist Rafael Lopez Valdés (1989, 1990) suggest that many Central African ethnic groups exerted influence in Cuba and it would be hard to point to one specific ethnic group for a specific dance. Thus the generalized nomenclature of *Central African, Bantu,* or *Kongo-Angolan* is preferred in Cuba. Jahn's (1961) focus, the Lake Chad area, seems very distant.

10. While it is known that dances of this type were found in Africa and transported to, as well as transformed in, the Americas, it was also possible for new American creations such as rumba to be transported to Africa much later (see Kubik, 1981).

11. In Cuba, people say the dance was taken to Spain first. For the Chicago Fair, see Benedict (1983:23). Jahn makes the interesting comment that with rumba's introduction in Chicago, the dance was danced for the first time without embarrassment.

12. Katherine Dunham distinguishes rumba de salón and del campo in her choreographies (personal communication, 1989); Clark and Wilkerson (1976). Also see Aschenbrenner (1980).

13. Several brief articles and a few books focus on dance in the Caribbean. Katherine Dunham (1947, 1969) and Fernando Ortiz (1950, 1951) are the major investigators who have published from an anthropological perspective on Caribbean dance, Haitian and Cuban respectively. Dunham and Ortiz have presented model ethnographies incorporating description and analysis of the major dance forms. These studies are based on field work that was completed more than fifty years ago, but they involve broad classifications of each island's dance. Dunham divides the Haitian dance world into secular, sacred, and marginal dance, then describes the actual dances, relates their origins, and discusses the function of dance, as was the focus of anthropology in her training years. She concentrates on religious forms associated with *Vodun*. While her divisions between the sacred and the secular are arguable, especially for an African-derived context, Dunham's work remains impressive, since she surveyed most, if not all, of the dances of that nation, described them as a dancer, and analyzed them as an anthropologist at a time when few conceived of dance analysis so seriously. Ortiz analyzes Afro-Cuban dance, but this is a formidable task, as most of Cuban dance is based on Afro-Cuban elements. Ortiz's ethnography publicly recognized the major contributions of Afro-Cubans in the formation of Cuban culture. Ortiz's research of dance is thorough and his early documentation assists modern research, especially on Yoruba chants and dancing, although he too can be criticized in retrospect for conjectured beginnings of dance and heavy reliance on the library research of Curt Sachs (1937).

Other Caribbean studies also are important to dance research. Edmundo Fuenzalida (1982) has pointed to the importance of dance in an interdependent world, specifically focusing on the Caribbean and Latin America. Lavinia Williams Yarborough (1958) wrote a short book which is an overview of the wealth of dances in Haiti and a documentary of her forty years developing Haitian dancers and spreading Dunham technique. Molly Ahye has addressed dance specifically in Trinidad and Tobago. She has presented a biography of Beryl McBurnie (1983), a leader in dance training and performance of folkloric dance from the English-speaking Caribbean. Also, Ahye has published an autobiographical account of her own dance company (1978) with some ethnographic information on Trinidad, Brazil, and Haiti. Margaretta Bobo Goins (1973) published a promising survey of African retentions in dance of the Americas. While this survey classifies Afro-American dance of the Caribbean area, it really points to the need for additional detailed studies.

More recently, sociologists have begun to comment on the importance of dance as well. Quintero Rivera (1986) has analyzed the Puerto Rican national anthem and has included important discussions of dance/music with regard to national identity. Likewise, in a sociological vein, Rex Nettleford's work (1985) on Jamaican dance documents the contributions of the National Dance Theater of Jamaica as a force of cultural resistence. A founder and the artistic director of this company, Nettleford has examined the dance company and theater artists at pivotal points in the process of nation building. His book describes and interprets choreographies that are predominantly based on folkloric elements and on choreographies that tend to have political and historical content. His work comes closest to the research of Ortiz and Dunham as another Caribbean dance ethnographer.

The works cited in the preceding paragraph are important for the field of dance; however, they are not detailed ethnographies of Caribbean dance, i.e., full descriptions of one or all the dances of a particular region and thorough analysis of the same. Unlike other works, such as Dunham's or Ortiz's undertakings on Caribbean dance, Hazzard-Gordon (1990) and Novack (1990) on United States dance, Cowan (1990) on Greek dance, Buonaventura (1990) on Arab dance, Guillermo-prieto (1990) on Brazilian dance, Azzi (1991) on Argentine dance, and Ness (1992) on Philippine dance, they do not thoroughly review the dances of a given society or culture in a systematic fashion. Neither do they thoroughly examine one dance, nor work from the perspective of both a dancer and an analyst as most of the aforementioned studies attempt to do. If dance study is to be of major consequence in anthropological theory, it will have to be predicated on and represented by dance ethnographies and problem-oriented research. If dance is to be considered in terms of social change, full pictures of dance culture need to be framed for comparative study. The present study seeks to add to the literature on Caribbean dance and, in more general terms, to the literature on African-derived movement in the Americas. Additionally, it gives Cuba an ethnographical text that includes the dancer's point of view (Ortiz was not a performer).

14. I had immediate, spontaneous, gracious, and favorable response to the video portion of my project from major dance masters and academic personnel in Cuba, including Fernando Alonso, Manolo Vazquez Robaína, Olavo Alén, Ordilio Urfé, Jose Millet, Nancy Morejín, and Ramiro Guerra, but I was permitted to film classes of Folk-lórico Nacional, the company I danced with daily, only on particular performance occasions and within limited time restrictions, i.e., only once during classes.

15. It is appropriate to state the conditions under which the investigation was made, at least form the etic or analyst's view. I acknowledge some biases, toward dance, rumba, and anthropology; however, the data are also influenced by the Cuban view of me, the anthropologist. (I am eternally indebted to Fredrik Barth whose inspiring words in the field on being an anthropologist helped me bridge dilemmas.) The current political situation between Cuba and the United States colors the way in which any North American is viewed in Cuba. Time is the only determinant that can prove what was actually happening during the fieldwork. From time to time I was convinced that Cubans understood me, my work, my regard for their culture, and my hopes for a respectable contribution both to anthropology and to Cuba. I was permitted to stay for a full year and to train and dance as a company member of a national dance company. Also from time to time, through my understandings of human interaction, I was convinced that I was distrusted, misunderstood, and placed in a more marginal position than was already the case. For example, I was offered shelter by the Episcopal diocese, yet I was not permitted to stay with church officials. Many were denied permission to film when I was allowed to film most dance classes, dance forms, or dance events throughout Cuba. I was allowed to interview and film national artists, such as Mendive and Zuñiga (national prize-winning visual artists), and permitted to study Haitian-Cuban dances (*gagá* with Grupo de Caidije and Cutumba), but I was limited in teaching dance, one of the few things that I had to give back to Cubans while I was in Cuba. I felt contradictions very often. I do believe that my marginality was imposed in part because of Cuban-American relations, but also by my intimate association with a black dance form that still has low status in the minds of many Cubans, my association with folkloric dancers who are not accorded high prestige as opposed to ballet or modern dancers, and my status as a black female researcher. I was a woman in a male domain, within a society full of machismo. I was a Berkeley researcher (University of California) who resisted the life of a tourist/researcher, for which Cuban officials were more prepared. Additionally, I am African-American, but often I appear to others as a Latina; this caused unexpected disclosures from those who were inadvertently confused about my identity. I have tried to retain an openness to see rumba and its consequences from all sides. I hope all readers, but especially Cuban readers, will appreciate my efforts. I trust most that

which I shared with my Cuban families and hundreds of dark- and light-skinned folk who often did not know me at all: warmth, congeniality, and a willingness, most of the time, to trust. My conclusions follow within the framework of these personal data.

16. To avoid the redundancy involved in the case of rumba, I report only the significant results of the data-organizing analysis. For another dance, such redundancy might not occur, and therefore all levels would be discussed fully. A display of what is actually happening in the body (physiologically) while dancing rumba and, more important, as the rumba event progresses (Snyder's final levels) would be quite informative to the present study and could assist my conclusions; however, I leave these for other specialists in physiology, kinesiology, and neuropsychology. I do comment fully, however, on the energy created and dissipated from the sociological and aesthetic points of view.

2. CUBAN DANCE CULTURE

1. Video examples that document Cuba's dance culture and visually display the review discussed in this chapter are available ("Cuban Dance Examples," Images, 11 Massasoit Street, Northampton, Mass. 01060).

2. The three arenas delineated in the world-view chart combine to form a general skeletal structure of Cuban social life surrounding the pivotal organization of political authority found in the leadership of Fidel Castro and the Communist party. The chart was compiled in the same vein as Alfonso Ortiz's figure for the Tewa (1969:18) as described and augmented by Snyder (1978).

3. Most observable was the minimal participation at formerly central religious sites, i.e., Catholic churches, and the constrained but fairly active participation in African religious ceremonies, including, for example, the masses of people who publicly participated in Obatala Day processions in Havana in 1986.

4. Martinez-Furé (1982, 1986) has organized most, if not all, of the Cuban folkloric dance traditions. He has written much of the underpinnings for teaching guides used in Cuban dance education. Unfortunately, however, the body of Martinez-Furé's thorough knowledge is not yet published. See María Teresa Linaris (1958, 1970), María del Carmen Hernandez (1980), and Graciela Chao Carbonero and Sara Lamerán (1982) for other types of Cuban dance organization.

5. Similar forms are found in the circum-Caribbean and Latin America. In Mexico and Nicaragua, for example, they are called *mitotes*; in Peru, *taquis*; in Jamaica and the Dominican Republic, *areítos*; and in other areas, *batocos*.

6. In Cuba and Spanish-speaking America, *mulatto* refers both to skin color and to a historical class (Martinez-Alier, 1974:71-76). In the nineteenth century, it designated the offspring of African and European parents; some mulattos were slaves and others were free, depending on the dispensation of the Spanish fathers and Spanish law (Martinez-Alier, 1974:27-33). In contemporary Cuban usage, *mulatto* refers to skin color that is darker than *blanca*, *trigueña*, or *morena* but lighter than *prieto*, *pardo*, or *negro*.

7. I use the term *Kongo-Angolan*, rather than the more common terms used in Cuba, *Congo* or *Bantu*, for western Central African influences in Cuba—the cultures from what comprises present-day Zaire and Angola. I leave *congo* for use as the name of the dance tradition of African heritage in Cuba in which rumba plays a significant part.

8. Several authors have done considerable research on the religions of Africa that are found in the Americas: M. Herskovits, 1941; M. and F. Herskovits, 1973; Bascom, 1950; Verger, 1957; Metraux, 1959; Bastide, 1978; Walker, 1980; Murphy,

1988; Cros Sandoval, 1989; Brown, 1991. So far, few exponents of dance anthropology have examined this vast reservoir of religious dance; the exceptions are Dunham, 1947, Courlander, 1960, and Deren, 1953 [1983].

9. *Carabalí* in Cuba most often refers to the Ngbe and Ekpe secret societies which were centered on the Calabar region of southeastern Nigeria during the height of the transatlantic slave trade. Elements of these organizations were transformed in Cuba as Abakuá or Ñañigo.

10. Here I will not review the tremendously important musical creations and their change. These elements have been thoroughly analyzed elsewhere (León, 1984a:232-314; Alén, 1984a:390-405; Linaris, 1958; Carpentier, 1946 [1979]). I firmly believe that music and dance are so interdependent that they should be conceived as one entity. Hence my special use of the virgule (dance/music and music/dance), which normally signifies alternatives, to indicate unity.

11. Son is found in Puerto Rico, the Dominican Republic, Mexico, and Latin America. Likewise, there are various Caribbean dance forms that evolved from son in similar ecological niches with parallel political and economic situations, e.g., *plena* of Puerto Rico, *meringue* of Haiti and the Dominican Republic, *tamborito* of Panama, *porro* of Colombia.

12. In summer 1991, Stanford University hosted the first Cuban dance exchange since the Revolution. Master teachers from Danza Nacional taught in Stanford's annual summer dance workshop. Manuel Vazquez Robaína (principal dancer, master teacher, and choreographer), Margarita Vilela Creagh (principal dancer, teacher), and Regino Jimenez Sáez (lead singer, master percussionist) worked in an intensive training program for dance teachers from across the United States. This occasion marked a historic meeting of Cuban dance and music specialists from the western United States who teach Cuban dance/music (Susan Cashion, Stanford University, son complex; Yvonne Daniel, Smith College, rumba complex, Yoruba, Arará, and Kongo-Angolan traditions; Catherine Evleshin, University of Oregon, Portland, comparsa, rumba, and Yoruba traditions; and Michael Spiro, performing artist and teacher of percussion, San Francisco, rumba, comparsa, and batá traditions). During the fall of 1992, Cuba's Ministry of Culture permitted two other interchanges of Cuban dance. Lourdes Tamayo of Conjunto Folklórico Nacional conducted a two-week workshop at Smith College, and Los Muñequitos de Matanzas made a national tour of the United States. Both events were well received by students and enthusiasts of Cuban dance and music. Plans were also under way for two major workshops and festivals: the Colorado Dance Festival and the Banff Center for the Arts in Canada. Both venues anticipated an exchange of Cuban artists for summer 1994 projects.

13. Both Haitian migrations transported the artistically rich and profoundly important dance tradition of *Vodun*. The dance tradition from this religious system, like the traditions from Yorubá, Arará, Kongo-Angola, and Abakuá, has its history and contemporary meaning connecting dance of Africa and Haiti to Cuba; however, one cannot comfortably include the dances of Vodun as part of Cuban dance at this moment. While Vodun dancing exists in Cuba, it does not embrace Cuba as much as it reaches for Haiti. Unlike gagá and tumba francesa, it remains within the boundaries of a closed, religious, very Haitian culture found within Cuban society. Tumba francesa and gagá, on the other hand, have permeated Cuban cultural boundaries while maintaining their French or Haitian heritage. They are Cuban as well as Haitian forms in this case. Vodun dancing, on the contrary, is Haitian only (Dunham, 1947; Deren, 1953; Daniel, 1980). The Haitians with whom I had contact in Cuba generally had a Haitian-born relative or several community members who were born or raised in Haiti (those who left between the ages of two and eleven years old). All seemed to identify very strongly as Hai-

tians. It will be interesting to see if young Cubans of Haitian descent guard the dances and the practice of Vodun as these elders have done so far.

14. Pro-Arte Ballet has changed names over the years: Ballet Alicia Alonso in 1948, Ballet de Cuba in 1956, Ballet Nacional de Cuba in 1959. It has remained under the artistic vision of the Alonso family, however. Fernando Alonso left in 1967 to become director of Ballet de Camagüey, the only other national ballet company in Cuba to date.

15. A glaring example of distortion involves Desi Arnaz (alias Ricky Ricardo, a native Cuban musician, husband, and co-star with Lucille Ball of "I Love Lucy" television fame) singing a stylized chant for Babaloúayé as his theme song for a comedy show. Babaloúayé is a deity in Santería belief.

16. Modern dance and jazz music are the two indigenous expressive forms of the United States. Both have antecedents, as well as offsprings, in other cultures; they were first formed in the continental United States, however, and are fundamentally "American" (as North Americans would say).

17. Martha Graham was the most public and most acclaimed modern influence; however, Doris Humphrey became professor of dance at the Juilliard School of Music in New York and wrote what is now a classic for dance composition (1953).

3. CUBAN PEOPLE AND RUMBEROS

1. This impression was colored by the presiding attitudes of the Cold War era and the Republican and conservative media of the 1980s that most Americans from the United States were subject to, including myself. I must admit also that I did not try to know and understand Soviets while in Cuba, although I did observe them. It was difficult enough to manage relations with Cubans. I spent one day sunning on the shore behind my apartment with a rather fascinating Soviet woman, an army sergeant and grandmother away from her beloved home, but I never saw her again.

2. I was often annoyed at Cuban bureaucracy and irritated with its inefficiency, but I was painfully concerned for the Cuban people and embarrassed by the U.S. blockade that indirectly impacted Cuba's food supply.

4. PERFORMANCE OF RUMBA

1. No one seems to know why these names came into being. Most drummers and Latin music enthusiasts in the States are well acquainted with guaguancó as a particular rhythm; however, many of them do not know of it as a part of the rumba complex. In Cuba, guaguancó is the most commonly recognized type of rumba also, but many Cubans know of the other rhythms and dance types. They may not as easily associate it with rumba choral singing; Urfe describes that type of rumba which involves choral singing and not dance (1977:183; also discussed later in this chapter).

2. A distinction is made here between those enslaved Africans who were born in Africa and those born in the Americas, all of whom were African. Note that the term *creole* signifies both black and white persons in the Cuban context at this particular historical period and accordingly I have used *European-American* or *creole colonial* to designate white creoles.

3. A pattern of work and nonwork, off-work, personal time, or recreation time is concluded with nonwork time as the seminal time of rumba development. I recognize the difference between ideal statements of behavior and the reality of practice, but most of the historical research supplies evidence that the nature and

character of Cuban conditions at this time, while not rigidly nor unanimously applicable to prevailing law, were generally consistent with the ideal, especially until large-scale sugar manufacturing enforced plantation conditions almost totally throughout the society.

4. Ortiz uses *Lala* as a prime example of the deformation of Afro-Cuban folklore by means of commercialism. Jahn uses rumba as a particular reference to the transformation of African principles to the Americas.

5. Another old rumba, *la bañista*, depicts a woman taking a shower. The woman carries her bucket, soap, and a towel. A very small space is delineated and the woman lets down her hair, pretends to undress and pour water over her body. As she dresses, she sees the peeping Tom of the neighborhood and chases him away. This rumba is most suggestive, as the imagination is swept away conjuring the nakedness of the dancer's body as she ripples and sways in the steps of rumba. *A pilar del arroz* is another popular rumba del tiempo de España in which a woman recounts in gesture and within the rumba step the many stages of hulling and preparing rice. She carries great sacks on her head; she moves equipment around; she shakes the rice through a sieve or sifter; she pounds rice with an imagined mortar and pestal, etc. The dancer creates the illusion of a rural female worker in the hot fields. Galiván is another choreographed rumba del tiempo de España that includes a large group pantomime with a theme of blackbirds and hunters. There are several couples, apparently farmers, dancing and flirting in a typical country scene. The couples are attacked by blackbirds. The men go for their rifles and hunt the birds. The birds swarm the women, and the men kill several birds. One bird, however, begs to be spared. He cries, hugs the women, and hides behind their skirts. The riflemen begin to shoot and the blackbird pretends a delayed death. The ending varies: at times the blackbird is shot and carried off or, on other occasions his appeals work and the whole group dances rumba as they exit.

6. Giribilla developed musically with the expert musicianship of Cuban drummers and the increasing influence of North American musical styles. Giribilla as it exists today is an augmentation or elaboration of guaguancó, but may mark the beginning of a new musical form.

7. Other dancers spoke of giribilla when referring to rare dances performed only in Matanzas, "like giribilla, *reseda*, and *bríkamo* [a female form of Abakuá]."

8. Some evidence points to the traditional performance of rumba outdoors and the performance of other dances indoors during a Rumba event. Certainly in the nineteenth century rumba was not always considered proper or acceptable for salon dancing and was reserved for the barrio. However, within the barrio, rumba was performed outdoors first and then other dances, like danzón, were performed afterward indoors, according to older informants in Matanzas Province.

9. The labanotation in the appendix was notated in 1989 by Luana Silverberg-Willis, a dance graduate student, and checked by Maryann Kincaid, a Labonotation Bureau certified teacher. Sharon Arslanian, also a certified labanotation teacher, transcribed the notation in 1994 onto a computer using the Labanwriter program, which was created and supplied by the Ohio State University Dance Notation Bureau Extension. The notation, achieved from multiple videotapes of rumba, has integrated the characteristic steps as a composite for the analysis; thus many repetitions and variations have been excluded.

10. In Cuba, drummers from Matanzas used the words *tumbador* or *conga* while Habaneros used *hembra* and *salidor* most often.

11. This drum is also referred to in Spanish as *dos o tres golpes*, "two or three hits." I rarely heard this name in Cuba, although it is found in the written literature and used frequently in the United States.

12. *Catá* may also come from an African language, perhaps from a Kongo-

Angolan caja drum. It may come from the Spanish prefix *catá*, meaning "against," because of its polyrhythmic function or differing register in relation to the drums. The cata is also called *guagua*, which may be reduced from the Kongolese instrument played with sticks, *guácara* (Barnet in Chao Carbonero and Lamerán, 1982:92). Currently, *guagua* in Spanish means "bus," which may suggest that the guagua keeps a repeated rhythmic *ostinato*, just as Cuban buses keep traveling on and on (*ostinato* is a musical definition of a repeated melodic and rhythmic line, usually in the bass.)

13. These citations refer to drummers, practicing artists who earn their living through their intimate knowledge of rumba and their specialized techniques in percussion playing in general. I was assisted in the musical notation by Sandi Garcia of Afro-Cuba and Augustín Díaz and Jesús Alfonso of Los Muñequitos in Cuba, and in the United States by Michael Spiro, an American percussionist who specializes in ethnomusicology of Cuba, especially rumba and batá drumming styles.

14. All combinations are possible, e.g., three conga drums (quinto, seis por ocho, and conga) with the *iyá* leading, or the three bata drums (*iyá, itótole,* and *okónkolo*) with the quinto leading. In batarumba, all drummers may compose melodies with all nine drum heads available to them. In effect, this invites intra-African mixtures, as well as, intra-African/European blendings. Interpenetration of differing traditions is a tendency in popular music, but it is the very essence of creole artistic forms.

15. African master drummers have a repertoire of tonal rhythmic patterns with literary sources, and often proverbs are alluded to and presented in musical form.

16. I was assisted in the translations of lyrics by Jose Luis Gomez and Denora Rodrigues, who are both Cuban. Both have relationships to rumba. It became obvious that translations of rumba songs depend not so much on understanding Spanish or even Cuban idiomatic Spanish, but more so in understanding rumba. Gomez was raised in Cuba and sings the songs in a San Francisco-based ensemble specializing in Cuban folklore (with director John Santos).

17. National companies have expanded since the Revolution, but each has a limited number of dancers that can be hired. Newly graduated professional dancers who do not secure employment in the national companies must find positions within the casa de cultura system of the Ministry of Culture or risk leaving their profession for alternative employment. In directing these teachers and culture house programming, the ministry oversees amateur dance and dancers as well. The ministry directs all professionals and students in the professional training schools (enseñanza artística), including youngsters (from eight-year-old ballet students in Oriente and from ten-year-old students of other dance styles) who show promise and interest in serious dance training. Additionally, the ministry oversees several theaters that are used as "home" spaces for opera, ballet, modern dance, classical music, popular music, drama, and folklore companies. There are six professional dance companies each with approximately forty dancers, twenty musicians, and twenty support staff (lighting crew, costume designers, staging experts, sound technicians, and administrators).

18. Keen competition between professional companies reveals historical jealousies between the capital and other cities. The national company in Havana has seniority, secures more opportunities to perform, particularly internationally, and receives more financial and prestigious support than companies outside of Havana. Underlying much of this is the long and continuous battle between Havana and Santiago de Cuba and Oriente, which is the area of many historic and revolutionary events. There is often comment criticizing Havana's disregard of the many intellectual, technical, and artistic specialists from the eastern provinces. Habaneros refer

to any place outside of Havana as "the interior," as if it were a jungle. This friction between the capital and other large cities is not uncommon in Caribbean history wherein the colonial government had close ties to the capital as the major source of commerce and administration (see e.g., Quintero Rivera, 1986:50-51, 60; Williams, 1970:58-68).

19. I had few opportunities to see and observe clubs and hotels. My comments are limited to about ten occasions, mostly in Havana, with a few in Matanzas, Camaguey, and Santiago de Cuba. Rumba was performed only once on the program of shows that I saw.

20. Usually the public is free to dance after the show and most of this dancing is not rumba. Shows feature variety and spectacles with Mexican, Brazilian, Panamanian, Yoruban, Congolese, and Cuban choreographies. The most outstanding is Tropicana in Havana; this nightclub resembles a Las Vegas or five-star night club (but it is also possible that Las Vegas has emulated the extravaganza approach of the original outdoor, tropical entertainment of Havana).

21. The concepts of ritual intensity and public display are taken from Jill Sweet's revision (1976) of Herbert Cole's analyses of Ghanaian festivals (1975). For rumba analysis, public display conforms to Sweet's usage, i.e., the numbers of people attracted by multisensory stimuli of the dance event. Ritual intensity here expands Sweet's usage and is concerned with performers' interest, involvement, and concentration, in addition to the heightened interest and activity of the group as a result of sound, color, odor, and movement. While complete statistical data were not gathered in the rumba case, similar results accrue from the composite rumba models.

5. SYMBOLIC ASPECTS OF RUMBA

1. Admission of all dancers, irrespective of previous training or ability, could be viewed in a positive educational and philosophical manner. However, the desperate economic situation of Cuba obviously influences every opportunity for possible financial gain. This is felt profoundly when less-experienced dancers and musicians are permitted to take advanced classes simply because they have paid for that level, which is generally more costly.

2. In his transcription of "Rumbitas de Chango," Ortiz (1951 [1985]:460) negates the relationship between rumba and the sacred. He says the song is improperly named.

3. From 1986 in Cuba, I viewed the mixture of batá and rumba as innovative development of rumba (Daniel, 1989), because that was what Cubans declared. So it was surprising to learn in the U.S. that there had been an earlier mixture of the same two traditions that was documented in the songs of Celia Cruz with Sonora Matancera (Gonzalez, in Boggs, 1992:295).

6. SOCIAL AND AESTHETIC CHANGE IN CUBA

1. The Cuban dances chart outlines many dances that I researched, but there are several others that I did not find adequately examined, e.g., the dances of Haitian-Cubans (babul, yuba, cate, tacona or mason), the Arará tradition (solli, afrekete, gebioso, etc.) the dance of female societies (brikamo), the dance of spiritists (de Cordon), etc. As elsewhere, Cuba has a rich repository of dance information that can yield a deeper understanding of dance as universal and particular behavior.

Bibliography

Ager, Lynn Price
    1975 Eskimo Dance and Cultural Values in an Alaskan Village *in* Dance Research Journal, vol. 8, no. 1, pp. 7-11.

Ahye, Molly
    1978 Golden Heritage: The Dance in Trinidad and Tobago. Trinidad: Heritage Cultures.
    1983 Cradle of Caribbean Dance. Trinidad: Heritage Cultures.

Alén, Olavo
    1984a Géneros de la música cubana. Havana: Editorial Pueblo y Educación.
    1984b La tradición popular y su significación social y política *in* Musicologiá en Latinoamérica, ed. Zoila Gómez García, Havana: Editorial Arte y Literatura, pp. 390-405.
    1987a La música de las sociedades de tumba francesa en Cuba. Havana: Casa de las Américas.
    1987b The Rumba, manuscript. Havana, July.
    1987c The Son, manuscript. Havana, July.

American Rumba Committee
    1943 The American Rumba, a Textbook of the Cuban Dance and Its Newest American Developments. New York: Rudor.

Appadurai, Arjun, ed.
    1986 The Social Life of Things—Commodities in Cultural Perspectives. London: Cambridge University Press.

Aschenbrenner, Joyce
    1980 Katherine Dunham: Reflections on the Social and Political Contexts of Afro-American Dance, Dance Research Annual 12, New York: CORD.

Astaire, Fred
    1955 The Fred Astaire Dance Book: Rhumba with Basic Mambo. New York: Arrowhead Books.

Azzi, María Susanna
    1991 Antropología del tango. Buenos Aires: Ediciones de Olavarría.
Barnes, Sandra, ed.
    1989 Africa's Ogun: Old World and New. Bloomington: Indiana University
         Press.
Barnet, Miguel
    1961 La religión de los Yorubas y sus dioses in Actos del Folklore, Havana:
         Instituto de Etnología y Folklore, January.
    1982 Distintas sectas: Briyumbas, Mayombes, Kimbisas y otros in Folklore cu-
         bana I, II, III, IV, Graciela Chao Carbonero and S. Lamerán, Havana:
         Editorial Pueblo y Educación, pp. 86-87, 91.
Barrows, Anita
    1984 Mao Tem Tempo: Domestic Organization and Migratory Patterns of
         Afro-Brazilians in São Paolo and New York. Ph.D. dissertation, Univer-
         sity of California, Berkeley.
Bascom, William
    1950 The Focus of Cuban Santería in Southwestern Journal of Anthropol-
         ogy, vol. 6, no. 1, pp. 64-68.
    1952 Two Forms of Afro-Cuban Divination in Acculturation in the Americas,
         ed. Sol Tax, Proceedings of the 29th International Congress of Ameri-
         canists, vol. 2, pp. 169-79.
    1960 Yoruba Concepts of Soul in Selected Papers of the Fifth International
         Congress of Anthropological and Ethnological Sciences, ed. Anthony
         Wallace, Philadelphia: University of Pennsylvania Press, pp. 401-10.
    1969 Ifa Divination: Communication between Gods and Men in West Africa.
         Bloomington: Indiana University Press.
    1972 Shango in the New World. Occasional Publication of the African and
         Afro-American Research Institute, no. 4. Austin: University of Texas.
    1980 Sixteen Cowries: Yoruba Divination from Africa to the New World.
         Bloomington: Indiana University Press.
Bastide, Roger
    1978 The African Religions of Brazil. Baltimore: Johns Hopkins University
         Press.
Behague, Gerard
    1979 Music in Latin America, an Introduction. Englewood Cliffs, N.J.: Pren-
         tice-Hall.
Benedict, Burton
    1983 The Anthropology of World's Fairs. London and Berkeley: Scholar
         Press.
Berreman, Gerald
    1979 Caste and Other Inequities, Essays on Inequality. Kailash Puri, Meerut,
         India: Ved Prakash Vatuk Folklore Institute.
Black, George
    1988 Cuba: The Revolution: Toward Victory Always, but When? in Nation,
         October, pp. 373-85.
Blacking, John
    1973 How Musical Is Man? Seattle: University of Washington Press.
Blier, Suzanne Preston
    1980 Africa's Cross River Art of the Nigerian Cameroon Border Redefined.
         New York: L. Kahan Gallery, African Arts, pp. 3-26.
Bloch, Maurice
    1974 Symbols, Song, Dance and Features of Articulation: Is Religion an Ex-

treme Form of Traditional Authority? *in* Archives Européennes de Sociologie, vol. 15, pp. 51-81.

Boggs, Vernon, ed.
1992 Salsiology. New York: Glenview Press.

Bolívar, Natalia Arostegüi
1990 Los Orishas en Cuba. Havana: Ediciones Unión.

Bonachea, Rolando, and Nelson Valdés, eds.
1972 Fidel Castro: Revolutionary Struggle, 1947-1958. Cambridge: MIT Press.

Bonachea, Ramón, and Marta San Martín
1974 The Cuban Insurrection, 1952-1959. New Brunswick, N.J.: Transaction Books.

Bourdieu, Pierre
1977 Outline of a Theory of Practice. Cambridge: Cambridge University Press.
1984 Distinction: A Social Critique of the Judgment of Taste, trans. Richard Nice. Cambrige: Harvard University Press.

Bourguignon, Erika
1976 Possession. San Francisco: Chandler and Sharp.

Bremer, Fredrika
1851 (1980) Cartas desde Cuba. Havana: Editorial Arte y Literatura.

Buonaventura, Wendy
1990 Serpent of the Nile: Women and Dance in the Arab World. New York: Interlink Books.

Cabrera, Lydia
1954 (1983) El Monte. Miami: Colección del Chichereku.
1957 Anagó: Vocabulario Lucumí. Havana: Ediciones C.R.
1958 (1970) La sociedad secreta Abakuá. Miami: Ediciones C.R.
1974 Yemayá y Ochún. New York: Colección del Chichereku.
1979 (1986) Reglas de Congo, Palo Monte Mayombe. Miami, Ediciones Universal.

Canet, Carlos
1973 Lucumí: Religión de los Yorubas en Cuba. Miami: AIP.

Carpentier, Alejo
1946 (1979) La música en Cuba. Mexico City: Fondo de Cultura Económica.

Cashion, Susan
1980 Educating the Dancer in Cuba *in* Dance, Current Selected Research, ed. Lynnette Y. Overby and James H. Humphrey, New York: AMS Press, vol. 1, pp. 165-85.
1982 La Danza de los Tastoanes: Festival of Santo Santiago in San Juan de Ocotán, México. M.A. thesis, Stanford University.
1983 Dance Ritual and Cultural Values in a Mexican Village: Festival of Santo Santiago. Ann Arbor: University Microfilms; Ph.D. dissertation, Stanford University.
1986 A Taxonomy of Cuban Dances, unpublished chart.

Castro, Fidel
1968 A New Stage in the Advance of Cuban Socialism. New York: Merit.
1984a Cuba Cannot Export Revolution, Nor Can the United States Prevent It, Speech, Santiago de Cuba, January 1. Havana: Editora Política.
1984b The World Crisis; Its Economic and Social Impact on the Underdeveloped Countries. London: Zed Books.

1985a Fidel y la religión; Conversaciones con Frei Betto. Havana: Oficina de Publicaciones del Consejo de Estado.

1985b If a Solution Isn't Found for the Economic Crisis, There Are Going to Be Widespread Revolutionary Outbreaks, Speech, March 1983. Havana: Editora Política.

1985c Our Struggle Is That of Latin American and the Third World. Havana: Publicación del Consejo de Estado.

Chao Carbonero, Graciela
1980 Bailes Yorubas de Cuba. Havana: Editorial Pueblo y Educación.

Chao Carbonero, Graciela, and Sara Lamerán
1982 Folklore Cubano I, II, III, IV. Havana: Editorial Pueblo y Educación.

Christopher, Luella Sue
1979 Pirouettes with Bayonets: Classical Ballet Metamorphosed as Dance-Drama and Its Usage in the People's Republic of China as a Tool of Political Socialization. Ann Arbor: University Microfilms; Ph.D. dissertation, American University.

Clark, VeVe, and Margaret Wilkerson, eds.
1978 Kaiso! Katherine Dunham, an Anthology of Writings. Berkeley: Institute for Study of Social Change, CCEW Women's Center, University of California.

Clifford, James
1988 The Predicament of Culture: Twentieth Century Ethnography, Literature, and Art. Cambridge, Mass.: Harvard University Press.

Cohen, Erik
1988 Authenticity and Commoditization in Tourism in Annals of Tourism Research, vol. 15, pp. 371-86.

Cole, Herbert
1975 The Art of Festival in Ghana in African Arts, vol. 8, no. 3, pp. 12-23.

Cole, Johnetta
1980 Race toward Equality: The Impact of the Cuban Revolution on Racism in Black Scholar, vol. 11, no. 8, pp. 2-24.

Copeland, R.
1978 Why Cuba Champions Ballet in New York Times, June 11, sec. 2, pp. 1, 9, 13.

Cowan, Jane
1990 Dance and the Body Politic in Northern Greece. Princeton, N.J.: Princeton University Press.

Cuyás, Arturo, and Antonio Cuyás
1982 Grán Diccionario Cuyás. Havana: Editorial Pueblo y Educación.

Dailey, Maurice Cecil
N.d. Spiritism and the Christian Faith. M.A. thesis, ca. 1950, Union Theological Seminary, Department of Missions, Matanzas.

Daniel, Yvonne
1980 The Potency of Dance: A Haitian Examination in Black Scholar, vol. 11, no. 8, pp. 61-73.

1983a Dancing Down River: A Presentation on the Dance of Suriname in Dance Ethnologists, University of California at Los Angeles, vol. 7, pp. 24-39.

1983b Dancing Up River: An Analysis of Afro-Surinamese Dance, lecture, Mills College, October.

1984 What is Ethnic Dance? in Ethnic Dance Festival Program, San Francisco, City Celebration, pp. 14-15.

1990a Economic Vitamins from the Cuban Aesthetic System or Commoditization and Cultural Conservation in Cuban Tourism *in* Tourism and Music, The World of Music, vol. 10, ed. Tomoaki Fujii, trans. Nobukiyo Eguchi, Osaka: Museum of Ethnology and Tokyo Shoseki Press, pp. 126-52.

1990b   In the Company of Cuban Women *in* African Commentary, vol. 2, no. 7, pp. 16-19.

1991   Changing Values in Cuban Rumba, a Lower-Class Black Dance Appropriated by the Cuban Revolution *in* Dance Research Journal, vol. 23, no. 2, pp. 1-10.

Davis, Wade
1988   Passage of Darkness: The Ethnobiology of the Haitian Zombie. Chapel Hill: University of North Carolina Press.

Departamento de Historia
1986   La esclavitud en Cuba. Havana: Editorial Académia.

Deren, Maya
1953   (1963) Divine Horsemen, the Living Gods of Haiti. New York and London: Thames and Hudson.

Deschamps Chapeaux, Pedro
1971   El negro en la economía habanera del siglo XIX. Havana: Premio Unión de Escritores y Artistas de Cuba.

Deutschmann, David, ed.
1987   Ché Guevara and the Cuban Revolution: Writings and Speeches of Ernesto Ché Guevara. Sydney: Pathfinder/Pacific and Asia.

Dirección Política de las FAR
1971   Historia de Cuba, vol. 1. Havana: Instituto Cubano del Libro.

Drewal, Margaret Thompson
1975   Symbols of Possession: A Study of Movement and Regalia in an Anago-Yoruba Ceremony *in* Dance Research Journal, vol. 7, no. 2, pp. 15-24.

Duarte Jiménez, Rafael
1988   El negro en la sociedad colonial. Santiago de Cuba: Editorial Oriente.

Dunham, Katherine
1947   Las danzas de Haití *in* Acta Antropología, vol. 2, no. 4, pp. 1-64.
1969   Island Possessed. Garden City, N.Y.: Doubleday.

Emery, Lynne Fauley
1972   (1988) Black Dance in the United States from 1619 to 1970. Palo Alto: National Press Books.

Erisman, H. Michael
1985   Cuba's International Relations: The Anatomy of a Nationalistic Foreign Policy. Boulder Colo.: Westview Press.

Evleshin, Katherine
1989   Dance in Cuban Carnival, paper delivered at the Congress on Research in Dance (CORD) Conference, Williamsburg, Va., November.
1991   The Changing Form and Function of Carnival in Havana, video lecture, Stanford University, Cuban Dance Seminar, July.

Faílde, Oswaldo Castillo
1964   Miguel Faílde, creador musical del danzón. Havana: Editorial del Consejo Nacional de Cultura, pp. 83-99.

Fanon, Frantz
1963   Wretched of the Earth. New York: Grove Press.

Farris, James
1979   The Productive Basis of Aesthetic Traditions: Some African Examples *in* Art in Society, ed. Megaw and Greenhalgh, London: Duckworth.

Feijóo, Samuel
  1986 Mitología Cubana. Havana: Editorial Letras Cubanas.
Feinsilver, Julie
  1989 Cuba as a "World Medical Power" in Latin American Research Review,
       vol. 24, no. 2, pp. 1-34.
Feld, Steven
  1982 Sound and Sentiment. Philadelphia: University of Pennsylvania Press.
Fernández, Armando
  1986 La historia de los haitianos en Cuba, lecture series for La Casa de Las
       Américas, Havana, October.
Fernández de Oviedo, Gonzalo
  1851-55 Historia general y natural de las Indias, Islas y tierra-firme del Mar
          Océano, 4 vols. Madrid: Real Academia de la Historia.
Frank, Andre Gunder
  1969 Latin America: Underdevelopment or Revolution. New York: Monthly
       Review Press.
Freire, Paulo
  1970 (1982) Pedagogy of the Oppressed, trans. Myra Bergman Ramos. New
       York: Continuum.
Fuenzalida, Edmundo
  1982 Dance as a Cultural Expression in an Interdependent World in Asocia-
       ción Nacional de Grupos Folklóricos, vol. 6, no. 1, pp. 24-27.
Fusco, Coco
  1988 Drawing New Lines in Nation, October 24, pp. 397-400.
Geertz, Clifford
  1973 Deep Play: Notes on the Balinese Cockfight in The Interpretation of
       Cultures. New York: Basic Books.
Giurchescu, Anca, and Lisbet Torp
  1991 Theory and Methods in Dance Research: A European Approach to the
       Holistic Study of Dance in Yearbook for Traditional Music, vol. 23,
       pp. 1-10.
Gleason, Judith
  1987 Oya: In Praise of the Goddess. Boston: Shambhala.
Goins, Margarette Bobo
  1973 African Retentions in the Dance of the Americas in Dance Research
       Monograph 1, 1971-1972, New York: CORD, pp. 207-229.
Goldberg, Alan
  1982 Play and Ritual in Haitian Voodoo Shows for Tourists in The Paradoxes
       of Play, ed. John Loy, West Point, N.Y.: Leisure Press, pp. 24-29.
Gordo, Isabel
  1985 Configuraciones de los Haitiano-Cubanos en la cultura cubana, manu-
       script. Havana: Instituto de Ciencias.
Graburn, Nelson
  1970 Art and Pluralism in the Americas in Anuario Indigenista, December.
  1986 Cultural Preservation: An Anthropologists' View in Problems in Cul-
       tural Heritage Conservation, ed. P. Brown et al., Honolulu: Hawaii
       Heritage Center, pp 39-46.
  1977 Takujaksak: An Exhibition of Inuit Arts as an Experiment in the Cen-
       tral Canadian Arctic, paper presented at the Annual Meeting of the
       Canadian Ethnology Society, Halifax, Nova Scotia, February.
  1984 The Evolution of Tourist Arts in Annals of Tourism Research, vol. 14,
       no. 1, pp. 393-420.

1989 Tourism: The Sacred Journey *in* Hosts and Guests, ed. Valene Smith, 2d ed., Philadelphia: University of Pennsylvania Press, pp. 21-36.

Graburn, Nelson, ed.
1976 Ethnic and Tourist Arts: Cultural Expressions from the Fourth World. Berkeley: University of California Press.

Greenwood, Davydd
1977 Culture by the Pound: An Anthropological Perspective of Tourism as Cultural Commoditization, *in* Hosts and Guests, ed. Valene Smith, Philadelphia: University of Pennsylvania Press, pp. 129-138.
1989 Culture by the Pound: An Anthropological Perspective of Tourism as Cultural Commoditization, in Hosts and Guests, ed. Valene Smith, 2d ed., Philadelphia: University of Pennsylvania Press, pp. 171-186.

Guedes Hernandez, Haydee, and Mara Galvez Abrahantes
1983 La rumba columbia: Proyecto de grado, curso de instructores de arte, Matanzas.

Guerra, Ramiro
1968 Apreciación de la danza. Havana: Editorial Letras Cubanas.
1989 Teatralización del folklore y otros ensayos. Havana: Editorial Letras Cubanas.

Guerra y Sanchez, Ramiro
1938 (1971) Manual de historia de Cuba. Havana: Editorial de Ciencias Sociales.
1964 (1970) Azúcar y población en las Antillas. Havana: Editorial de Ciencias Sociales.

Guillermoprieto, Alma
1990 Samba. New York: Knopf.

Hanna, Judith
1979 To Dance Is Human. Austin: University of Texas Press.
1984 The Performer-Audience Connection: Emotion to Metaphor in Dance and Society. Austin: University of Texas Press.

Hazzard-Gordon, Katrina
1990 Jookin': The Rise of Social Dance Formations in African-American Culture. Philadelphia: Temple University Press.

Henriques, Fernando
1949 West Indian Family Organization in America *in* Journal of Sociology, vol. 55, no. 1, pp. 30-37.

Hernandez, María del Carmen
1980 Historia de la danza en Cuba. Havana: Editorial Pueblo y Educación.

Herskovits, Frances, ed.
1966 New World Negro. Bloomington: Indiana University Press.

Herskovits, Melville
1937 Life in a Haitian Village. New York: Knopf.
1941 The Myth of the Negro Past. New York: Harper.

Herskovits, Melville, and Frances Herskovits
1934 Rebel Destiny among Bush Negroes of Dutch Guiana. New York: McGraw-Hill.
1947 Trinidad Village. New York: Knopf.
1973 Retentions and Reinterpretations in Rural Trinidad *in* Work and Family Life, ed. D. Lowenthal and L. Comitas, New York: Anchor.

Hintzen, Percy
1978 Myth, Ideology and Crisis in Plantation Society: The Guyanese Example *in* Working Papers in Caribbean Society, Skrikia, no. 4, October–November.

1982a Class, Ethnicity and the Political Economy, manuscript. University of California, Berkeley.

1982b Developmental Crises in Small Ex-Colonial States, manuscript. University of California, Berkeley.

Hobsbawm, Eric, and Terence Ranger, eds.

1983 The Invention of Tradition. Cambridge: Cambridge University Press.

Holloway, Joseph, ed.

1990 Africanisms in American Culture. Bloomington: Indiana University Press.

hooks, bell

1990 Yearnings: Race, Gender and Cultural Politics. Boston: South End Press.

Horner, Alice

1990 Conceptualized Tradition: Intellectual Approaches in Assumptions of Tradition: Creating, Collecting, and Conserving Artifacts in Cameroon Grassfields (West Africa), Ph.D. dissertation, University of California, Berkeley.

Jahn, Janheinz

1961 Muntu: The New African Culture. New York: Grove Press.

James, Cyril Lionel Robert

1938 (1963) The Black Jacobins, Touissaint L'Ouverture and the San Domingo Revolution. New York: Vintage Books.

Kaeppler, Adrienne

1967b The Structure of Tongan Dance. Ann Arbor: University Microfilms, Ph.D. dissertation, University of Hawaii.

1973 Polynesian Dance as Airport Art in Dance Research Annual 8, New York: CORD, pp. 71-85.

1986 Cultural Analysis, Linguistic Analogies, and the Study of Dance in Anthropological Perspective in Explorations in Ethnomusicology: Essays in Honor of David P. McAllester, ed. Charlotte Frisbie, Detroit Monographs in Musicology, no. 9, pp. 25-33.

1991 American Approaches to the Study of Dance in Yearbook for Traditional Music, vol. 23, pp. 11-22.

Kealiinohomoku, Joann

1965 (1973) A Comparative Study of Dance as a Constellation of Motor Behaviors among African and United States Negroes in Dance Research Annual 7, New York: CORD, pp. 1-181.

1967 Hopi and Polynesian Dance: A Study in Cross-Cultural Comparisons in Ethnomusicology, vol. 11, pp. 343-357.

1969-70 An Anthropologist Looks at Ballet as a Form of Ethnic Dance in Impulse, Extensions of Dance, pp. 24-34.

1974 Dance Culture as a Microcosm of Holistic Culture in New Dimensions in Dance Research: Anthropology and Dance, the American Indian, Proceedings of the Third Conference on Research in Dance, New York: CORD, pp. 99-106.

1976 Theory and Methods for an Anthropological Study of Dance. Ann Arbor: University Microfilms, Ph.D. dissertation, Indiana University.

Kincaid, Maryann

1982 Elementary Labanotation. Palo Alto: Mayfield.

Klein, Herbert

1967 Slavery in the Americas: A Comparative Study of Virginia and Cuba. Chicago: University of Chicago Press.

1986 African Slavery in Latin America and the Caribbean. New York: Oxford University Press.
Knight, Franklin
1970 Slave Society in Cuba during the Nineteenth Century. Madison: University of Wisconsin Press.
1978 The Caribbean: The Genesis of a Fragmented Nationalism. New York: Oxford University Press.
Kubik, Gerhard
1981 Neo-traditional Popular Music in East Africa 1945 in Popular Music, vol. 1, pp. 83-104.
1979 Angolan Traits in Black Music, Games, and Dances of Brazil: A Study of African Cultural Extensions Overseas. Lisbon: Junta de Investigacoes Cientificas do Ultramar.
Kurath, Gertrude
1949 Dance: Folk and Primitive in Dictionary of Folklore, Mythology and Legend, ed. Maria Leach and J. Fried, New York: Funk and Wagnalls, vol. 1, pp. 277-296.
Kurath, Gertrude, and Antonio Garcia
1970 Music and Dance in Tewa Plaza Ceremonies, New Mexico. Santa Fe: University of New Mexico Press.
Kurath, Gertrude, and Samuel Marti
1964 Dances of Anahuac: The Choreography for Music of Precortesian Dances. Viking Fund Publications in Anthropology, no. 38, New York: Wenner-Gren Foundation.
Labat, Père
1724 Nouveau voyage aux Isles de l'Amérique, trans. Anthony Bliss. The Hague.
Lachatánere, Rómulo
1961 Tipos étnicos africanos que concurrieron en la amálgama cubana in Actos del Folklore, vol. 1, no. 3, pp. 5-12.
Laguerre, Michel
1975 The Impact of Migration on the Haitian Family Household Organization in Family and Kinship in Middle America and the Caribbean, ed. Arnaud Marks, Leiden: Institute of Higher Studies and Department of Caribbean Studies, pp. 446-81.
Langer, Susanne K.
1953 Feeling and Form. New York: Scribner.
Larose, Serge
1975 The Haitian "La Kou": Land, Family, and Ritual in Family and Kinship in Middle America and the Caribbean, ed. Arnaud Marks, Leiden: Institute of Higher Studies, pp. 482-512.
Leo Grande, William M.
1988 Cuba: The Democrats: A Party Divided and Paralyzed in Nation, October pp. 395-97.
León, Argeliers
1955 El ciclo del danzón in Nuestro Tiempo, vol. 2, no. 4.
1984a Del canto y el tiempo. Havana: Editorial Letras Cubanas.
1984b La música como mercanciá in Musicología en Latinoamérica, ed. Zoila Gómez García, Havana: Editorial Arte y Literatura, pp. 406-28.
Levine, Barry B., ed.
1983 The New Cuban Presence in the Caribbean. Boulder, Colo.: Westview Press.

Lewis, Gordon K.
1983 Main Currents in Caribbean Thought. Baltimore: Johns Hopkins University Press.

Linaris, María Teresa
1958 Ensayo sobre la influencia española en la música cubana in Pro-Arte Musical, Havana.
1970 El sucu-sucu de Isla de Pinos. Havana: Instituto de Etnología y Folklore.

Lopez Valdés, Rafael
1986 Hacia una periodización de la historia de la esclavitud en Cuba in La Esclavitud en Cuba, Instituto de Ciencias Históricas, Havana: Editorial Academia.
1988 Una muestra de la composición étnica y el matrimonio de africanos en la Habana entre 1694 y 1714 in Revista Cubana de Ciencias Sociales, no. 17, p. 1.
1990 Africanos de filiación Bantú en Cuba, 1521-1898, manuscript.

MacGaffey, Wyatt
1986 Religion and Society in Central Africa. Chicago: University of Chicago Press.

Mahler, Elfrida, Ramiro Guerra, and Jose Limón
1978 Fundamentos de la danza. Havana: Editorial Orbre.

Mandela, Nelson
1991 How Far We Slaves Have Come! South Africa and Cuba in Today's World, Nelson Mandela and Fidel Castro. New York: Pathfinder.

Maquet, Jacques
1971 Introduction to Aesthetic Anthropology. McCaleb Module, Reading: Addison-Wesley, pp. 3-36.
1986 The Aesthetic Experience: An Anthropologist Looks at the Visual Arts. New Haven: Yale University Press.

Mariana, Myriam Evelyse
1986 A Portrayal of the Brazilian Samba Dance with the Use of Labananalysis as a Tool for Movement Analysis. Ann Arbor: University Microfilms, Ph.D. dissertation, University of Wisconsin, Madison.

Marks, Arnaud, ed.
1975 Family and Kinship in Middle America and the Caribbean. Leiden: Institute of Higher Studies and Department of Caribbean Studies.

Martinez-Alier, Verena
1974 Marriage, Class and Colour in Nineteenth-Century Cuba: A Study of Racial Attitudes and Sexual Values in a Slave Society. Cambridge: Cambridge University Press.

Martinez-Furé, Rogelio
1961 El bando azul in Actos del Folklore, vol. 1, no. 7, Centro de Estudios del Folklore del Teatro Nacional, Havana.
1982 La rumba in G. Chao Carbonero and S. Lamerán, Folklore Cubano I, II, III, IV, Havana: Editorial Pueblo y Educación, pp. 114-17.
1986 La rumba. Havana: Conjunto Folklórico Nacional de Cuba, pp. 1-3.

Mason, John
1985 Four New World Yoruba Rituals. Brooklyn, N.Y.: Yoruba Theological Archministry.
1992 Orin Orisa. Brooklyn, N.Y.: Yoruba Theological Archministry.

Matas, Julio
1971 Theater and Cinematography in Revolutionary Change in Cuba, ed.

Carmelo Mesa-Lago, Pittsburgh: University of Pittsburgh Press, pp. 427-46.

Mernissi, Fatima
1975 Beyond the Veil. New York: Schenkman.

Mesa-Lago, Carmelo, ed.
1971 Revolutionary Change in Cuba. Pittsburgh: University of Pittsburgh Press.

Metraux, Alfred
1959 Voodoo in Haiti. New York: Schocken.

Meyer, Leonard
1956 Emotion and Meaning in Music. Chicago: University of Chicago Press.

Millet, José, and Rafael Brea
1989 Grupos Folklóricos de Santiago de Cuba. Santiago de Cuba: Editorial Oriente.

Mintz, Sidney
1964 Foreword in Ramiro Guerra y Sanchez, Sugar and Society in the Caribbean, New Haven: Yale University Press, pp. xi-xliv.
1975 Slavery, Colonialism and Racism. New York: Norton.

Moliner, Israel
1986 La rumba. Matanzas: Ministerio de Cultura.
1987 La rumba in Del Caribe, vol. 4, no. 9, pp. 40-47.

Moore, Carlos
1989 Castro, the Blacks, and Africa. Los Angeles: Center for African American Studies, University of California.

Moreau de St.-Méry, Méderic Louis Elie
1796 (1976) Danse: Description topographique physique, civile, politique et historique de la partie française de l'isle le Saint-Domingue, trans. Lily and Baird Hastings. New York: Dance Horizons.

Moreno, José A.
1971 From Traditional to Modern Values in Revolutionary Change in Cuba, ed. Carmelo Mesa-Lago, Pittsburgh: University of Pittsburgh Press, pp. 471-97.

Moreno Fraginals, Manuel, ed.
1977 (1984) Africa in Latin America: Essays on History, Culture, and Socialization. New York and Paris: Holmes and Meier.

Murphy, Joseph
1988 Santeria: An African Religion in America. Boston: Beacon Press.

Needham, Rodney
1978 Primordial Characters. Charlottesville: University of Virginia Press.

Ness, Sally
1992 Body, Movement, Culture: Kinesthetic and Visual Symbolism in a Philippine Community. Philadelphia: University of Pennsylvania Press.

Nettleford, Rex
1985 Dance Jamaica: Cultural Definition and Artistic Discovery. New York: Grove Press.

Nketia, J. H. Kwabena
1965 The Interrelations of African Music and Dance in Studia Musicologica 7, pp. 91-101.

Novack, Cynthia
1990 Sharing the Dance: Contact Improvisation and American Culture. Madison: University of Wisconsin Press.

Orovio, Helio
1987a En el yambú no se vacuna in Revolución y Cultura, no. 3, p. 46.

1987b Unión de reyes llora *in* Revolución y Cultura, no. 12, pp. 39-42.
Orozco, Danilo
1984 El son: ¿Ritmo, baile o reflejo de la personalidad cultural cubana? *in* Musicología en Latinoamérica, ed. Zoila Gómez García, Havana: Editorial Arte y Literatura, pp. 363-89.
Ortiz, Alfonso
1969 The Tewa World: Space, Time, Being, and Becoming in a Pueblo Society. Chicago: University of Chicago Press.
Ortiz, Fernando
1926 (1986) Los negros curros. Havana: Editorial de Ciencias Sociales.
1940 (1963) Contrapunteo cubano del tabaco y el azúcar. Havana: Consejo Nacional de Cultura.
1950 La africanía de la música folklórica de Cuba. Havana: Educaciones Cárdenas.
1951 (1985) Los bailes y el teatro de los negros en el folklore de Cuba. Havana: Editorial Letras Cubanas.
1974 La música afrocubana. Madrid: Ediciones Júcar.
Patterson, Orlando
1969 The Sociology of Slavery: An Analysis of the Origins, Development and Structure of Negro Slave Society in Jamaica. Rutherford, N.J.: Fairleigh Dickinson University Press.
Paulston, Rolland G.
1971 Education *in* Revolutionary Change in Cuba, ed. Carmelo Mesa-Lago, Pittsburgh: University of Pittsburgh Press, pp. 357-98.
Pedro, Alberto
1967 La semana santa haitiano-cubana *in* Etnología y Folklore, no. 4.
1986 Lectures on Haitian populations in Cuba, for La Casa de las Américas, October 16-20.
Pratt, Mary Louise
1992 Imperial Eyes. London: Routledge.
Price, Sally, and Richard Price
1980 Afro-American Arts of the Surinamese Rain Forest. Los Angeles: Museum of Cultural History and University of California Press.
Primus, Pearl
1969 Life Crises: Dance from Birth to Death *in* American Therapy Association, Proceedings from the Fourth Annual Conference, Philadelphia, pp. 1-13.
Quintero Rivera, A. G.
1986 Ponce, the Danza and the National Question: Notes toward a Sociology of Puerto Rican Music *in* Cimarrón, New Perspectives on the Caribbean, vol. 1, no. 2, pp. 49-65.
Randall, Margaret
1974 Cuban Women Now. Toronto: Women's Press.
1981 Women in Cuba: Twenty Years Later. New York: Smyrna Press.
Ranger, Terence O.
1975 Dance and Society in East Africa, 1890-1970. Berkeley: University of California Press.
Reed, Gail, and Joe Walker
1976 Solidarity in Cuba *in* Center for Cuban Studies Newsletter, vol. 7, no. 1, pp. 29-33.
Rigal, Nieves Armas
1991 Los bailes de las sociedades de tumba francesa. Havana: Editorial Pueblo y Educación.

Roberts, John Storm
    1979 The Latin Tinge. Tivoli, N.Y.: Original Music.
Rockefeller, Michael C.
    1968 The Asmat of New Guinea: The Journal of Michael Clark Rockefeller,
        ed. A. A. Gerbrands, New York: Museum of Primitive Art.
Rosaldo, Michele, and L. Lamphere
    1974 Women, Culture and Society. Stanford: Stanford University Press.
Royce, Anya
    1977 The Anthropology of Dance. Bloomington: Indiana University Press.
    1984 Movement and Meaning: Creativity and Interpretation in Ballet and
        Mime. Bloomington: Indiana University Press.
Saco, José Antonio
    1932 (1946) La vagancia en Cuba in Cuadernos de Cultura, no. 3, Havana:
        Ministerio de Educación.
Salvador, Mari Lyn
    1975 Molas of the Cuna Indians: A Case Study of Artistic Criticism and
        Ethno-Aesthetics. Ph.D. dissertation, University of California, Berkeley.
Schlegel, Alice
    1977 Sexual Stratification: A Cross-Cultural View. New York: Columbia Uni-
        versity Press.
Schneebaum, Tobias
    1975 A Museum for New Guinea in Craft Horizons, vol. 35, p. 2, vol. 36,
        pp. 88-89.
Serviat, Pedro
    1980 La discriminación racial en Cuba, su origen, desarollo y terminación
        definitiva in Islas, vol. 66, May-August.
Simey, T. S.
    1946 Welfare and Planning in the West Indies. London: Oxford University
        Press.
Simpson, George
    1978 Black Religions in the New World. New York: Columbia University
        Press.
Slocum, Sally
    1975 Woman the Gatherer: Male Bias in Anthropology in Towards an An-
        thropology of Women, ed. R. Reiter, New York: Monthly Review Press.
Smith, Michael G.
    1962 West Indian Family Structure. Seattle: University of Washington Press.
Smith, Raymond T.
    1965 The Negro Family in British Guiana. London: Routledge & Kegan
        Paul.
Smith, Wayne
    1988 Cuba: The Diplomacy: Accommodation Is in the U. S. Interest in Na-
        tion, October, pp. 386-88.
Snyder, Allegra Fuller
    1974 The Dance Symbol in Dance Research Annual, vol. 6, pp. 213-24.
    1978 Levels of Event Patterns: An Attempt to Place Dance in a Holistic Con-
        text, paper presented for Joint American Dance Guild and Congress
        on Research in Dance Conference, University of Hawaii, August.
    1988 Levels of Event Patterns: A Theoretical Model Applied to the Yaqui
        Easter Ceremonies in The Dance Event: A Complex Phenomenon,
        proceedings of ICTM Study Group for Ethnochoreology, Copen-
        hagen.

Solien, Nancy
1971 Household and Family in the Caribbean *in* Peoples and Cultures of the Caribbean, ed. Michael Horowitz, New York: Natural History Press.
Sosa, Enrique
1984 El Carabalí. Havana: Editorial Letras Cubanas.
Spencer, Paul, ed.
1985 Society and the Dance. Cambridge: Cambridge University Press.
Steward, Julian
1948 The Circum-Caribbean Tribes, Handbook of South American Indians, vol. 4. Washington, D.C.: Government Printing Office.
Stone, Elizabeth, ed.
1981 Women and the Cuban Revolution: Speeches and Documents by Fidel Castro, Vilma Espín, and Others. New York: Pathfinder Press.
Sudarkasa, Niara
1980 African and Afro-American Family Structure: A Comparison *in* Black Scholar, vol. 11, no. 8, pp. 37-60.
Sweet, Jill
1976 Space, Time and Festival *in* Asociación Nacional de Grupos Folklóricos, vol. 6, no. 1, pp. 1-13.
Szulc, Tad
1986 A Critical Portrait: Fidel. New York: Avon Books.
Thomas, Clive
1988 The Poor and the Powerless: Economic Policy and Change in the Caribbean. New York: Monthly Review Press.
Thompson, Robert Farris
1974 African Art in Motion. Berkeley: University of California Press.
1981 The Four Moments of the Sun: Kongo Art in Two Worlds. Washington, D.C.: National Gallery of Art.
1983 Flash of the Spirit. New York: Random House.
1990 Kongo Influences on African-American Artistic Culture *in* Africanisms in American Culture, ed. Joseph Holloway, Bloomington: Indiana University Press, pp. 148-84.
Torres Rivera, Alejandro
1993 Defendiendo una revolución: La organización sindical y la participación de los trabajadores en la economía cubana *in* Pensamiento Crítico, vol. 16, no. 73, pp. 18-48.
Trinh T. Minh-ha
1989 Woman, Native, Other: Writing Post Coloniality and Feminism. Bloomington: Indiana University Press.
Turner, Victor
1969 The Ritual Process: Structure and Antistructure. Chicago: Aldine.
Turner, Victor, ed.
1982 Celebration: Studies in Festivity and Ritual. Washington, D.C.: Smithsonian Institution.
Turner, Victor, and Edith Turner
1978 Image and Pilgrimages in Christian Culture: Anthropological Perspectives. New York: Columbia University Press.
Urfé, Odilio
1948 La verdad sobre el mambo *in* Invertario, no. 3, Havana.
1977 Music and Dance in Cuba *in* Africa in Latin America: Essays on History, Culture and Socialization. New York and Paris: Holmes and Meier, pp. 170-88.
N.d. Rumba *in* de Música y Folklore, Havana: Ediciones del CNC, pp. 9-16.

Valdés, Oscar, and Hector Vitria
    N.d. Rumba. A film produced in Havana and distributed in New York, Center for Cuban Studies.
Van Gennep, Arnold
    1909 (1960) Rites of Passage, trans. Monika Vizedom and Gabrielle Cafee. Chicago: University of Chicago Press.
Verger, Pierre
    1957 Notes sur le culte des Orisa et Vodun a Bahía. Dakar: Ifan.
Walker, Sheila
    1972 Ceremonial Spirit Possession in Africa and Afro-America. Leiden: E. J. Brill.
    1980 African Gods in America: The Black Religious Continuum *in* Black Scholar, vol. 2, no. 8, pp. 45-61.
Williams, Eric
    1970 (1984) From Columbus to Castro: The History of the Caribbean 1492 to 1969. New York: Vintage Books.
Wilson, Olly
    1981 Association of Movement and Music as a Manifestation of a Black Conceptual Approach to Music Making *in* Essays on Afro-American Music and Musicians, ed. Irene V. Jackson, Westport, Conn.: Greenwood Press, pp. 1-23.
    1983 Black Music as an Art Form *in* Black Music Research Journal, pp. 1-22.
Yarborough, Lavinia Williams
    1958 Haiti: Dance. Frankfurt am Main: Bronners Druckerei.
Zimbalist, Andrew
    1987 Cuba's Socialist Economy Towards the 1990s. Boulder: Lynne Rienner.

Index

Abakuá: African influence on Cuban dance, 36-37; rumberos and religion, 58; columbia variation of rumba, 79
Affranchis (French-Haitian dance), 38
Africa: cultural origins of rumba, 17, 18-19, 168n.9; influence on development of Cuban dance, 33-37; rumba and national identity of Cuba, 118, 119
Ahye, Molly, 169n.13
Alén, Olavo, 17, 28, 130
Alfonso, Jesús, 175n.13
Alonso, Alicia, 42, 64
Alonso, Fernando, 173n.14
Anthropology: research on dance in Caribbean, 20-21, 169-70n.13; methodology for dance analysis, 21-25
Arará (Cuban dance tradition), 6, 35
Los areítos (indigenous dance form), 28-29
Arslanian, Sharon, 174n.9
Arts and artists: and Cuban world view, 51; Cuban government support of, 92; Cuban-Marxist view of, 113; status of in contemporary Cuba, 143

Baile de palo (African dance), 79
Ballet: in prerevolutionary Cuba, 16; in contemporary Cuba, 42-43; rumba in repertoires of, 64
Bandamban (Suriname, dance), 18
Bantu, African heritage of rumba, 64
Barth, Fredrik, 170n.15

Batarumba: as variation of rumba, 68, 72-73, 74; rhythm of music, 83-84; religious and secular elements in, 134; drumming in, 175n.14
Bausa, Mario, 83
Behavior: patterns of produced by Cuban world view, 45-57; and gender in contemporary Cuba, 123-24
Bloch, Maurice, 112
Bourdieu, Pierre, 134
Burdsall, Lorna, 43-44

Cabildos (homogeneous African ethnic groups), 34
Carabaí culture: influence on development of dance in Cuba, 35, 36; and rumba, 79; use of term, 172n.9
Caribbean area studies, anthropological research on dance, 20-21, 169-70n.13
Cáscara, instrumentation of rumba music, 81
Cashion, Susan, 28, 168n.5
Casino (Cuban dance), 141
Castro, Fidel, 144
Catá, instrumentation of rumba music, 81, 174-75n.12
Catholic Church, influence on development of Cuban dance, 32. See also Religion
Chaconas (Cuban dance form), 32
Children: Spanish influence on Cuban dance, 33; patterns of Cuban life, 55;

establishment of, 59; versions of rumba and performance practices of, 100; rumba as politicized activity, 118; community members as *informantes*, 167n.1

National identity, and politicization of rumba, 117-24. *See also* Cuba

Native Americans, indigenous culture and dance in Cuba, 28-29

Ness, Sally, 142

Nettleford, Rex, 169n.13

Nigeria, origins of rumba, 18

Noriega, Elena, 44

Ortiz, Alfonso, 171n.2

Ortiz, Fernando, 17, 18, 36, 44, 70, 114, 168n.9, 169n.13, 174n.4, 176n.21

Palo (Cuban dance tradition), 6

Pantomime, types and variations of rumba, 70-71, 174n.5

Papolote, pantomime form of rumba, 71

Pedro, Alberto, 130

Perez, Dolores, 67

Performance, rumba: evolution of, 63-67; dance forms, types, and variations, 67-79; structure of music for, 79-91; personnel for, 90-91; practices of contemporary, 91-100; spontaneous and prepared, 101-105; ritual intensity of, 105-106, 109-11; political reality of, 119-20; organic change in traditional dance, 139

Piliabena, Nurudafina, 131

Politics: world view of Cuban workers and students, 49; development of rumba and, 65; rumba as Cuban national symbol, 117-24. *See also* Ministry of Culture; Revolution

Porro (Colombia, dance), 18

Price, Sally and Richard, 140

Primus, Pearl, 22

Professionalization: of rumberos in postrevolutionary Cuba, 58-61; structure of rumba in postrevolutionary Cuba, 65; performance practices of contemporary rumba, 92-94; and traditional rumba performances, 98-100; Cuban dance companies and change in performance of dance traditions, 139

Public: performance practices of contemporary rumba, 95-98; spontaneous rumba as type of performance, 101-104

Puente, Tito, 83

Race: political reality of rumba, 120; rumba and social change in Cuba, 145, 147. *See also* Class

Raíces Profundas (dance company), 94

Regionalism: impact on Cuban world view, 46; competition among Cuban professional dance companies, 175-76n.18

Religion: Cuban world-view chart and, 27; differing African traditions of, 36; Cuban world view and, 50; rumberos and, 58; symbolic movements in rumba, 78; public performances of rumba, 100; secularization of modern rumba, 132-35

Revolution, Cuban: rumba as national symbol, 16-17; world view of Cuban workers and students, 48; professionalization of rumberos, 58-59; and gender equality, 122, 124

Rhumba, as style of ballroom dancing, 18

Rhythm, structure of rumba music, 81-84

Ritual. *See* Intensity, ritual

Rivera, Eduardo, 41

Rivera, Quintero, 169n.13

Rodrigues, Denora, 175n.16

Las rondas infantiles (Cuban-Spanish dance), 33

Rumba: description of performance by National Folkloric Company, 2-7; description of performance in Matanzas, 7-13; development of from Revolution to present, 13-17; types of, 17-20; and yearly cycle in Cuba, 27; evolution of in nineteenth-century Cuba, 40-41; life of rumberos, 57-62; international interest in, 61-62; evolution of performance practices, 63-67; dance forms, types, and variations, 67-79; structure of music, 79-91; performance practices of contemporary, 91-100; spontaneous and prepared performances of, 101-105; ritual intensity of performance, 105-106, 109-11; symbolism and restaging of meaning in, 112-17; politicization of, 117-24; commoditization of, 124-32; secularization of, 132-35; as structured communitas, 135-36; process of change in, 140-42; and social change in Cuba, 142-48; future of, 148-49. *See also* Dance; Rumberos

Rumba (film), 7, 20, 168n.3

Rumbas del tiempo de España: as variation of rumba, 68, 70-71; professional performances of, 99

Rumberos, pattern of life, 57-62

Russia. *See* Soviet Union

Sachs, Curt, 169n.13

Salsa (Cuban dance), 40, 168n.4

Samba (Brazilian dance), 18, 79

Santeria (Afro-Cuban religion), 58

Seduction, as theme in rumba, 63, 69, 136

Yvonne Daniel teaches dance and anthropology at Smith College and the Five College Consortium in Massachusetts. She is the author of articles on Haitian, Cuban, Brazilian, and Surinamese dance traditions that have appeared in *Dance Research Journal, Black Scholar,* and *Dance Ethnology.*